CRITICAL ACCLAIM
FOR BOOKS BY MARYBETH BOND

A Woman's World

"*A Woman's World* is not just a book for 'Everywoman'.... It's also a book for 'Everyman.' It shows how women travel through the world and how the world relates to them."

—*The New York Times*

"*A Woman's World* not only gives us a special sense of place and a glimpse into the women traveling through it, but also insight into ourselves. The book is packed with stories of courage and confidence, independence and introspection; if they don't inspire you to pack your bags and set out into the world, I can't imagine what would."

—*Self Magazine*

A Woman's Europe

"Delicious adventures remembered by women who love to travel with their hearts and minds wide open."

—*Daily Herald*

Gutsy Women

"Packed with instructive and inspiring travel vignettes and tips."

—*Boston Globe*

"Essential reading for women travelers of any age."

—*Chicago Tribune*

A Woman's Passion for Travel

"Reading this book is dangerous. You'll quit your job. You'll cash in your savings—or take out a loan. At the very least, you'll ache to follow in the footsteps of these fine writers on their exciting travels."

—Lucy Jane Bledsoe, author of *Working Parts*

A Mother's World

"Heartwarming and heartbreaking, these stories remind us that motherhood is one of the great unifying forces in the world."

—*San Francisco Chronicle*

A WOMAN'S ASIA

TRUE STORIES

TRAVELERS' TALES

A WOMAN'S ASIA

TRUE STORIES

Edited by

MARYBETH BOND

Series Editors

JAMES O'REILLY AND LARRY HABEGGER

TRAVELERS' TALES

PALO ALTO

Credits and copyright notices for the individual articles in this collection are given starting on page 295.

We have made every effort to trace the ownership of all copyrighted material and to secure permission from copyright holders. In the event of any question arising as to the ownership of any material, we will be pleased to make the necessary correction in future printings. Contact Travelers' Tales, Inc., 853 Alma Street, Palo Alto, California, 94301. www.travelerstales.com

Art Direction: Michele Wetherbee/Stefan Gutermuth
Cover Photograph: © Index Stock. Thar Desert, Rajasthan, India.
Interior Design: Kathryn Heflin and Susan Bailey
Page Layout: Patty Holden using the font Bembo

Distributed by: Publishers Group West, 1700 Fourth Street, Berkeley, California 94710.

Library of Congress Cataloging in Publication
    Available upon request

First Edition
Printed in the United States
10 9 8 7 6 5 4 3 2 1

*For my husband Gary, and
my daughters, Julieclaire and Annalyse,
and for all the gutsy women travelers
whose stories inspire us.*

Table of Contents

A Woman's Asia: An Introduction

I went to Asia for the first time when I was twenty years old
and a student in Paris, but my fascination with the Orient had
begun much earlier, when I was a child. Our elderly next-door
neighbors had lived in Singapore, Malaysia, and Sri Lanka (but
they had always called it Ceylon). I was enthralled with their
tales about life on the rubber plantations and adventures in the
jungle. They punctuated their stories with props: stuffed cobras,
elephant toenails, embroidered slippers, and magenta silks
pulled from an ornate leather trunk stashed in the basement.
During my time in Paris the lure of the East grew stronger.
The French romanticize their former colonies in Indochina,
and my friends in France often referred to ancient Siam and
the Khmer civilizations. When one said she was planning a trip
there I jumped at the chance to head for the jungles of
Malaysia, the golden Buddha temples in Bangkok.

It wasn't the grand tour of the Orient. We ate pork buns,
satay, and fresh mangoes on the street; in modest guesthouses
we laid our heads on hard cots, enveloped in a cocoon of
mosquito netting beneath whirling ceiling fans. From Kuala
Lumpur we traveled upcountry and upriver to trek in the
primeval beauty of Taman Negara National Park, where the
sun rarely penetrated the thick jungle canopy. In hothouse
conditions we hired a Dyak guide, indispensable because there
was no trail system. Using a machete to clear a path, our guide
made loud grunts and whistles to locate a nomadic aboriginal
tribe. When we entered a clearing where a small group of abo-

rigines were resting, a young hunter, clad in a loincloth, returned with a monkey and his blowgun over his shoulder. His hand-made poison darts were stored in a quiver. We traded cigarettes and a lighter for a blowgun and some untreated darts.

In Bangkok we floated through the *khlong* waterways and wandered through golden temples where I was initiated into the sensual pleasure of my first massage. I reclined, fully dressed, on a straw pallet on the cement floor of the School of Traditional Thai Massage in the gardens of Wat Po, the Temple of the Reclining Buddha. I was disturbed by the moaning of a corpulent Chinese man on the pallet next to me, who had a thumb-length hair protruding from the mole on his chin. I was thrilled—the more exotic, the better.

In the garden of the dilapidated, unrenovated, colonial Raffles Hotel we split a Singapore Sling and I wore the orchid from the swizzle stick in my hair. We wandered through the night market and watched people buy live bullfrogs, snakes, and crickets to add to their dinner menu. It didn't matter that very few Asians spoke English or French. Smiles, nods, and gestures welcomed us and made us feel safe.

But I did not feel comfortable. For the first time in my life, I felt off-balance. I could understand, at many levels, Western European culture and life. At some subliminal level, Asia befuddled me and shook the very foundations of my belief system. Why? Why were the people I met so seemingly satisfied and happy? Was it their religion, or perhaps family, friends, and community that was central to their lives? I had more questions than answers.

Fragrances of frangipani and jasmine, the aromas of ginger and lemongrass worked their way under my skin and into a deeper consciousness. The impact of traveling off-the-beaten path in the Orient was like the reverberating gong of a temple bell. I had fallen under the spell of Asia, and I knew I would always want more.

Ten years after my first journey there, I left my corporate job, bought a one-way ticket to Bangkok, and traveled alone for a year. I went to many of the remote places I had dreamed about as I sat in my cubical at work. For four months I trekked in Nepal, in the Everest, Annapurna, and Langtang areas. Although I feared India, I was seduced for five months—I trekked in the Kashmiri and Ladakhi Himalayas, meditated in a Buddhist temple, rode trains, camels, and rickshaws. Elephants carried me through the forests that are home to the tribes of northern Thailand, and I explored the shores and cultures of Sri Lanka, the Maldives, Bali, and southern India. What great truth did I learn? You will get diarrhea and you may, or may not, find God.

One truth is certain: Asia gets into your bloodstream. It was true for Joseph Conrad, Somerset Maugham, Noel Coward, Graham Greene, John le Carré, James Michener, and it is true for me. We are drawn to the Orient for the timeless possibilities it holds—for culture, spiritual awakening, romance, adventure, and fabulous food.

On that second trip, I met my future husband, an American trekker, in Kathmandu. Since then I've returned with friends and my own family more than two dozen times, and I hope to return another dozen times. My yearning for Asia has not been dulled by marriage, mid-life, motherhood, or menopause.

It's true that life is a journey, and for me, travel is a catalyst for change. After I appeared on the *Oprah Winfrey Show* with my book *Gutsy Women*, I renewed my efforts to urge women to take time off to revive themselves. As demonstrated throughout this book, many women use travel as the cocoon stage in which to grow, discover themselves, and make changes that would be harder to make at home.

When I went to Asia alone at thirty years old, I was called a "gutsy woman," and I wear this badge, then and today, with pride. Gutsy does not mean foolish or arrogant. It means being savvy, strong, and courageous. And I am not alone. Many other courageous, adventurous, and, yes, gutsy women are out there, in Asia, traveling right now.

We love to travel because it feeds our curiosity as well as the desire to see and connect with other cultures. When we travel, we bring home a bit of the world. We know how important it is to care for our brothers and sisters, worldwide, regardless of religion or politics. Upon my return from each trip to Asia, I realize I have found another soul mate: Made from Bali; Ringee, Namdu, Pertemba, and Olga from Nepal; Anita and Mandip from India. The list goes on and on and I am deeply enriched by these friendships.

Most recently, for our Christmas holiday, my family and I went to southern Thailand where the weather is almost always sunny and deliciously warm. The ocean is calm and clear. "Why are you traveling so far for Christmas?" friends and family asked. "Because we *love* Asia; its food, culture, natural beauty, and most of all, its people." Of course, those who haven't experienced Asia wonder why Hawaii or the Caribbean isn't good enough. I reply to my friends, "Thailand deserves its reputation as 'The Land of Smiles.' The people are sweet, kind, patient, and fun-loving."

We had the usual plans for a vacation in southern Thailand. We wanted to snorkel, dive, sail, kayak, and relax. We had no idea we were headed towards the worst natural disaster in modern times. My family's December holiday to this favorite destination transformed into a lesson in life, as the Land of Smiles was filled with terror and tears.

The story of our close call with the tsunami is included in this collection. It was written by our sixteen-year-old daughter, Julieclaire.

Of course, the scenes of the tsunami remain etched in my mind. Today, as I sit at my desk writing to you, I count my blessings as I struggle to cope with my family's survival and the death of so many innocent people. My heart goes out and remains with the people there. The earth can tremble and we can vanish in an instant. Life is fragile. San Francisco has earthquakes, New York City had the 9/11 terrorist attacks, Florida has hurricanes, but we return to these wonderful places. And so when asked, "Would you return to Thailand?" I answer unequivocally, "Absolutely, tomorrow, given the opportunity."

My experience with the tsunami solidified my passion for Asia and my deep connection with the people, culture, and religions. My close call in southern Thailand has brought me, symbolically, closer to Asia, closer to life.

Join me and the women in this book to share adventure, romance, healing, self-discovery, intellectual and spiritual explorations, escape, and pilgrimages. May our stories open a door, and give you courage, confidence, and wisdom.

—MARYBETH BOND

PAULA McDONALD

Waltz at the End of Earth

*Amazing things happen when you journey
to the edge of the map.*

TWO OF US WERE ON OUR WAY TO "END OF EARTH," THE MOST
remote beach on remote Hainan Island, the farthest south in a
string of Chinese islands in the South China Sea. A ridiculous
place to want to go; there's nothing there. But the ancient
Chinese believed the earth ended at the southern tip of this
largest of China's islands. Thus, to journey to "End of Earth"
was to show great "strength and courage," qualities of utmost
importance to the Chinese. To journey to "End of Earth" was
to bring great good fortune to yourself. In such a strange way,
my journey did.

Getting to Hainan Island from Guangzhou isn't easy.
Eighteen-hour village-bus rides through the mountains with
the inevitable breakdowns in the middle of the night are
followed by tedious ferries, incomprehensible transfers, and
more tedious ferries.

But, we found our way to "End of Earth" eventually, a
peaceful, serene place with an aura of great continuity. Beyond,
with quiet waves lapping at our feet, the sea seemed to stretch

forever. Like the ancient Chinese, who could know what was out there? Or what would come next?

In a village nearby, we stopped for lunch at a roadside house, a hovel actually, one of those one-room shacks that serve as home, restaurant, and mini-zoo, a combination so common in rural China.

Joanne Turner, my fellow traveler, and I had eaten in many similar places in the few weeks since we'd met and completed a stint together as volunteers on a scientific project meant to catalog China's southern rainforests. We'd camped on remote mountaintops, sea kayaked the uninhabited Outer Islands, trekked through leech-filled jungles, and eaten, standing up, in every street market in Southern China it seemed.

Along the way, we'd become expert pantomimists, ready smilers, and absolute gourmands on the street-food scene. The shabbiness of the shack didn't bother us. The luxury of eating from an actual table instead of a rock seemed rather civilized, in fact.

This particular shack was poor even by Chinese standards though. It held only the bare wooden table, a rope bed, and several cages full of eight- and ten-foot snakes. The dirt floor was swept clean, and an old bicycle hung on the wall. Nothing more adorned the place. Cooking, as is customary in the countryside, was done out back on an empty oil drum with a wood fire below.

The eighty-year-old owner and her granddaughter immediately began to display their snakes. Out they came from their cages and were handed to us, one by one. Which did we want for lunch? We tried to pantomime that it was very hot, that we weren't very hungry after all, and that the snakes were very large. There would be so much waste.

Perhaps rabbit would be better, suggested our hosts. Or so we assumed as they took us to a shed in back where three rabbits were caged. Unable to look any bunny in the eye and then eat it, we politely tried to say that the rabbits were also too big. The only other choice seemed to be an old chicken pecking at the edge of the dirt lane, so we opted for him. Least of all possible sins, or so we thought.

Twenty minutes later, the food began arriving: the usual Chinese mystery soup, followed by several courses of vegetables, rice, and endless pots of steaming tea in the 100-degree heat. Finally the meat arrived.

It was unmistakably rabbit! Oh, lordy, where had we gone wrong? Perhaps we should have drawn pictures instead of doing charades. We ate it, of course. With grace and a good deal of hard swallowing. Not to would have caused a loss of face for the two gracious women whose humble hospitality we shared.

The heat was oppressive that day, as it is all over southern China in May, and even to sit still was to sit and drip. During lunch, the old woman kept smiling at me as if to say, "I forgive you for sweating in my house. There is no loss of face in this," and fanning me with a marvelously ingenious fan made completely of feathers. I had never seen anything like it.

Since there was literally nothing else in the one-room house, not even a change of clothes, and the fan seemed to be her only possession besides an old watch, I was careful not to admire it openly. Chinese custom demands the giving to guests of whatever they admire. But despite my intentional disregard of the fan, I was immensely grateful for the momentary illusion of coolness each *whoosh* brought.

Perhaps because I was trying so hard to ignore the feather fan, what happened next caught me completely by surprise.

Suddenly, for no apparent reason, the old woman broke into a great grin, hugged me hard, handed me the fan, and then hugged me again. I was stunned. It was obviously a gift, but her generosity, under the circumstances, was astonishing. What had prompted the act? What could I, a lanky, perspiring stranger with a sunburned nose, in her life for so short a time, have possibly done to deserve the gift of one of her few possessions? Nothing that I could conceive of, but something had changed dramatically in the little room. The old woman now sat smiling beatifically as though I had pleased her more than I could ever imagine. But I couldn't, for the life of me figure out how.

Despite the baking heat inside the house, we lingered awhile after lunch and drank more tea just to stay and not seem to rush away. And then, to our amazement, when her granddaughter finally left to take care of other chores, the old woman began to speak in halting English, obviously a language she had not used for decades. Bit by bit, straining to understand the stumbling words, we learned her story.

Her husband had been imprisoned under Mao for being a follower of Chiang Kai-shek and had died a prisoner. She had watched as he was led away. She never saw him again.

Before the Cultural Revolution the woman had been a teacher, the daughter of educated diplomats, one of the new regime's despised intellectuals. After the Communist victory in China, she had been exiled from Shanghai to the remote island village for the double sins of being educated and being the wife of a political enemy. She had lived in the isolated village for decades surviving as best she could by cooking and selling the snakes and rabbits she and her granddaughter were able to trap.

Her story, told with no rancor, captured our hearts, and despite the need to get on, we stayed. The long-forgotten English words seemed to get easier for her as we asked questions about her life and encouraged her to reminisce. She told us of her childhood, of traveling and learning English at embassies as a youngster. Memories of another, so very different life. Yet, for all her losses, she truly seemed to have no bitterness. With one strange exception. When I asked her directly if she had regrets, she could think of only one: that she had never learned to waltz.

One of her most vivid childhood memories was of being taken, as a young girl, to a grand ball in Hong Kong where there were many English guests in attendance. The music was international that night, the first time she had heard anything besides the harsh, sharp cacophony of China's music, and suddenly the ballroom was filled with swirling skirts and the sweetest sounds she had ever heard. Couples were waltzing, and, to the young Chinese girl, it was the most beautiful sight in the world. Someday she would grow up to become one of those graceful waltzing women.

She grew up, but China changed. There were no more waltzes. And now there were no more illusions in her life.

In the silence that followed the story, I took her hand across the table. Then I quietly asked if she would still like to learn to waltz. Here. Now.

The slow smile that spread across her face was my answer. We stood and moved together toward our ballroom floor, an open space of five feet of hard-packed dirt between the table and the bed. "Please, God," I prayed, "let me remember a waltz. Any waltz. And let me remember how to lead."

We started shakily, me humming Strauss, stepping on her toes. But soon we got smoother, bolder, louder. "The Blue Danube" swelled and filled the room. Her baggy Mao pajama pants became a swirling skirt, she became young and beautiful again, and I became a handsome foreigner, tall, sure, strong…perhaps a prince who carried her away. Away from her destiny at "End of Earth."

The feather fan hangs on my office wall today, next to her picture. Next to our picture. The two of us, hands clasped, smiling strangers from such different worlds, waltzing around a steaming hut in a forsaken spot I visited by chance that day. That day I met strength and courage at "End of Earth."

Paula McDonald lives on the beach in Rosarito, Mexico. On the clearest of days, if she squints, she can almost see China's "End of Earth." When the waves are quiet, she can certainly hear Strauss.

MARJORIE HAMLIN

✶

The Gift of Beggars

Her travel motto: Look beyond appearances.

OUTSIDE OUR HOTEL IN HO CHI MINH CITY, AN ANCIENT woman on crutches waited by the door with her hand outstretched. Every day I put my hand in hers as our eyes met. She never failed to return my smile, my grasp, and my "*Sin chao*" greeting.

John Cowper Powys has assured me that "No one can consider himself wholly civilized who does not look upon every individual, without a single exception, as of deep and startling interest." She was a beam of light in a shadowy doorway.

The last day of our visit to Vietnam, I found myself alone, on a busy street corner across from our hotel. Bicycles and motorbikes careened in front of me. We had been advised to walk straight through the teeming traffic without looking right or left. Let them avoid us. We had proved it possible, but tonight I was by myself, and felt inadequate to face the torrent of vehicles. As I hesitated on the curb, I felt a hand on my elbow, and looked down to see the smile of my small beggar friend looking up at me. She nodded her head toward the street, indicating that she would take me across. We moved slowly into the chaos together as she gently prodded me forward. When we reached the center of the crossing, I looked down at her again, and couldn't resist exclaiming,

"You have the most beautiful smile!"

She obviously knew little English, but must have recognized the tone, for she threw both arms and crutches around me in a genuine hug, while the traffic streamed by us on both sides. Then we moved on toward the sidewalk, where she pulled my face down, kissed me on both cheeks, and limped away, still smiling and waving back to me.

I had not given her a single coin. We had shared something vastly more important—a warming of hearts in friendship.

Mother Teresa suggested, "If you cannot do great things, you can do small things with great love."

To look beggars in the eye and smile, thus acknowledging their existence, is a small thing. Putting a hand into another's outstretched hand and holding tight for a moment is also a small thing. Learning to use a greeting in the local language is not too difficult. Yet fear seems to distance us from one another, and we lose something precious.

There are many reasons why giving money is not the best response to an outstretched hand. Many world rovers have discovered that the greatest gift we have to give while traveling is our time and friendship. Everyone needs recognition, to be seen as worthy of attention, to feel appreciated and loved.

Traveling with Americans in poorer nations, I have witnessed a variety of ways in which they deal with beggars. The most common response of tourists when faced with the poverty-stricken is to ignore their very existence, focusing eyes elsewhere. I have seen Americans push away an outstretched hand in angry annoyance. A few guilty tourists will hastily drop a few coins into a beseeching hand, and then execute a quick exit, in hopes that another twenty ragged pursuers won't immediately appear.

My life continues to be enriched by connecting with the humanity surrounding us. In astonishment, I discover that what I have been given is far beyond monetary value.

There was the legless man sitting by a road at the Pushcar Camel Fair in India. I sat down beside him, and we began to communicate in the kind of sign language and laughter one learns while vagabonding the world. Where does such joy come from? Moments before, we were total strangers, and suddenly we are cemented in a friendship born of our common existence in this world. His eyes shone as we exchanged names. Vidur confirmed what I have discovered, the special beauty of a new relationship. "Speak to the king, and the king will come forth."

When Vidur's smile lured me to join him, I was returning to our tent with my tape recorder replaying the exotic music that I had just captured of the dancing men of Pushkar. After mimicking the whirling skirts and sticks, I showed Vidur how my tape recorder worked. He motioned for me to give it to him. I hesitated only a fleeting moment. After examining it carefully, he began to sing a hauntingly beautiful song, indicating that he wanted me to take it home as a memory of our time together.

Why do we ever hesitate to share?

I did hesitate outside of a Vietnamese temple one day when a teenaged boy aggressively thrust a very deformed hand into my face. I pushed him away and entered the temple, where beggars were not allowed. Feeling pangs of guilt, I prepared myself to face him again when I emerged. I reminded myself of Jesus's words, "As ye have done it to the least of these my brethren, you have done it unto me."

Goethe came to mind as well, with his, "To see a man as

he is, is to debase him. To see him as he ought to be is to engrace him."

I became determined to see the king, trusting the king to come forth. Sure enough, the hand was in my face again as I moved out of the temple. I looked past the ugliness into the determined boy's eyes, and asked him if he knew any English. He responded with a hesitant nod, so I started telling him how handsome he was, and how he could use his other hand, the good one, in the future. An education would help to lead him toward new creative ideas. Slowly his smile responded to mine and the misshapen hand totally disappeared as we became involved in a lively discussion in rather muddled English. I learned his name and age and dreams. He learned something about Americans.

When my transportation honked, we had to say goodbye. I reached into my pocket and retrieved a limp 2,000-dong note. I gave it to him, saying "This is not because you were begging, but because you are my friend, and I know you can start something good with it." He quickly put his good hand into his shirt pocket and pulled out a dime and two nickels. "What these?" he asked. I told him and we both laughed that his American coins had exactly the same value as the Vietnamese bill I had given to him. I reached out to put them back into his pocket, and this time he pushed my hand away, saying "No, you keep. We are friends."

After learning a greeting in any new language, I learn the word for "friend." I wear an elaborately beaded Masai necklace, given to me in Kenya as the result of my knowing the Swahili word for "friend." When Maria heard the word "*rafiki*," her skinny begging hand disappeared immediately, and she took my hand to lead me to her selling stall, where I was decorated with delight, and at no charge. Yet another friend had come into my life. Maria and I had our picture taken together, and my daughter brought a copy of the photo back to Kenya a year later. When Maria saw it, she burst into tears, hugged my daughter and put one of her beautiful handcrafted necklaces around her neck. "*Zawadi*" (gift), she exclaimed. "*Rafiki*."

I continue to learn about giving from the world's most hopeless. Rich in humanity, they have hearts yearning to be affirmed, and oh-so-ready to respond.

The great Russian writer, Dostoevsky, has told us, "To love a person means to see him as God intended him to be."

Everyone is worthy.

Worth knowing!

Marjorie Hamlin, eighty-three years young, has long been fascinated by the diversity of cultures and the variety of perceptions in our world and travel has reinforced that belief. She lives in St. Louis, Missouri.

KATHRYN KEFAUVER

* * *

The Beginner's Gift

Teaching and learning take place in an unbroken circle.

"WHAT'S IT LIKE," A FELLOW VOLUNTEER IN LAOS ASKED ME, "teaching one of the last communist governments on earth?"

"It's hard," I said, "to make them do homework." I didn't say, "Probably because I've confused them too much." Just the thought "Intermediate English" left a cramped, wiggly feeling in my throat, like a small frog there trying to get out.

My classroom at Communist Party Headquarters in Vientiane was the size of a one-car garage. Four windows framed a yellow blazing sun, a profusion of coconut palms, and fuchsia orchids on a chain-link fence.

A rickety green fan wobbled overhead as the Intermediate English Class—twelve middle-aged men in gray uniforms and three women in ankle-length silk skirts—filed into the U-shaped configuration of desks. Their rubber flip-flops flapped, chairs scraped the floor, papers rustled. I pushed my round metal glasses high on my nose, hoping the frames lent maturity to my face. It was my third week teaching; I needed all the props I could get.

"We'll review the verb 'to be' again," I said.

I put my notebook behind a brown ceramic vase which held a bouquet of white plastic flowers. With a sigh, I reread my motto for the class, "If it's not a disaster, it's a success." Since day one, I had floundered. The perfect lesson, recycled from the Beginners' Class, had ground to a halt in eight minutes flat. To fill the queasy void, I'd babbled an ad-lib grammar lesson. Weeks later, I was still struggling to clear their confusion in a stunning act of teaching triage.

Sipachan, one of the three women and immensely pregnant, stared at me like I had a noodle trapped in my teeth. Sometimes I directed my lecture at her, dividing my focus to pray, *Oh please have your baby now oh please have your baby now.*

"These are the tenses of the verb 'to be'," I said, boring even myself.

"This is the present, for today, now." I translated a little into Lao, as the marker squealed across the board, "and the past. We *did* these last week."

This failed to stir the quicksand in their eyes.

"And next is the past perfect, that you use when…" I squinted through a column of sunlight, wishing it would beam me upward, as in an Italian painting.

"Mr. Kamfan," I said, "please read the rule for past perfect. Bottom of the page."

I forgot that three of the men were named Khamfanh, Kamfanh, and Khamfan. In Lao, a tonal language, they sounded different.

"Kam-fan," I said again.

The trio conferred in whispers.

One of them looked up, "Me?"

"Yes, you."

A Lao man with black, square glasses read the rule in halting, tense English.

"O.K., do you all understand that?"

Silence.

"I want you to work in pairs," I said, "on exercise three."

They gazed at me, motionless.

"O.K.," I relented, "we'll continue together."

I had them read from the book, just to hear English from their mouths. My cheeks burned, a seam of dew dampened my hairline. Outside, a mutt chased two squawking chickens. The dog let them go every time, more interested in the havoc than actual capture.

"Any questions?" I said at the end of class.

One of the Kamfans raised his hand.

"Teacher, can you explain the verb 'to be'?"

"That's what we covered in class today. Anything else?"

"How old are you?"

"Um, I'm...older than you think."

For the first time, they smiled, as if forgiving me the very immaturity I'd hoped to conceal. They gathered up their books and walked out, the flapping of flip-flops fading into the hall.

"Goodbye, teacher," they called. I winced at the word.

I might have resigned myself to failure if it hadn't been for the Beginners' Class an hour later. They spoke no English beyond what we'd covered in Unit One, which they breezed through: greetings, names, introductions. I felt a proprietary affection toward them, *my* students. Maybe it was their curiosity, the spark of pure intention that was the beginner's gift. I wished I could always glimpse this newness in others. They took notes in labored, neat print with pencils so sharp I could almost see lead dust floating off the tips. Their textbooks were open to Unit Two.

"'He,'" I said, "is for a man. 'She,' is for a woman."

The Lao language had only "*lao*" for "he" and "she," and

these learners often ignored the distinction, just as most foreigners wanted to gloss over tones in Lao.

"*He* is Mr. Duangta," I gestured with an open palm, suspecting it was impolite to point, and "*she—*"

My hand smacked the glass of water on the desk. It was airborne for a quiet moment before shattering on the floor. Everyone, including me, was shocked by this spasticity. Except when driving, the Lao seldom mustered enough velocity to smash anything.

"Too much iced coffee this morning," I said in Lao, "please forgive me."

Then, with the same suddenness of the breaking glass, everyone exploded into laughter.

"*Bo penn nyang,*" they said, *Don't worry.*

The air in the room seemed charged with delight as the lights behind their faces switched on. There was a universal quality to physical humor, the banana peel, the loss of dignity. Or maybe their own language, from my foreign face, made me easier to see. Laughter needed no translation.

After class, Siban lingered. In Lao she said, "There is so much I want to ask you, so much I want to *ask…*"

I thought of what we might say if we could close the gap of language. Still, the absence of our ability exposed the deeper impulse, to simply speak, to know and be known, and the expression of that was in some ways more profound. It sanctified my effort, my struggle to teach. There was so much I wanted to ask her, too.

The next day, Sipachan, grasping the beach ball contour of her middle, lowered herself into her chair with a grimace.

"No grammar books today," I said, unable to add to her affliction.

Everyone, including me, waited to see what would happen next. I burrowed in my bag for glossy photos clipped from

People magazine.

"Choose a picture and pass the rest."

Then I wrote on the board: name, age, job, family, the things they would not discuss on the first day.

"Write four sentences about the person in the picture," I said.

As I turned to the board, my hand smacked the brown vase. It twirled, skidded, then plunged to the floor. Ceramic bits and fake flowers scattered.

Sipachan covered her mouth. I stared at the mess, as if to blame the flowers. No one else moved.

"*Jai hon, no?*" I said. *Hot hearted, hurried, no self-control.*

Like the other class, they erupted with laughter. It was almost a relief; any sound from this class. I laughed, too, crouching to pick up the bits of vase while one of the Kamfans hurried for a broom.

When the class settled, students burrowed in their dictionaries. Sipachan giggled uncontrollably at the photo in her hand. It was the first I'd seen her smile.

"What?" I asked.

She pressed her finger on the image of a pale, long-haired "computer geek." Suddenly I saw how freakish foreigners appeared in this homogeneous, closed society.

They delivered their magazine biographies in front of the room.

Phuvieng drifted to the front and solemnly held up his picture of O. J. Simpson. "His name is Xai. He is twenty-six years old. He has seven children. He is a farmer."

In the next twenty minutes, Elizabeth Hurley became a tour guide, Natalie Merchant a seamstress, and the redheaded technical geek a referee. When they finished, I was suddenly filled with gratitude just to be there. If O. J. could become a farmer in Laos, surely I could teach.

On the board I wrote, "Khamfanh, Kamfan, and Khamfan."

"Please," I said, "can you help me?"

They laughed as I botched their names in a variety of ways, but finally began to hear. My students looked surprised when the hour was up.

"Goodbye, Ajaan." *Ajaan* was teacher in Lao.

The teaching textbooks advised an "ice-breaker"—but breaking glass worked, too. Perhaps the willingness to be a fool was a kind of teaching in itself. Perhaps my students would see in me the pure spark of intention that was the beginner's gift.

The next morning, there was a new vase on the desk, this one blue, with a mess of fuchsia orchids tumbling over the sides.

Kathryn Kefauver is completing her Masters of Fine Arts in Creative Writing at the University of San Francisco. Her work has been published in The Christian Science Monitor, San Francisco Examiner, *and the* South Florida Sun-Sentinel. *She lives in San Francisco.*

* * *

Taken for a Ride

Come on in where it's warm.

"TELL THE TAXI-*WALLAH* TO CROSS THE YUMANA RIVER USING Matura Bridge, *not* any other bridge. After crossing, tell him...." Sujata's rhythmic right, left, right instructions left me dizzy.

"They'll take advantage of you," she continued in her sing-song cadence. "You foreigners don't know taxi drivers like we do."

"Don't worry, Sujata, no one is going to take advantage of me," I said, but that's what I and other foreigners fear daily when we live abroad.

Sujata, a fellow editor at the wire service where we both work, had invited me to dinner with her family. I'm an American who had been living and working in New Delhi for a year, but this would be my first trip across the tea-colored river.

I knew she had legitimate concerns. Taxi and auto rickshaw drivers in New Delhi had devilish reputations. Since first moving to India, I'd heard all the stories of taxi-*wallah* ripoffs: their meters didn't work; their meters were rigged to tick faster than allowed by law; they refused to activate their meters, preferring instead to negotiate outrageous sums before setting off. But their main scam, according to foreigner's urban legend, is to chauffeur wide-eyed tourists around in circles, raking up the miles and money when the destination is just a few rupees ride away. A young German couple once told me that when they first arrived in New Delhi an auto rickshaw-*wallah* offered to take them from the train station to their hotel in the travelers' ghetto Pahar Gang for fifty rupees. They readily agreed, thinking they'd met the only honest driver in Delhi; climbing in to his contraption, they tugged their rucksacks onto their laps. Their driver putted his smoking three-wheeler out of the gravel parking lot and twenty feet across the street, then stopped and announced, "Here is Pahar Gang." No, I was too sharp for this to happen to me, been here too long to be taken for a ride.

"I'll be fine, Sujata."

"You do not understand. It is different coming to the east side of Delhi. Foreigners do not come across the river. Taxi-*wallahs* will know you do not know your way. You must be very careful."

"I'll be careful. I've got your instructions, nothing will go wrong."

As I hung up I wondered if Sujata's fears were for my safety. There were always reports of bad things happening to women in taxis. Her words, her subtle suggestions played in my mind, and deep inside I began steeling myself for what might come.

When it was time to leave for Sujata's house that evening, I wrapped a silk shawl around my shoulders, confirmed I had her directions, and headed for the taxi stand near my home. It was cold and I quickened my pace as I passed my neighbors' homes warm with light and guarded by walls embedded with shards of glass along the top. As I approached a group of taxi-

wallahs huddled around a glowing twig fire, one young man jumped to his feet.

"Yes, madam. This way, madam."

The thin teenager ushered me to a black Ambassador and tugged open a screeching back door. I climbed in. Once slumped inside the leathery womb, smells of damp tobacco and sweat from former passengers assaulted my nose. For a brief moment, I wondered if this was where the driver slept, folding his thin legs to his birdlike chest in a fetal position, letting his heavy eyelids fall shut till dawn. But before I followed the fantasy into his life, I heard both front doors open and looked up to see the driver sliding in behind the wheel while another smaller man eased into the passenger's seat.

"Co-pilot, madam," my driver said, grinning and bobbling his coconut-oiled head.

"Oh, no, tell your friend to get out," I said, Sujata's other warning ringing in my ears, *"Never get into a taxi with two men."*

His face clouded as he looked from me to his friend. The friend sat silent, innocent as a six-year-old, and I felt silly. The two of them together would barely equal my size and weight. What could they do to me?

"O.K. but no funny business," I said.

"Yes, madam. No funny business."

Adopting a low, authoritative *memsahib* tone of voice was one of the first things I learned upon moving to India. I didn't really like it but preferred sounding like a stern maiden than to be seen as a sex maven. It's not that I am sexy or dress provocatively, but I am a tall, blonde Western woman living in a country where men and women are segregated and the men's opinions of foreign women are formed from watching *Baywatch*.

I had planned to dole out Sujata's directions turn-by-turn, but since I couldn't see my notes in Delhi's soot-filled air, I gave the driver her address. As soon as he heard East Delhi he jiggled the stick shift into first and popped our weighty vehicle over the curb. We lurched into traffic with the horn blaring and me sitting rigid in the back while the two men up front navigated in silence.

My suspicions soared immediately. They were too quiet. Why was the co-pilot along if not to chat with the driver? Stories of women being abducted by their drivers while riding in taxis never leave the minds of women traveling alone, and now I thought of all those headlines I'd read. Even though my driver and co-pilot weren't big men, my alertness was imperative. I watched for secret signals or missed turns as we passed street vendors selling *paan*, newspapers, fruit. There were none. I snatched glimpses of Sujata's directions each time we rumbled under one of Delhi's dim yellow street lamps. I found the drive took the exact route Sujata had wanted, rumbling past the zoo, the crumbling red walls of Firoz Shah Kotla, and the formidable *Times of India* news offices. He created no shortcuts of his own, drove without excessive speed, and within twenty minutes stopped in front of my destination.

"Press Apartments," he said, grinning and jerking his head to indicate a row of gray cinder-block buildings.

"Oh! Fine," I said, a little startled by his swiftness, his competence. How could it be this simple, this uneventful? "How much do I owe you?"

He walked to where the ticking meter sat welded on the front fender of the taxi and put his eyes close to the numbers.

"Eighty rupees."

Eighty? Fifty maybe, but eighty rupees? I wondered. Still, I reached into the little purse dangling from my shoulder and pulled out a one hundred rupee note; this is less than $5. He grinned. Big.

"Sorry, madam. No change."

"No change?" Ah, so this was his ruse, to take a fat tip on

top of his inflated meter reading. I wasn't surprised but I wasn't prepared for this old trick either. Delhi's taxi-*wallahs* reputedly never carried change for their passengers. While I'd encountered the situation before, it wasn't limited to foreigners. My former landlord, Mr. K. N. Gupta, used to complain at length about the taxi-*wallahs* lack of change. "They are thieves," he would rumble, shaking his gray head. "They will never admit to having small bills for change."

Now, here was my driver insisting, rather gleefully in my opinion, that he had no change.

O.K., I thought, watching the driver and co-pilot exchange covert glances. This hostage situation required some balance.

"Give me your sweater, please," I said, *memsahib* superiority dripping from my words.

"What, madam?"

"Your sweater. Please, give me your sweater."

A befuddled expression replaced his grin and his wide eyes slid to his partner in crime. I could almost hear the wheels of his brain singing, *Foreign woman wants me to remove my clothes!!!* as he tugged the sweater over his head. The co-pilot remained speechless.

The driver handed me his heavy, crew-neck sweater and I saw that beneath it he wore only a thin t-shirt worn thinner with holes.

I should have seen where things where headed, but I felt sure he had change. I took the sweater and got out of the taxi. I wasn't going to be duped by these clever taxi-*wallahs*.

"When you find the change you owe me, come and get your sweater," I said, shoving the door shut.

I got as far as the iron gate to Sujata's building before hearing the rubber-slapping sound of two men's sandals as they ran up behind me.

"Madam, madam. I need my sweater."

"Yes, madam, he needs his sweater," the co-pilot confirmed, uttering his first words in halting English.

"Yes, and I need my change," I countered. My eagerness to play the *memsahib* should have concerned me, but it didn't.

They looked at each other, and another telepathic message crackled between them. To prove he had no change, the taxi-*wallah* slid his hand into his tight, hip-hugger jeans and pulled out several one hundred rupee notes. Then he turned out his other pockets, proving big bills were all he had.

"Please, madam, no change. You look for change."

I didn't want to believe him, preferring instead to maintain my cynicism. Taxi-*wallahs* have a wealth of hiding places for small change. It's well known. The glove compartments of their cars, little pockets in the door panels, and maybe in this case, the silent co-pilot.

Twenty rupees was an insignificant sum of money to me, but it wasn't the money I was after, it was the upper hand. While in India I'd felt powerless. The locals spoke the language. The shopkeepers sold the goods. The taxi-*wallahs* drove me places. If a local didn't want to talk, he walked away. If a shopkeeper didn't want to sell me something, he turned his back on me. If a taxi-*wallah* didn't want to drive to the part of town I wanted to go, he steered his taxi out into traffic and left me standing on the side of the road. I had no power or control. But not now, now it was my turn.

During my year in the subcontinent my faith in others took a beating, becoming frayed and tattered. Not by big incidents, but rather little ones, like the shopkeeper charging me more than anyone else or the man who pretended not to see me as he stepped in front of me in line. These things wore my patience and darkened my view of humanity so slowly that I didn't see it happening. I'd chosen to view these as slights against me — a foreigner. But the looking glass is two-way, and seeing the skinny driver shiver I wondered who was being taken advantage of. In the black velvet night, I suddenly saw a new truth. He had no change, and I no compassion.

As a child, my brother and I played a game every Christmas that was supposed to teach us compassion for those who had less than we had. My mother had grown up poor and she knew the cruelty of others; her children would have compassion. Pretending to be orphans, we would go outside without our coats and look in at our beautifully decorated pine tree, glimmering with silver tinsel, bejeweled Styrofoam ornaments, and glowing red, white, and green lights. Shivering in the snow, we'd whisper, "Isn't it beautiful. Maybe there is a lady inside who will be kind to us." Then our mother would appear at the door and say, "Oh, you poor children. You have no coats. You must be freezing. Come inside and I'll get you some hot chocolate." And in we would go, stepping back into our privileged lives.

I still had a privileged life, as do most foreigners who can afford to live abroad, while the driver's clearly wasn't. Most likely he came from a village to work in the city, slept in his cab, and owned only the clothes on his back. We foreigners lived in pristine houses with marble floors and had servants clean and cook for us. It's the way things were; not to hire a maid would keep someone unemployed. But our opulence can blind us, making it easy to get caught up in the he-done-me-wrong stories we feed ourselves, losing sight of the truths before us. Ashamed of my behavior, I searched inside for that girl who learned compassion on those long ago winter nights and handed him his sweater.

The driver could have hurled ugly insults or muttered obscenities that I'd tried to cheat him, but he didn't. He smiled and quickly pulled the black, diamond-patterned sweater over his shivering back. I started to slink away, wondering when I'd stopped seeing with my heart and became the one who took advantage, when I heard the taxi-*wallah* call out, "Madam, shall we wait for you?"

Yes, I thought, please wait for me. I've got some changing to do.

Connie Stambush has lived, worked, and traveled in seventeen countries in six years. She lived for four years in India and rode a Royal Enfield Bullet solo around the subcontinent in 1997, even though she'd never ridden a motorcycle before and is currently working on a book about this motorcycle journey. Her work has appeared in Cosmopolitan, Chicago Tribune, Far Eastern Economic Review, *and other publications.*

LAUREN CUTHBERT

* * *

Up Mandalay Hill

In the hands of the Buddha goes the traveler.

WHEN I WAS A CHILD, I WAS FASCINATED BY MAPS, EVEN MORE by the names on the maps.

Antigua, Jakarta, Zanzibar, Shanghai.

Mellifluous, mysterious words, words full of promise, words that beg to be read aloud. They slip off the tongue, as smooth and rich as a fine wine, hanging lightly in the air, a liquid song, seducing first the ear, then the mind.

Bahia, Sahara, Kashmir, Calais.

My grandmother, who lived in India in the 1930s and who traveled by ship from San Francisco to get there, stopping at nearly a dozen ports along the way, encouraged my verbal wanderlust.

For my eighth birthday she bought me a stand-up globe, brightly colored and bumpy with topographical markings. I spent hours spinning it round and round, my index finger lightly pressed against the plastic so that the Himalayas, the Andes, the Rocky Mountains massaged the tip as they whirled by. Once the orb slowed to a halt, I'd lift my finger and pronounce the name of whatever lay below—spinning again if I landed on water or someplace I already knew—twisting my tongue around the unfamiliar, tasting the sounds.

Madagascar, Mykonos, Sofia, Versailles.

But the name that called out to me most, soft poetry in its voice, was Mandalay. I loved the feel of the word as much as its lyrical sound, the way it rolled along my tongue, languid and delicious.

Looking at Mandalay on the globe, set smack dab in the middle of upper Burma, I determined to visit one day. And I knew, as only an eight-year-old can know such things, that I would love it.

But when I finally got to Mandalay, some twenty years later, I did not love it at all.

The country's second largest city, Mandalay was the site of the last royal capital before the British colonized Burma—now called Myanmar by its military government—in 1885. Today it remains the nation's cultural center, the most "Burmese" of cities.

When I arrived, however, culture was the last thing on my mind. Much of my body was covered with the red, itchy rash of prickly heat (the result of four glorious but baking-hot days cycling the pagoda-speckled plain of ancient Pagan) and I cared only about finding an air-conditioned hotel. There is little treatment for prickly heat beyond transfer to a cool climate. In mid-July, Mandalay, sprawled across the dusty region of the upper Irrawaddy River, is anything but cool.

Worse, by the time I collected my bag from the airport tarmac and headed out to find a taxi, there were none left. Unlike the other tourists on the flight from Pagan to Mandalay, all of whom were met by officials of Myanmar Travels and Tours, the government tourist agency, I was traveling independently—not the easiest way to get around.

I approached one of the airport officials. Where could I find a taxi?

"No taxis," he said. "They are all taking tourists to their hotels."

Would they return to the airport when they were done? He shook his head no; they would not return again until the following day.

He suggested I hail a passing bus. "Maybe one will take you to your hotel."

I stood under the blazing noon sun along the dusty road outside the airport, my backpack slumped against the trunk of a withered palm tree. I saw nothing that looked like a bus, only modified vans, belching smoke and heavy with human cargo. People stared as they passed. A trail of sweat inched down my back. My rash burned an angrier shade of red.

Soon enough, curiosity got the better of two pedestrians. They wandered over and one of the men spoke to me in Burmese. I pulled out my map and pointed to the location of the Mandalay Hotel, my best bet, I'd been told, for air conditioning. The man motioned back toward the airport.

"Taxi," he said, smiling heartily. I shook my head no.

The two conferred a moment. Then, with another big smile, the man stepped out into the street and flagged down one of the passing vans.

It was crammed well beyond capacity, easily one of the most crowded I'd seen. People hung off the back. They spilled from the sides. Five or six men were balanced on the roof, fingers wrapped around frayed ropes tied to the side of the truck.

The man consulted with the driver. He, in turn, stuck his head out of the window and called out to the back of the truck. A loud chorus ensued. Suddenly a shaved head popped out from the rear of the vehicle.

"Where you go?" asked the monk, in broken but definite

English. I told him. He yelled to the driver. The driver yelled back. More deliberation. Finally the monk turned to me again, waving a bare, tattooed arm.

"Come," he said. "The driver will take you."

Given the discussion that had greeted my answer, I very much doubted that the hotel was on the regular route, but I wasn't about to argue. A man standing on the pavement grabbed my pack and threw it onto the top of the truck. I headed for the back of the truck but was waved away and ushered to the cab. One of the three men seated there hopped out and clambered up onto the roof. With much grinding and clanking, we set off.

Twenty minutes later, the truck pulled up outside my hotel. I paid what seemed a paltry sum for door-to-door service and checked in. After a cold shower—generally the only kind in Burma, though in my case it was welcome—I set out to see the city.

I toured the remains of the reconstructed Royal Palace, which burned to the ground in 1945 when British troops bombarded the fortress, then held by the Japanese. I admired the Shwenandaw Monastery, part of the old Palace complex, and one of the few original wooden buildings still standing. I visited the Mahamuni Pagoda, Mandalay's most important religious structure, and watched the faithful paste tissue-paper-thin strips of gold leaf to the twelve-foot-high Buddha housed within, adding to the two-inch-thick layer that already coated the image.

Midway through the second day, however, I gave up. Despite the many sights left to see, my fiery skin dictated leaving for a cooler locale. The next morning, I decided, I would do as the colonial British had done and escape to the old hill station of Maymyo, set high in the foothills of the Shan Plateau.

So, as the afternoon drew to a close, I headed toward

Mandalay Hill, the city's most famous attraction. It was from the top of the hill that the Buddha was said to have prophesied that a great city would be founded below. It is also the only site offering a wide-angle view over the otherwise pancake-flat terrain.

Climbing almost 775 feet above the surrounding plain, Mandalay Hill is cut by covered stairways, each with numerous small temples scattered along the path. Under the stern gaze of the carved white *chinthes*—talisman griffins that guard all temples, ensuring, among other things, that visitors remove their shoes before entering sacred ground—I slipped off my sandals and headed for the stairs. Seated on a stone bench at the base of the path was a lone, saffron-robed monk. He stood as I started up the stone stairway and fell into step beside me.

After ten days in Burma, I was used to uninvited company. The country is not often included on the itinerary of travelers to Southeast Asia; those who do visit attract considerable attention. As a woman traveling alone, I attracted even more.

This time, however, I preferred to walk by myself. I increased my pace. Without seeming to hurry, my companion matched my step. I gradually fell back. So did he. I stopped, pretending to retrieve something from my bag. He stopped, too, and waited, still as a photograph, a few steps above.

At this, I looked at the monk more closely. He was tall and gaunt, with sunken cheeks and deep-set eyes. His shaved skull showed the shadow of a few days' growth, his face recorded only a few lines and no furrows. He could have been thirty, he could have been fifty. Black tattoos adorned his hands and arms, which were bone-thin and strong. A snake curled across the back of his left hand; a five-point star, pierced by two arrows, hung in the smooth underside of his forearm; a band of small dots ringed each wrist like two narrow bracelets.

Something about those tattoos struck me as familiar. I

looked again at the narrow face, looked into the quiet Burmese eyes. With a start, I realized he was my savior from the day before. I smiled sheepishly. The monk grinned back in forgiveness, displaying a gap-toothed smile stained betel-nut red. Such smiles are common throughout Burma, the result of chewing the copper-colored nut, which is said to evoke a mild sense of euphoria.

"I walk Mandalay Hill every day," he explained, in answer to my unspoken question. "I knew you come one day. All visitors watch the sun go down from Mandalay Hill."

Despite the 1,729 steps, the half-mile walk to the top of Mandalay Hill is not difficult. A wood roof shading the open-air stairway keeps the stone path cool. The monk maintained an unhurried, even pace, taking the smaller steps two at a time. Every so often, without slowing, he would place a plug of betel in his mouth, chew a while, then spit the red juice off to the side.

We climbed in silence, past the souvenir vendors and palm readers stationed along the path, past old women resting on stone benches, chomping on fat, green cheroots. Midway up the hill, the monk halted at a large temple and motioned me inside. Inside were the so-called "Peshawar Relics," three bones of the Buddha.

Though the relics housed within may actually be real, they receive little attention from the Buddhist faithful. Much more venerated, for some reason, are the countless (and often suspect) Buddha hairs and Buddha teeth scattered throughout the world. Save for one small, grizzled man bowed low before the shrine, we were the only visitors to the temple.

Near the top of the hill we stopped once again, this time alongside a statue of a woman kneeling before the Buddha, offering him her severed breasts. Legend holds that the woman was once a terrible ogress who, upon hearing the words of the Enlightened One, was so overwhelmed that she immediately changed her ways and devoted the rest of her life to following his teachings. As a symbol of her devotion, she sliced off her breasts.

The view from the top of Mandalay Hill extends far across the Irrawaddy plain, its flat surface and occasional jutting hill studded with the gold and white spires of pagodas and temples. In the waning light of late afternoon, they glittered like jewels lain across the throat of a beautiful woman. To the north stretched the rice paddies of the upper Irrawaddy. Spread out to the south was the golden city for which the hill is named, dominated by the enormous palace fortress. To the east, toward China, rose the purple outline of the Shan Plateau. To the west flowed the Irrawaddy River, its slow-moving waters framed by the gleaming hills opposite.

We sat down, my monk friend and I, to watch the sun set over the river. Since monks in Burma are forbidden to take anything directly from the hand of a woman, I placed my notebook and pen on the bench between us and asked him to write out his name for me. He did, neatly filling the right-hand corner of a page in my journal with the charming bubbles that make up Burmese script. Opposite, I penned its phonetic translation: Oo Te Tee La. We watched as the butter-dipped sun dropped low in the sky, watched as it slipped behind the thin clouds stretched across the horizon. Its angled rays painted the sky—first lavender, then peach—before melting into the pink waters of the Irrawaddy. As the last glow of day headed into night, the monk stood to go. He raised his hands palm-to-palm beneath his chin and bowed slightly. "Good-bye, Lo Ren," he said. "I hope you come again to Mandalay."

He turned and walked away, back toward the stairs we had so recently climbed together. I watched his angular form disappear from sight. Yes, I thought. I will come again to Mandalay.

Lauren Cuthbert turned three in Japan, four in Las Vegas, nine in Mexico, and sixteen in Spain. Thereafter, she determined to spend as many birthdays as possible on the road. She was a reporter for the South China Morning Post *and her travel stories have appeared in numerous publications, including the* San Francisco Examiner, Atlanta Journal-Constitution, *and* Fort Lauderdale Sun-Sentinel. *She was both a contributor to and publishing partner of* Wild Writing Women: Stories of World Travel, *where this piece first appeared. She lives with her family in Northern California and still dreams of returning to Mandalay.*

TARA AUSTEN WEAVER

✦

Cycling Shikoku

An island pilgrimage yields wisdom and insight.

THE SLOW BOAT FOR SHIKOKU DEPARTS HIROSHIMA AT EIGHT A.M. Early one cloudy May morning, my cycling companion and I carefully wheel our heavily loaded mountain bikes onto the lower deck of the small, rusty ferry. Tent poles and sleeping mats sprout from the side-bags of our bicycles, rain jackets are strapped to the rear. Our plan is to spend ten days riding the salty ups and downs of the Shikoku coastal route, a much-needed break from everyday work and life in Japan.

Shikoku is a mystical place, a large island just off the coast of the Japanese mainland. It is mere miles from the skyscrapers and pulsating, technology-fueled nightlife of Osaka, but in all other ways Shikoku is a universe apart. In an increasingly modern and mechanized country, Shikoku is an island that has remained as it was. Dense foliage blankets the island's steep hills, shadowing thatch-roofed farmhouses and terraced rice paddies, and in weather-battered fishing villages clinging to the coast, old men continue to eke out a meager existence from the sea.

Boarding the ferry this morning I feel as if I am escaping. The spring has been hard. Recent staff transfers in the Japanese office where I work have thrust me into a job I am neither trained nor qualified for. I try to *gaman*—to persevere—as is the Japanese way and work hard to make up for the deficiencies, but I am worn to the breaking point from constant failure and lack of sleep. Shortly before leaving for Shikoku, I receive a letter from my best friend. Standing in the small, cramped entryway of my apartment I hungrily read the letter and her words—so kind and comfortable—bring me to tears. What am I doing here, I wonder, so far from those I care about?

Three years of living in Japan has caused all the edges of my life to blur. From the beginning I wanted to experience the country and culture as deeply as possible—to become part of it. I didn't want to leave Japan laden with photographs of festivals but with no real understanding of the why behind the culture. If Japan is an enigma, as is often said, I wanted to get as close as possible to its enigmatic heart.

In my attempt to become part of Japan, I seem to have lost part of myself. Three years of living here have gifted me with insight into the Japanese way of doing things. By birth and upbringing I understand the *gaijin*—the Western—way, but I no longer know where I belong. I now fall somewhere between the two extremes, a place where there are no clear rules. My manner of dress, body language, and sense of humor have all been toned-down in order to render them understandable and acceptable to my Japanese colleagues and friends. The end result leaves me feeling like a pale, washed-out version of who I really am.

A week before the planned trip I come down with a *kaze*— a virulent Japanese cold. Feverish and coughing up small pieces of what feels like my lung, I consider staying home to use this precious time to rest and recuperate. I quickly reject

the idea. I need to go, I need to get away. The word *escape*
frequently crosses my mind; I am escaping to the island
of Shikoku.

Most visitors to Shikoku are pilgrims who come to walk
the eighty-eight temple circuit established in the year 880 by
Kobo Daishi, the founder of Shingon Buddhism. The pilgrims
circle the 1,000-kilometer course in hope of gaining inner
peace and karmic merit. Some pilgrims leave their jobs and
families to complete the two-month pilgrimage, others take a
few days each year covering as much distance as possible in
time stolen away from commitments and careers.

Pilgrims are far from my mind this May morning. As our
boat draws near, the island emerges out of the mist: emerald
green mountains rising from clear waters. The mountains are
impossibly steep, like ancient scroll paintings of rocky cliffs
studded with pine branches in an Asian art museum. I had
always thought the steepness an artistic device.

The mountains become my challenge. The side-bags on my
bike weigh heavily as I slowly pedal up near-vertical inclines.
The hills never seem to end. I'm coughing badly and breathing is difficult. Every mountain pushes me further than I
comfortably want to go. I consider turning around, going
home, but the idea of re-climbing the mountains already
climbed is heartbreaking. I decide life must be lived in the
forward direction, at whatever speed I am capable of.

While every incline tests me, I am rewarded and the payoff
is worth the struggle. To stop pushing, to simply coast down
thrilling, spiraling hills from summit to sea, wind streaming
past my face and tugging my hair out from beneath my helmet
is perhaps as close as I will ever get to the joy of natural flight.
I feel like a bird, like a child on a swing set with the world
rushing up to meet me. I shout out my joy to the empty green
canyons and it echoes back at me and all around.

I am riding back through time to a Japan unknown to the children of today living in cement apartment blocks in the urban sprawl. I cycle through misty, jungle-like ravines, past terraced rice paddies aflock with white cranes, and hillsides covered with blooming orange trees, their heady perfume overwhelming the senses. At night we camp on deserted beaches, the sound of waves invading our dreams and wake to the noise of villagers on their way to harvest seaweed from the rocky shore. I am struck by the beauty of this ancient life and reminded of why I was drawn here.

Sticking to the coast we pedal our way through towns bypassed by the speedy new highway. It is May and the tiny villages where we buy food are festooned with colorful carp banners hung to celebrate the upcoming Children's Day holiday. The bright, fish-shaped flags dance merrily on the ocean breeze, the only visible movement in many of these faded, sleeping towns. We ride past local festivals and through a blessing ceremony for a new house. The Shinto priest and members of the family throw pieces of celebratory *mochi* to the villagers assembled in the street below. Wrapped in brightly-colored kitchen towels, the balls of *mochi* go sailing by on the spring breeze, only to be snatched up by the wrinkled hands of the practical *oba-chans*, the village grandmothers. Once they see us, we are inundated by offers of these colorful parcels. Uncooked, the *mochi* tastes like glue and sticks to our teeth. We tell them it is delicious and they laugh, delighted.

The unlikely sight of two foreigners on bicycles livens up most places we pass through and we become the center of attention wherever we stop. Where are we going? Where are we from? Where will we sleep tonight? We answer their questions, doing our best to wade through the unfamiliar local dialect, and in return they give us gifts of food for our travels. We receive so many oranges, the local specialty, that by the third day we are forcing them down and swearing off all citrus fruit for months to come.

The kindness of the local people is touching. One night it begins to rain and, when the locals in the public bathhouse where we've gone to bathe, discover we are planning to camp, a playful argument erupts over who will get to take the foreigners home. Not wanting to impose, we ask the owner of the bathhouse if we may pitch our tent in the covered parking area after the baths are closed. Instead she takes us to a small shed built on the roof of the bathhouse. It is filled with tatami and evidence of a late-night card game, but it is dry and comfortable. In the morning we offer her money, but she refuses. Other pilgrims have stayed there before, she says.

The pilgrims are always with us. Carrying wooden walking sticks, and dressed in traditional white clothing and pointy straw hats, they plod along the pilgrimage course. We exchange greetings of "*ganbatte*" (do your best) when we pass them on our bikes. In ancient temples along the route, their chanting blends with the scent of burning incense and wafts by on the wind. What lives have they left behind them, I wonder, and what they are searching for?

Days spent on the bike leave me with time for thinking. Realizations dawn slowly, the result of hours of uninterrupted cycle meditation. While never a disciple, like all travelers I too am searching; however, it is not karma I hope to gain. Through my travels and my life in Japan I am searching for new horizons and challenges. I want to push myself beyond what is comfortable—both mentally and physically—in order to test my own spirit. I want to discover myself: my boundaries, strengths, and weaknesses. It is not the succeeding lifetimes that concern me, I want to fully experience the present and to discover new vistas, not only around me, but within me as well.

Shikoku is the answer I seek. Amidst early morning climbs

up steep ravines and adrenaline-filled, late afternoon sprints along a rocky coastline, I find my stride. Sweat-stained and dirty with bike-chain grease decorating my calves and sore from days riding and nights sleeping on the ground, I am happier than I have been in months. The mountains—along the road and in my life—no longer seem overwhelming, and I am excited about the surprises that lie around the next curve. I lose the feeling of being lost between two worlds. I am not lost, I am simply in a place I have never been before.

One morning late in the trip, I slip outside the tent to watch the sun rise. Sitting on a sandy beach, so like the beaches of my childhood, I look past the small, offshore islands cloaked in mist and across the ocean towards the country that is my home. Soon I will return to my job and the small apartment that is home for the moment. My job will not have changed. I will still be faced with the challenge of balancing who I am with what is acceptable and appropriate in this traditional society. However, Shikoku has left me with a clarity of vision and a sense of self I had not known before. I am a bridge connecting two worlds—one the world of my birth and another, more ancient world I have sought to understand and come to love. I may always feel this conflict, this fear of losing what I was, but I am compensated by the process of learning another way of being. I will never fit entirely in either world, but I have the gift of being able to connect the two and find parts of myself in each.

The sun begins to break through the mist and glints off calm waters. I fill my hands with the sand of Shikoku and watch as the grains slip slowly through my fingers. The early morning sunlight begins to warm me and I realize what I had thought of as an escape was really a search. As the Japanese dawn breaks in all its fiery brilliance, I realize I too have been on a pilgrimage and, like the pilgrims of Shikoku, I have found the peace and knowledge I was looking for.

Tara Austen Weaver is a San Francisco-based writer and editor specializing in travel, cultural issues, and adventure sports. She is the coeditor of two Travelers' Tales anthologies, Tuscany *and* Provence, *and lead author for the guidebook* Art/Shop/Eat San Francisco. *She has lived in four countries on three continents, including five years spent in the mountains of central Japan, and likes to cycle whenever and wherever possible.*

JENNICA PETERSON

⋆ ⋆ ⋆

Bathing with Elephants

Asia both toughens and softens your skin.

THE SAPPHIRE WINGS OF A KINGFISHER CUT ACROSS THE SKY, then folded as the bird dove into the brown waters of the Rapti River. In these 100-degree temperatures, I also wanted to dive from my position on top of an elephant into cool water.

I was sitting in a corner of a wooden box-shaped frame that was strapped unevenly to the elephant's back, my legs draped over onto its shoulder. My boyfriend, Mike, provided my only back support. The sharp edges of our crude carriage dug into my thighs and ribs as we lumbered across the river and headed to the grasslands to search for one of the most famous residents of Nepal's Chitwan National Park—the greater Asian one-horned rhinoceros. As we leaned left, then right, then left, with each giant step, I was reminded of my first boat trip on the ocean and how I tried to overcome my nausea by catching the ocean's elusive rhythm. Now I was trying to understand a completely different rhythm, not only that of the elephant, but that of this totally foreign part of the world and my place in it.

During the past week and a half of my first trip to India and

Nepal, my appearance as a tall, blond, American woman made it clear that I didn't belong. Finding commonalities with the locals normally delighted me on my travels. On this trip, I felt a need to create physical and emotional space between those around me and myself. Now as I searched the thick grasslands for a rhino, I knew I was looking for an armor-like hide not unlike the one I had formed around my heart.

Our trip had begun in Kolkata (formerly Calcutta), India. As soon as we exited the airport, a stout man with greasy black hair approached and offered his services. We quickly bargained and followed him past a row of polished yellow-and-black cars that seemed transported from the fifties. I wasn't expecting such style for my ride into town, nor was I expecting the lingering fingers of the taxi driver as he brushed past me. It was one of those touches that might have been accidental, but my inner radar told me it wasn't. I didn't say anything, not ready for a confrontation in my first five minutes out of the airport.

During the ride into town, I stared out the window, entranced by the images that flew by: naked boys playing under the gush of a broken fire hydrant; women covered in sheer cloth the colors of desert flowers standing next to businessmen in black suits and shiny shoes; skinny cows wandering the dirt streets in a daze; juice carts, fruit carts, milk carts, meat carts; scenes that I had never seen or imagined growing up in Nebraska.

Our taxi dropped us off in the middle of the tourist section of the city. Trash littered the street and hotel signs cluttered the sides of the buildings. The air smelled like spoiled milk and overripe fruit. Taxis raced by, horns honking at everything and nothing.

As we entered hotel after hotel, searching for a place to sleep that didn't look like a prison cell, I noticed the strange way the men looked at me. It wasn't like they saw *me*, just my chest. It was as though they could see right through my high-necked loose shirt. I wished I had something extra to wrap around me, even though I was dripping with perspiration. I quickly understood the practical nature of the women's saris that cover the body and then cover it again. I put on my darkest sunglasses so I wouldn't have to worry about returning the men's stares. I walked in front of Mike so I wouldn't be groped from behind. Finally, I slid my pearl ring off my third finger and onto my fourth. I was temporarily eloping from all of the feminist ideals I had been raised with that told me I didn't need a man to protect me, that I belonged to no one. I knew from the blatant stares that I had better belong with another man, or I would be considered unclaimed property.

The next night we headed to the train station bound for the cooler tea-covered hills of Darjeeling. We bought folding wooden fans at the terminal since we had unwisely planned our trip during India's hottest season. Spaghetti straps and shorts were called for, but I tried to completely cover my body like every Indian woman I saw. I soon realized the fan doubled as a shield between my chest and the ogling eyes of the men studying it. Happy with my new tool, I fluttered it under my face like an overheated geisha.

We baked inside the train until it began to chug north through the Indian night. Mike and I had seats across from each other that would later fold into a set of bunk beds. I heard the universal whoop of a salesman and a jangle like Dickens' Ghost of Christmas Past from the next car down. We had wanted to buy a chain and lock for our baggage, and purchased a set at the first price offered by the salesman—$1. It surprised me that these items would be sold so casually, with the overt purpose of protecting luggage while sleeping. That unguarded property was anyone's property was a matter of fact. I wondered how to guard my own body from harassment while I slept.

Mike came up with the idea of hiding me behind the multi-purpose sarong I carried in my backpack. Even though it had only cooled to around 90 degrees Fahrenheit, and the cloth would block the air from the overhead fan, I relished the idea of being hidden from intruding eyes and hands. An Indian man in a collared shirt and pressed slacks nodded when Mike began to clip the sarong to the bed frame with clothespins. He looked me over and told us in English that this was smart. I chained my luggage to a pole, then lay down on my top bunk while the man I love and one I didn't know pinned the fabric around me until I could no longer see their faces. I welcomed the barrier between me and the rest of the world, and slept unbothered behind my curtain.

The next day we bought two seats on a shared jeep for the final three-hour ride from New Jalpaiguri up the mountain roads to Darjeeling. We waited in the stuffy cargo area for half an hour for the jeep to fill with passengers. We needed just one more, but the driver wouldn't leave until all the seats were taken. There were already six adults in the front two seats; the final person would have to bend yoga-like to sit beside Mike and me. Finally, the doting husband of a woman wearing designer sunglasses and at least forty sparkling bracelets suggested that every passenger contribute ten rupees to pay for the missing passenger so we could leave. After arguing with our fast-talking, beady-eyed driver, the deal was made. Mike and I would have a small amount of "extra space," even though we were both already hunched over and looking for somewhere to stretch our legs.

This "extra space" seemed to weigh on the driver's mind as we rode farther and farther up the mountain and the road narrowed. He kept glancing back at us with an annoyed look as though we were keeping him from earning his full share for the day. He took out his frustration by speeding up as we reached switchback turns and pounding to a stop when we rounded a corner to face another vehicle. He would play "chicken," forcing oncoming cars to pull over to the very edge of the now one-lane road. Finally, the desire to fill that extra space conquered our driver; he pulled over quickly, striking a fast deal with three sari-clad women. Before I had time to protest, I found myself forced to put my arms around and overlap legs with the new passengers like old friends.

The driver dropped the women off in the next village, and we were able to spread out again. By this time, Mike had become pale and sweaty with motion sickness and had laid his head down on my lap. Then I saw two men flagging our driver from the road ahead. The jeep pulled over, but I pushed the lock switch down. "No more," I said with a shaky voice. "We paid for this extra space." One of the men from outside the car tried the door, but couldn't get in. I looked in his eyes and shook my head, angry—not at him, but at everyone since the driver at the Kolkata airport who had invaded my space, my body, and my sanity. The fortitude it took to lock that door also cemented a bitter wall inside of me that protected my deepest self from the ongoing intrusions, but kept the beauty and significance of all that I saw from coming in.

I spent the next week in Darjeeling sick with a cold, longing to go home. Instead, we decided to leave the crowded cities of India for rural Nepal, booking our elephant safari in Chitwan National Park.

After two hours of sailing above the grasslands on our gray, four-legged vessel, my attempts to anticipate the elephant's rhythm had earned me only bruises on my chest and thighs from rubbing against our carriage. My face burned from sun and sweat. The elephant kept stopping to sweep in bushel-sized mouthfuls of grass with its trunk. We told our guide we were ready to return to our lodge, rhino-less.

As we started back, the guide spotted a break in the grass in the distance. He shouted at our elephant, gave him several hard kicks behind the ears, and hit his bristly forehead with a stick. The elephant began to run towards our target, a female rhino and her calf. We bounced along uneasily, trying to grab our cameras, pointing and shouting in excitement. As we approached, the mother ushered her baby away from us and disappeared into taller grass. After looking for my own ways to hide for the past week and a half, I didn't blame her.

Following the hour-long ride back, Mike was tired and ready for a nap. I was, too, but I didn't want to miss seeing the elephants get their daily bath as our guidebook described. I would have to go down to the river by myself.

I sat down on the riverbank to watch the safari elephants get scrubbed down by their lifelong caretakers, or *mahout*s. A sinewy Nepali man straddling an elephant's back called from the river.

"Come help!"

I looked around, not believing that his invitation could be directed at me. I was alone on the riverbank. The *mahout* called again and nodded his head when I pointed to myself. I shook my head no, wary of joining the men in the water, but my stomach lurched as I realized how much I wanted to do this. I felt like a child at the circus who gets called down out of the audience to take part in an act. How could I miss this opportunity? When the *mahout* waved to me once more and smiled, my gut told me he had only good intentions. I took off my shoes, then waded off through the strong current past one towering elephant to another with pale pink freckles on her ears and trunk.

I didn't know how to bathe an elephant, and half expected the *mahout* to hand me a gigantic bottle of bubble bath.

Instead, he slid off the elephant's back into the water and then shouted a command. I stepped away nervously as the massive creature rolled onto her side so that only her round belly and the side of her head stuck out of the water like boulders. Bubbles poured to the surface from the trunk below. The *mahout* pointed at me and the elephant's stomach and gestured that he wanted me to climb on top. Unsure of how to accomplish this unusual task, I stood on my toes and reached as far as I could over the wet, loose skin of the belly. Then the *mahout* boosted me up so that I could swing one leg over and sit up. Suddenly, I heard another loud command, and the elephant slowly stood up, forcing me to reposition myself so that I was now straddling the elephant's back. I scooted up to the bridge of the neck, and leaned over to lay my head on top of the unlikely pillow of the elephant's skull. I felt tenderness towards this enormous animal who allowed me to rest on her neck while she continued to splash water on her legs and sides. She seemed to be enjoying herself, and didn't notice my weight.

The *mahout* shouted again, and the elephant shook her head fiercely from side to side. I tried to hold on, but couldn't get my hands all the way around the neck. I screamed as I fell down into the river. I fought against the current that pushed me towards the elephant's unpredictable legs, and swallowed a mouthful of the polluted water. When I was finally able to stand up, gasping for air, I found the *mahout* laughing and shouting at the other men about what had happened. My distrust raced back. Had this been a mistake? The *mahout* turned and looked at me straight in the eyes.

"Are you O.K.?" he asked softly.

I stared at him for a moment, weighing his behaviour against my experiences with other men on this trip. He continued to look only at my face, not at the rest of my body. His eyes shone with kindness. His wide, bright smile was innocent and reassuring. My initial intuition had been right—this man meant no harm.

"Yes, I'm fine," I said, and relaxed into my recovered trust.

"Again! Again!" he said.

"O.K.," I agreed. I was laughing, too. I now understood that my elephant bathing experience would have nothing to do with cleaning an elephant.

Over and over the *mahout* repeated his trick of having me mount the elephant, then commanding her to shake me off. Each time I tried to hold on longer, like a rodeo star. When I eventually fell, I would struggle to stand up with the *mahout's* help, and then laugh as he did when I broke the river's surface, happy to be breathing and alive. Every time I climbed back up the tough hide of the elephant, some of my internal hide loosened and fell away as I tumbled off into the water.

"Now try Nepali style," said the *mahout*, ready for some new amusement. He led me to the front of the elephant and told me to grab the ears.

I stood waist high in the muddy water of the river and took hold of the elephant's rubbery earlobes, one in each hand. In front of me dangled the trunk between a pair of surprisingly small, soft, gentle eyes with plumes of lashes. The *mahout* stood to my left and smiled in encouragement.

"Yes! Put your knee there," he said, and pointed to the middle of the trunk.

Before I could back out of the *mahout's* plan to have me mount the elephant the "real Nepali way," the *mahout* lifted me so I had to put my knee somewhere or fall back into the river on top of him. The elephant's long earlobes stretched with my weight, and then the trunk raised to support me. After one sharp command that sounded like, "Hut!" the elephant lifted me high above the water, pushing me up, up toward the sky.

In that moment, I forgot that I was a tall, blond, American

woman surrounded by short, dark-haired, Nepali men who trained elephants for a living. I forgot about concealing my body and keeping people out of my personal space. Outside of any place I had ever known, doing something I had never imagined I would do, I forgot that I didn't belong. I only knew that I was completely alive, soaking wet, and suspended in mid-air by the strength of an elephant's trunk above a wide river somewhere far from home.

Since she left Nebraska ten years ago, Jennica Peterson has traveled to thirty countries, worked in three national parks, and moved eighteen times. Currently she is an intern at VIA *magazine and is working toward a full-time career in writing and editing. She lives in Oakland, California with her husband, Mike.*

JAN MORRIS

* * *

Archipelago

Go to the islands for a taste of Old China.

HONG KONG INHABITS SEVERAL WORLDS. IT IS PART OF THE immense and incalculable Chinese world. It is a glittering outstation in the world of high finance. It is a prodigy of the Orient and a late anachronism of Empire. But it is also the center of a world that is all its own, consisting of 235 tightly grouped and variously fascinating offshore islands.

The chief of them is, of course, the island of Hong Kong itself, Asia's Manhattan, one of the most celebrated and astonishing of all the islands of the earth. But when in 1898, the British leased from the Chinese a slab of mainland to act as a *cordon sanitaire* for their island colony, they acquired at the same time the whole adjacent archipelago spilling through some 400 square miles of the South China Sea. Most of its islands are infinitesimal; one, Lantau, is bigger than Hong Kong itself. Some had immemorial histories, some were known only as pirate hideouts, and others had never been inhabited at all.

From the top of Victoria Peak, the crowning summit of Hong Kong island, where the financiers and the mandarins of government look down from their villas upon the splendid city-state below—from up there you may see the archipelago spread in the sea around you. Especially in the evening it is a wonderfully suggestive sight. Humped or supine in the setting sun, the islands seem to lie bewitched along the dim blue coast of China; and as the skyscrapers burst into blazing neon at the foot of the hill, and the riding lights twinkle from the hundreds of ships at their moorings in the harbor, sometimes it seems that those ethereal places out at sea, so silent against the blush of the evening, are not really there at all.

But they are, and one of the more seductive distractions of Eastern travel is to go a-sailing through the particular small world of the Hong Kong archipelago.

Swoosh! With an arrogant rumble of engines and a plume of spray the hydrofoil leaves the pier, on the waterfront of Hong Kong's financial district, in a wide, wide sweep for the islands of the west. Every kind of vessel plies between the islands of Hong Kong. A fleet of sensible ferries plods regular as clockwork between the main ports of the archipelago. An armada of homely *sampans* links the lesser islands, chugging up shallow creeks, calling at out-of-the-way settlements, with mother at the helm as likely as not, father down in the greasy engine room, and small children contentedly pottering, in the Chinese way, in and out of the wheelhouse.

There are sundry launches, too, and small shambled craft called *walla-wallas*, and posh motorized junks flying the flags of the great merchant houses, which take the rich, both Chinese and European, sybaritically toward distant pleasure places. And through them all from time to time, weaving a passage among the massed ranks of merchant men, one of those thundering hydrofoils launches itself spectacularly toward the outer islands.

The island waterways, then, are in a constant state of motion, edging toward congestion. You are never traveling alone—always, wherever you are sailing, a distant *sampan* is traveling in the same direction, a tug is towing a sluggish string of barges, a customs launch is watching, pacing you, or a group of country boats, piled high with nets, crates, dogs, pigs in conical wire baskets, and complacent old ladies in wide straw hats, is racing you to the harbor.

Yet when you disembark you may discover among the islands, just as that prospect from the Peak suggested, places of magical serenity. Of course development threatens all of them—nowhere in Hong Kong can be immune to progress and profit. Even so, most of the islands are uninhabited, mere protrusions of shingle, sand, and coarse grass unvisited from one year to the next except by picnicking weekend sailors. On others only a few fisher-families live huggermugger in their huts. Even on the bigger, well-frequented islands, a few short miles from the Peak and the skyscrapers, there remain unexpected expanses of open country—the nearest thing to pristine countryside left within the ferociously crowded limits of Hong Kong.

On the island of Lamma, for instance, half an hour in a *sampan* from Hong Kong island, there are wide tracts of green moorland, wind-swept and tangy above the sea. It is true that in the northwest the chimneys of a power station grimly protrude above the skyline, but there are only two small villages on the island, there are no cars, all is still and quiet, and the hill tracks that alone connect Yung Shue Wan at one end with Sok Kwu Wan at the other wind their way through landscapes almost Scottish in their exhilarating emptiness.

Better still is Lantau. This is the largest of all the islands, some fifteen miles from end to end—twice as big as Hong Kong itself, but with perhaps one-sixtieth of its population. Holiday villages and retreats for the bourgeoisie are sprouting on the coast of Lantau, but inland you may find yourself in proper mountain country, wild feeling even now, with few roads, fewer villages, and a grand sensation of space and liberty (though as it happens several of Hong Kong's penal institutions are ironically sited here). There is pony-trekking on Lantau. There is fine hill walking—well over the 3,000-foot mark. And in the wet, when these highlands are shrouded in damp white mist and the foliage shines with warm moisture and the boggy ground squelches beneath your feet, a proper sense of wilderness informs the place, and makes you feel you are a thousand miles from the nearest computer printout or the latest financial index, somewhere altogether indeterminate among the China Seas.

Over some of the islands an evocative air of antiquity impends. Nobody knows for sure who first lived in this archipelago, or what forgotten tribespeople carved the patterns to be seen here and there on rock faces and cavern walls. But even the recorded history of the islands is long enough, and often you may be reminded that long, long before the British reached these parts, a great civilization held sway here and quite another stately empire flew its flags.

Ceaselessly, all through the day, an elderly ferry, manually propelled, crosses and recrosses the saltwater creek at Tai O, on the western coast of Lantau. No cars enter the village, which straddles the waterway, so that life revolves around the navigations of that humble craft, backward and forward, backward and forward down the centuries, setting the pace of everything and dominating the style.

In this as in much else, Tai O is the very picture of a traditional Chinese settlement. Except perhaps in remoter parts of Taiwan, there are probably no other villages anywhere so redolent of the immemorial Chinese past. Tai O lives entirely from the sea, and its society is pungently amphibious—fishing boats moored in apparently inextricable confusion along that creek, houses projecting on wobbly stilts over the water, strong fishy smells wherever you go. In the morning the village streets are loud with the doings of open-air markets, in the afternoon they echo to the clack of *maj-jongg* counters from shady living rooms; everywhere joss sticks burn in small domestic shrines, and arthritic figures disappear into the recesses of wayside temples.

It is like China in a novel, China in somebody's memoirs; and in many another part of the archipelago, too, you may feel that here, and perhaps here alone, a tremendous culture is tenuously defying the passing of time and ideology. Scattered through the islands are settlements of fishing people, Tankas and Hoklos from southern China, with their intricately fretted and tangled *sampans*, their jumbled houses, their sweet, simple shrines to Tin Hau, goddess of the sea; and occasionally you may see gliding past a headland a genuine engineless sailing junk, its patched, thin sails ribbed like the skin of some ancient bird and its helmsman lolling at the tiller precisely as his forebears must have lolled through these seas for a couple of thousand years.

Though many a young person leaves the islands for more exciting opportunities elsewhere, still the traditional communities of the archipelago are full of gusto, and nothing is more fun than to sail to one of the remoter islands on a bright fall day, say, in search of Sunday lunch. Wherever there is a settlement in these waters—on Kat O Chau, Crooked Island, which is only a mile or two from the China coast, on Tap Mun in Mirs Bay, where the deep-water fishermen live, on the inaccessible Sokos or the Po Toi islands in the south—wherever there is life there is almost sure to be a restaurant. To sit out there at a gimcrack table on the waterfront, shaded by tarpaulins, watching the activities of boat people and eating mussels and stewed eel, or clams with ginger, is to share in one of the most fundamental of all Chinese pleasures, pursued in absolutely the same way, without benefit of microwave, deep freeze, or for that matter dishwasher, as it was in the days of the Celestial Emperors.

And the Emperors are present, too, if only in memorial, for distributed through the islands are the forts, watchtowers, and customhouses of their lost authority. One of the best preserved is the fortress of Tung Chung on Lantau. There the Imperial Chinese Government maintained a naval base, and its formidable stone walls stand in the lee of a wooded ridge, looking over marshy flatlands to the sea. Once this stronghold, as an offshore outpost of the Middle Kingdom, specialized in accepting homage from tributary nations; now it has been taken over by a local school, and when I was there, poking about its courtyard and inspecting the old guns that still line its ramparts, the schoolroom burst into sudden song.

The words of the song were Cantonese, and beyond me, but the tune, though sung in a mournfully approximate kind of singsong, seemed vaguely familiar; and as I left the fortress to catch my ferry at the harbor I found myself singing, more or less in harmony with the exotic rendition that pursued me through the gate: "Just remember the Red River Valley, and the cowboy who loved you so true."

Even more evocative of past time, past values, are the holy places of the archipelago, which are myriad. There are Taoist temples and family shrines wherever you go, some unobtrusive in village streets, like shops, some lonely on promontories where fishermen pause to pray for luck on their way to sea.

The island of Cheung Chau is by no means among the most otherworldly of the islands. Thickly populated, easily accessible, it is popular as a weekend resort for Europeans living in Hong Kong. Nevertheless its one great moment of the year is essentially a spiritual occasion—the event known to foreigners as the Bun Festival, which is centered upon the temple of the sea god Pak Tai. Then for three days the island becomes a place of pilgrimage, as hundreds of boats swarm in with devotees, sight-seers, or mere merrymakers from all over Hong Kong and beyond. Amazingly recondite processions move through the cramped village streets, and beside the temple three gigantic towers of buns are erected, said to be for the pacifying of hungry ghosts but eventually, on the last day of the celebration, eaten one and all by mortals.

For the rest of the year the temple of Pak Tai dozes in a kind of timeless haze, oblivious to change. It is everything you expect a Chinese temple to be. The interior is dark, but flickering with candles. It is incense-fragrant, image-littered. At tables beside the door elderly caretakers sit, sometimes caressing the temple cat, sometimes eating rice from metal bowls, and now and then villagers wander in, in the casual Chinese way, to light a joss stick or say a prayer. And though in fact the building is little more than 200 years old, it feels utterly beyond calendar, as though the very same caretakers have been stroking the very same cat more or less forever.

Holy places of another kind survive among the rough hills of Lantau, for it has always been an island of monasteries. One of them, the Buddhist shrine of Po Lin, is very famous, very rich, very spectacular, and is visited by thousands of tourists on day trips from Hong Kong—it has a splendidly showy modern temple, all golds and crimsons, in the best Hong Kong style, the largest image of the Buddha ever made.

Other Buddhist monasteries are less ostentatious. They are hidden away among the moorlands, to be reached only by arduous footpaths, or they meditate the years away on hillside terraces—a shrine, a cluster of houses, an eating room, a garden from whose purlieus, when the wind is right, you may hear the haunting rise and fall of sacred chants and the jingle of prayer bells.

And on the island's eastern shore, high on a ridge above the sea, there stands a Christian holy place, the Trappist monastery of Our Lady of Joy. You can reach it only by walking over the hills behind, or by taking a sampan from the nearby island of Peng Chau; whichever way you go, once you enter its presence you will feel yourself almost eerily encapsulated. A church crowns the little settlement, with living quarters around it and fishponds and pleasant gardens, and it is inhabited by a handful of Chinese monks, ejected from the mainland years ago, and an English abbot, all of them living in perpetual silence.

Far in the distance you may see the white concrete towers of Hong Kong. The spectacle thrills me always, for if there really is a spell over these islands, as it seemed from the Peak, it is the spell of that astonishing city itself. As the skyline of Manhattan is to Queens and Brooklyn, Hong Kong is to the archipelago, and sailing back to the city from Lantau or Cheung Chau is a never-failing wonder. It may sadden you at first, as the green calm shapes of the islands slip behind your stern, to feel that you are returning from fantasy to reality, from almost imaginary places to a place unquestionably, unforgivingly true.

But then, as that terrific mass of shipping closes all around your boat, as the skyscrapers rise higher and higher against the hills, as the roar of the city traffic reaches you over the water, mingled with the thumping of steam hammers, the shriek of sirens or the shattering blast of a passing hydrofoil, it will dawn upon you that sometimes, in worlds of travel as in realms of literature, fact is more extraordinary than fiction.

Jan Morris has been wandering the world and writing about her experiences for more than forty years. She is the author of numerous books and her essays on travel are among the classics of the genre. She lives in Wales.

✦ ✦ ✦

Mr. Handsome

He took her for quite a ride indeed.

"VERY GOOD DRIVERS," SAID MR. TAM, OUR VIETNAMESE motorbike guide. We weren't convinced. Instead of the expert hosts we had expected, the drivers looked like a college football team coming off a losing streak. They huddled in a circle as if seeking protection from the rain that beat down with ferocity. Mr. Tam began the introductions. Under his encouraging wave, each driver stepped forward to be paired with his rider.

One woman from Manchester got "Most Experienced." Everyone looked envious.

Then, Tomo, a woman from Japan got "Most Kind." She moved off to the side like an Academy Award recipient.

Next, stepped out "Most Responsible." The recipient, a burly man from Australia, looked puzzled but relieved.

There were only a few drivers left. I wondered what personal qualities could possibly remain. Then, with a flourish, stepped forward my driver—"Most Handsome."

Under his blue poncho that hung like a recycling bag, it was hard to tell. But, I stood tall with pride at my good fortune and stepped forward to claim the helmet he held out like a prize. Fortunately it fit.

Others were less fortunate. One woman from Manchester received a helmet with a strap that barely reached her chin. Her eyes were squeezed together in a painful squint. Even worse, the easy-going Aussie with a wide face received a Viet Cong pith helmet—with a brim like a fried egg, it was shallow and camouflage green. He had no rain gear so he was also given a poncho—in hot pink. I swear I saw Mr. Kind stifling a laugh behind his nod of encouragement. I hoped the Aussie didn't pass a mirror.

With a sputter and a few roars, we headed out—in a perfect single-line formation. Like a Hell's Angels family—admittedly of a skinny variety—my biker buddies and I were hitting the open road, bound on a tour of Hue, Vietnam's Imperial City. We streamed past the stone walls of its center, the Forbidden City, and I revelled in the perfect symbolism of it all. The rain had become a Vichy shower—light and warm on my face. I was happy to be living life to its fullest. Then, like a reality slap to the face, Mr. Handsome's poncho flapped back in the wind and began strangling me.

Like a nightmare my mother had warned me against, it was as though I'd stuck my head inside a dry-cleaning bag. The harder I sucked for air, the closer the thin plastic wrapped around my lips. Then, I did what we'd been warned against and let go of the handlebars. I pried the film—now a soggy dental membrane—out of my mouth and it whipped off to the side. The drool was barely noticeable in the rain. He thrust the throttle open to full speed and the bike lurched forward.

We were traveling so fast that I didn't know what to hang on to. The filmy blue poncho was clearly inadequate as a life-saving device. So, on a particularly sharp corner I let go of the bar behind my seat and boldly grabbed in the general region of Mr. Handsome's waist. He didn't swat me, so I hung on even harder.

Horns blaring around us, we swerved to avoid a bicycle laden with squealing pigs and jumped the curb onto a narrow sidewalk. Tidy white stucco homes lined the pathway like sugar cubes. We slowed and I could see smoke from incense sticks curling upward into the gray sky. We brushed past white jasmine bushes that released an inspiring scent. Orchids hung from terracotta pots. Just as I relaxed my grip to drink it all in, we skirted a bend in the trail and again hit open ground. Like raging bulls released from a pen, we roared past a pond of water buffalo who gazed in sleepy puzzlement at the ripples our snorting exhaust pipes created. Our wind tunnel turned a few chickens into whirling dervishes before their very eyes.

Then, just when I was ready to leap off and walk back, we turned a corner and, looming out of the mist like the Leaning Tower of Pisa was Thien Mu Pagoda. I struggled off the bike, arms tangled in the poncho and knees shaking. Mr. Handsome undid my helmet and, to his credit, averted his eyes from my flattened hair. The woman from Manchester looked equally disheveled and by the edge of the Perfume River, the man from Australia shone like a neon-pink billboard. We stumbled up the hill as a group.

"Have you ever seen Vietnamese smooching in public?" Tam asked the group. "Not polite. But in here," he said, pointing to a bronze bell the size of a Volkswagen, "it is O.K."

Cast in 1710, the bell weighed 2,052 kilograms and was once used to shelter Buddhist monks from persecution.

"Big enough to hide inside," said Mr. Tam ducking out of sight. He was back in a few moments, with a red face. Apparently it was already occupied.

An hour later, we were back at the motorbikes. As I eyed a waiting taxi, I could see Mr. Handsome removing a faded cloth from his pocket. He carefully wiped the rain off every inch of the back seat of the motorbike and held my helmet out. I looked around. No one else was bolting. The guilt of betrayal was too much. I climbed back on. The lady from Manchester was already perched on her seat. A crowd of laughing *sampan* ladies was pinching the Aussie.

"Lunch not far, " promised Mr. Tam, as we roared off. We passed a covered bridge, one of only three remaining in Vietnam.

"Also good for smooching," said Mr. Tam. I thought I heard Tomo and Mr. Kind's motorbike slow and make a stop behind us. Turning down a jungle path, we finally arrived at a nunnery. Three novices in long gray robes and woolen toques began serving us a traditional vegetarian lunch. Hardly a serious bunch, they took turns laughing and giggling as they tried to teach us how to say "Too cold" and "Too much rain." Their life, the gardens, the dark kitchen with its wood burning fire, the water that puddled in the orange dirt like paint in a child's paint box, I wanted to preserve it all in my memory. Leaving the group, I began carefully transcribing some words written on a wooden sign that led down the path to a garden of frangipani flowers. As I struggled with the lettering, Mr. Tam came along.

"Please translate the words for me?" I asked, expecting words of profound beauty. A few moments later, he passed my notebook back. There, the words on the sign were perfectly translated. They read, "Go this way."

Deflated, I climbed back on the motorbike. The afternoon sped by in a whirl of rain clouds, incense, and pagodas. There are over two hundred pagodas surrounding the city of Hue and I think we paid each one a visit. But Mr. Handsome and I were one on the motorbike, leaning hard into the curves, roaring across bamboo bridges, streaming past the tombs of royalty, and climbing riverbanks. At pit stops we shared mugs of rice wine dipped in the vats of backyard distilleries.

Miraculously, the weather began to clear as we neared the hotel. Parked back under the almond tree on the driveway, he steadied the motorbike and for the first time, removed his tattered blue poncho. Underneath was a brown leather bomber jacket much like the one worn by Charles Lindbergh. Striking a pose worthy of James Dean, he lifted his visor to reveal a truly handsome face. He was a dead ringer for Antonio Banderas.

Mr. Kind's motorbike was empty. Later that evening, rumor has it that Tomo, the woman from Japan, was seen carrying two mugs of tea down the hall to her room. It seems that the Forbidden City, once a place hard to enter, was now difficult to leave.

Michele Peterson has written for publications from Canada to South Africa including the Globe and Mail, The National Post, The Christian Science Monitor, NOW, *and* Transitions Abroad. *A recipient of a 2004 Award of Excellence from the North American Travel Journalists Association, she is also a contributor to* Sand in My Bra: Funny Women Write from the Road.

SHIRLEY-DALE EASLEY

* * *

All Night on the River Kwai

*History, the movies, reality — where does
one leave off and the other begin?*

THE BUS FROM BANGKOK IS LOADED TO THE HILT WITH
tourists. Not yet ten in the morning, the bald yellow sun beats
down on the highway and hot air wafts in the open windows.
The driver is cutting his fingernails as he swerves in and out
of traffic, passing on hills, bullying small cars into ditches,
running face-to-face with death and oncoming traffic. Yet,
nothing can daunt our spirits. We are on the three-hour ride
to Kanchanaburi, a small town on the banks of the River Kwai.

I have been traveling through Southeast Asia with my
friend, Sandra, who makes this part of the world her winter
home. Last night on a street corner it was she who first
spotted the sign, "Bus Leaves for River Kwai at 8 A.M." Two
weeks of Thailand's exotic and unfamiliar colors, tastes, sights,
and smells and finally a note that strikes home.

Everyone remembers the movie, *The Bridge Over the River
Kwai.* In the 1957 box-office hit, Alec Guinness and William
Holden dramatize the suffering of the prisoners of war who
were forced by the Japanese to build a railway between

63

Thailand and Burma. It was called the Death Railway. The film portrays the building of a bridge across the River Kwai. Sessue Hayakawa plays the part of the cruel and uncompromising Japanese Colonel Saito. This movie put the town of Kanchanaburi on the world map. Now it is a vacation place, a place where tourists go.

Although we know, vaguely, that there is a more callous story, we are filled with excitement and nostalgia. It is as if we have been asked to go behind stage, behind the set of the movie. We envision the steaming jungle where an amazing bamboo-and-wooden structure is going up over the river, which itself seems rocky and wild. Racing down hillsides, roaring through the jungle, in our minds the river is touched with peril and romance. Endless chain gangs of men, stripped to the waist, carry timbers on their backs in the sweltering sun. Driven beyond all human endurance, they are whistling in unison, "Colonel Bogey March."

The bus slows down. Kan, the driver, shouts and we pour out of the bus into the staggering heat at the entrance to a small open-air museum. Almost immediately the rest of the tourists dissipate, leaving only a handful of us behind.

The JEATH Museum is a replica of the detention camp at this actual spot during World War II. It is built like a henhouse, a long bamboo hut with an earthen floor. JEATH is an acronym for the nations involved (Japan, England, Australia, America, Thailand and Holland).

Inside, tables are loaded heavily with pistols, knives, helmets, water canteens, plates, and spoons. Boots, still caked with mud, lie haphazardly among the clutter. These are the items used by the POWs and impressed laborers from June 1942 until December 1943. On the floor is the blown-out shell of the bomb that supposedly downed the bridge over the River Kwai.

Moving slowly, we begin to read newspaper clippings from around the world carrying stories of the survivors and the dead. We read journals, diaries, letters that have been written home, and letters that have been received. There are letters of hope to parents and letters of pain and torture to friends. This is an incredible litany of abuse and suffering, courage and camaraderie. We are literally down on our knees reading.

Thousands of pictures fill the walls. Some photographs have been enlarged to fit from floor to ceiling. Faces look out at us, hollowed by starvation and grief. Swollen, sun-cankered lips. We can count their ribs. I stare into the face of a curly-haired youth. They were only boys, no older than our own sons.

Hours have passed and we realize that we are the only two people left in the place. We meet at the end of the last row, unable to speak. A small sign on the wall states: MAY PEACE ALWAYS CONQUER VIOLENCE. A lone monk holds out a pot for a donation at the door.

Blinded by tears, we step out into the sunlight. Birds are singing. Giant hibiscuses grow along the river. A ferry, laden with farmers, bicycles, and a few pickup trucks is plying a crossing.

Over 100,000 lives were lost here by hunger, beatings, malnutrition, disease, and heat. The graves of Allied prisoners are neatly laid out in two war cemeteries, one on each side of the river. There are 6,982 copper-plaque tombstones in one and 1,750 in another, with inscriptions such as, "Corporal Howard Johnston, Age twenty-two, Always Remembered by Mom." The impressed laborers from Southeast Asia were buried where they dropped.

We walk two kilometers down the main street along the river in silence, our throats too constricted to speak. It surprises us when we come upon a regular bridge crossing a regular river. Where is this phenomenal structure we saw in the movie? Surely this bridge, a concrete-and-steel structure, cannot be the strategic link in the 415-kilometer railway joining Thailand and Burma. Yet, a small plaque states that this is *the* bridge over the River Kwai. British engineers surveyed the terrain in 1905 for a projected rail route and declared it impossible. The Japanese predicted that the construction would take five years. Dismantled steel spans were brought over from Java and the POWs and laborers built it in eighteen months. It was completed December 25th, 1943. Christmas Day.

We walk the iron rails in the mid-afternoon heat, the temperature above 40 degrees Celsius. Our heads are light, our clothes drenched. Below us is the infamous Khwae Yai River. On and on it flows, gliding between its banks in silence. The mountains of Burma rise to the west. A floating market is inching its way up river, loaded with melon, guava fruit, coconut, and pineapple. Houseboats dot the weedy shores.

So this is where they were, these men. Bags of bones really. Driven by fear and cruelty, sweat dripping from their bodies, brains boiling in their heads.

I break the silence. "So where is the raging river? Shouldn't it be thrashing and beating against its bed?"

"I don't know, but I will tell you one thing," says Sandra. "There was no whistling."

A sign posted on the last span of the bridge reads "Elephant Rides 50 baht." Down below, in a small patch of trees, we see a group of tourists leaving, mounted on elephants. Wearily, the old animals stumble off, shuffling in the dust. There is a kind of *sow-jai* in their gait. A sadness.

A whistle is blowing from the Kanchanaburi side of the bridge. A group of tourists rushes past us and then another and another. Thinking it is a train on the rails, we move to the nearest lookout and wait. Nothing is in sight so we amble back across, arriving just in time to see the tail end of the last bus to Bangkok leaving town.

"*Rot meh,*" says an old lady under a tree, as she draws her hand across her neck, indicating that the bus is dead and gone. Or could it be that we are doomed.

"For thirty baht," I read from the guidebook, "we can stay on the river in a raft house." Sandra is sitting on the curb, elbows on her knees.

"Sam's place…a complex of floating rafts on the slow moving River Kwai," I read. Sandra is looking up and down the street, surveying the situation.

"Or for seventy baht, it says there are clean rooms near the bridge."

"We are not taking anything until we see it," she says.

Catching a *song-thaew*, a pickup truck with seats in the back, we get ourselves into the main part of town and begin the fruitless search for a raft house. Long rows of them line the shore, like floating motels, linked to each other with bridges and wooden walkways. They are perched on props less than a meter above the water. Even the smallest and most desolate is occupied for the night.

On the street, vendors are packing up and heading…where? The sun is collapsing into the horizon and we are considering following someone home. Limited in language to "hello, good-bye, please, thank you, excuse me, and it doesn't matter," we are tearing the book out of each other's hands to look for words in the waning light.

After some time, Sandra looks up and says, "Of course, there is only one answer. We need Singha." Thai beer.

At a booth near the end of the street, teeth red with betel nut, sits an angel. Bent over her wild onions, sweet rice wrapped in banana leaves, eels in plastic bags, and pink shrimp, is the lady at the bridge. Not only does she sell us Singha, sticky rice, and pineapple, she leads us, with her knobby claw-like hands, to her son Prae. He is sitting on a box carefully rolling betel nut in leaves, a touch of lime to bring out the red juice. Using English, Thai, and sign language, he tells us that his mother has been watching us. He tells us that things are busy tonight. He knows a place where we can stay. A houseboat, he says. On the river near the bridge. Not big. Not fancy.

The slippery mud path that leads to the river is narrow and steep. The smell of rubbish, riverweed, and thick water mixes with the sweet perfume of wild orchids and lilies as we skirt the shoreline. Tree branches, like moss-covered fingers, touch the water.

In a shallow inlet, we come upon the houseboat. It is a bamboo shack roped together with the most tenuous grasp on the land. It is as if it had come downriver in a freshet and lodged temporarily against the bare branches of the dead tree that holds it. A few planks reach out to a small sandy beach on the bank. At home this would be the equivalent of a woodshed, or an outbuilding slung up in a pasture somewhere.

Inside, the walls are at a slant, the floorboards soggy and uneven. The river comes in at places, runs across the floor and flows on out. There is a table, a few mat-like sleeping places, and some shelves. At the back, facing the river, is a verandah strung with two hammocks, the rope gray with age.

"Are we safe?" we ask.

Prae laughs.

"Are there water snakes?"

Prae laughs harder.

"Ghosts?" We act this one out.

Prae understands. "*Mai! Mai!*" he wails with laughter. He points to his house set back in the trees and we are almost sure that he is saying he will be there. Then he is gone.

And here we are. Thousands of miles from home, not only on the River Kwai, we are in it.

"What about rats?" I ask. "I read that raft houses are built up on stilts to keep out rats".

"Never mind rats," says Sandra. "What about this goddamn thing dislodging from the tree and taking off down river?"

"And where does this river go?" I wonder. "Did we read that anywhere?"

At this we dissolve into fits of hysterical laughter. Today we have been through the whole gamut of emotions.

The air is thick and warm and the first stars come out. We decide to stay out in the hammocks all night, being afraid to take our eyes off the river, sipping Singha and rocking.

We feel a steady thumping in the air, then a tremendous drumming. Down the river comes a floating disco raft, howling out rock-and-roll music, chock full of people, throbbing and blasting into the night. Luckily, it passes our inlet and fades into the distance. All is quiet again.

Then the insects arrive. Spiraling, turning and wheeling, buzzing and batting their wings in our faces. We find some pieces of black mosquito netting on a shelf and put it completely over our heads. Then, like old mourners, we return to our vigil in the hammocks. There is not a breeze on the river.

Night talk. The mind drifts to strange and convoluted things. We talk of our families at home in Canada, the ice that would be clinging to the highways, the heat of this Asian night, two geckos inside the door slapping their tails in combat.

The faces return. The faces on the walls of the museum. They are haunting us. Just before she drifts off to sleep, Sandra tells me she read this story on the wall: "There were always maggots in the food. One of the prisoners said, 'Jeez, I can't eat those maggots.' His partner said, 'Pass it over here mate, it's my ticket out of here.'" Her words filter away; she is sleeping.

Now it is just the river and me. I cannot sleep. I think I hear someone crying in the jungle. It comes closer, louder. It is only dogs. The wild dogs of Thailand. Their barking recedes, echoing toward the Burmese hills.

Rivers are like people. Some are feisty and loud, some babble and gush, some are lazy and slow, others are old and bent. But the Kwai Yai River is silent; as if its secrets are so deep it can never talk. Or whatever it once knew has gone on down the river.

I think of Corporal Howard Johnston and his mother: "Always Remembered By Mom." Then I think of Prae and his mother. She would have been a young woman when the POWs, as slaves, walked through her village to work on the Death Railway. Prae would have been a child. Perhaps some of their own villagers were with them. Did they hear the bomber that blew up part of the bridge in 1945? Did they shriek and run in terror? Is it possible that things can pass and leave no trace?

I must have slept because I jump with a start. The train is passing through on the Death Railway. It is still possible to get to Burma that way. It is said that the train hugs the mountain-side at a dizzy height, creeping over the same old, rickety World War II rail line, laid on the same creaking, wooden trestles. It is a well-traveled smuggler's route. This particular train would be carrying tourists who obtain a day visa to Three Pagoda Pass. It whistles as it thunders over the river and fades in the distance.

Mist is rising on the river. The arms of the old tree that holds our raft are bathed in the thin light of morning. A rooster is crowing. We arise stiffly from our perches, like two black ravens.

Already we can peel the heat from our bodies. A small craft, piled high with food, is moving up the river. A family comes down to wash clothes. The children swim. Men, waist deep in water, are fishing.

At the market, the tourists have come. It is the usual clamor of the morning. People are fixing up their stalls among the chickens and the dogs. We eat *pad thai* and sticky rice for breakfast. Children are selling key chains with helmets, guns, and bombs hanging from them. Magnificent flowers grow up through the garbage, flowers with huge, succulent mouths, in purple, crimson, and magenta. In the distance we see a long line of monks in their saffron robes walking barefoot toward the Wat Chaichumpal. Life is so continuous and simple.

We are looking for Prae. He is nowhere to be found. The first bus to Bangkok is ready to depart and we see his mother. We run to her and she holds us both for a moment in her bony arms, laughing through jagged teeth already dyed as red as blood.

"Money," we say. "Money."

She shoos us away. "*Mai pen rai! Mai pen rai!*" she laughs. Never mind. Never mind. We hold for a moment her bird-like hands and then run for the bus. She is still laughing and waving as we pass out of sight.

The bus is loaded to the hilt, this time with locals. I'm sharing a seat with a whole crate of chickens. Across from me an old man is holding the hand of his middle-aged son. Near the front I can see Sandra sitting on one of the crates in the aisle. People are laughing and talking, calling back and forth to one another. As the bus careens out of town, we catch one last glimpse of the legendary bridge over the River Kwai and I realize that we did get behind the set, after all. It was just not the same story.

Shirley-Dale Easley is an education consultant and a freelance writer living in Durham Bridge, New Brunswick, Canada. She has a special knack for getting herself in and out of unusual predicaments and places.

MEG PETERSON

* * *

Confrontation at
Xegar Checkpoint

Can you shift the balance of power?

"*NIMENDE HUZHAO!*" DEMANDED THE CHINESE GUARD AT Xegar Checkpoint, a small army outpost. It was the last one before leaving Tibet. He peered menacingly at the driver of our weather-beaten minibus.

"He wants your passports," translated Lapa, our Tibetan guide. Mentally, we jumped to attention and, with misgivings, handed over the documents.

We were a diverse group of eleven strangers from five countries who had met in Kathmandu and flown to Lhasa to begin our exploration of Tibet. All week long we had been captivated by the gentle monks, the ancient monasteries, and the turquoise mountain lakes. In the process, we had become friends.

The guard strode away from the bus, through a high gate emblazoned with red Chinese characters, and into a dusty courtyard. Lapa scurried after him. Another routine bureaucratic check, no doubt. We hoped this one would be quick like the other three. But there was something ominous in the way the guard's superior—a rigid, strutting little commandant—

peered out from under his military visor and waved his arms at Lapa. Was it conceivable that he would keep us here for questioning? This was, after all, the government of the Tiananmen Square massacre and the brutal, decades-long repression of Tibet.

Half an hour later, Lapa returned, extremely agitated. "They want to send us back to Lhasa," he announced, "but is not possible. Our group visa is good only for going one way."

"So what's the problem?" asked Arie, a middle-aged Israeli.

"Is Kristoff's passport," answered Lapa. "One of the numbers put on visa by Chinese Embassy is different from one on passport. They say he cannot go through checkpoint." Kristoff was a quiet, likable young German.

Lapa walked back through the gate. He pleaded and cajoled, but the officer remained intransigent. It was sad to see such a gentle man subjected to this humiliating game of cat and mouse.

"The Chinese will not forgive my country for its recent proclamation about human rights in Tibet," Kristoff said. "I'm sure the embassy in Kathmandu changed that passport number on purpose. But I will stay here. Please, you must go on."

"Never," said Arie, who had taken to walking back and forth outside the barbed wire, glowering at the commandant. "It's a disgrace! That man is a dictator. He's playing with us. How come we passed the other checkpoints without a problem? I want my passport, and I want my freedom. Now!" He pounded the air with his fists.

"Be still, Arie, or you'll get us all in trouble," said his wife, Anna. "You're not in Israel." Two hours passed. The sun beat down.

I retreated to the bus and tried to read. But nothing could alleviate my fears. How long would this petty tyrant hold us? There wasn't a phone in sight, and I couldn't speak the language. During the week we'd experienced some uneasy moments: bouncing over washed-out roads and being whipped by rain and waterfalls in an open truck. But that was adventure. This was frightening. We were seeing another Tibet. The Tibet that was held hostage—like us.

Outside my window, Anna was engaged in intense conversation with June, a French teacher from California, who'd recently been in China. "I have an idea," Anna said, reentering the bus and gathering the women around her. "For three hours the men have been trying to settle this, and they're getting nowhere. Why not try a different approach: quiet, friendly persuasion? We'll walk through the gate and speak to the leader face to face. It just might work."

We started, slowly, toward the compound and pushed the gate open. The commandant, who had been supervising a motley group of soldiers, backed up a little, his eyes wide, his arms akimbo. As we approached, he motioned for a chair and sat down in the middle of the dirt yard. Lapa made frenzied gestures in an attempt to stop us, then fled to a far corner.

Anna opened her arms and regaled the stunned officer. "We have only goodwill toward you, and we want to leave your beautiful country with friendly feelings." He listened intently. Did he understand English?

June knelt in the dust in front of him and tried her limited Chinese. "*Wo jiao June.*" (My name is June.) "*Nin guixing?*" (What is yours?) "*Women hen xihuan Zhongguo.*" (We like China very much.) Then she introduced us, one at a time.

Else, from Denmark, spoke next. "Sir, we can't go back, and you won't let us go forward. We all have families. I beg of you...."

"I love your country," Brigitte said. "But I must fly in two days from Kathmandu to Switzerland." She made the sound of a plane and spread her arms like wings, swooping, turning. No response.

Each of us tried to tap the man's innate humanity, to find a link between us, to give him a chance to save face. But it seemed hopeless. We were getting nowhere.

June tried again. "We are all friends," she said in Chinese, reading randomly and with great enthusiasm from her Chinese-English dictionary. "Where is the hotel? Please open the door. I must go to bed…. Oops! Wrong page." The commandant's dark eyes stared directly at June, and the serious face cracked just alittle.

Encouraged, June tried again, in Chinese: "What are we having for dinner tonight? Can I camp here? Which way to the bathroom?"

In an instant, the curtain lifted from the frozen countenance and a smile appeared. Then full-throated laughter. He rose from his chair. "O.K., O.K., you may go." What? Did I hear English?

All inhibitions evaporated in that moment of intense relief. Joyously we surrounded the officer, clapped him on the back, and shook his hand. Lapa stood open-mouthed. He seemed to be in a state of shock.

As we drove off, cheers erupted. The crisis at Xegar Checkpoint was over. With satisfaction we reviewed our success in softening the stance of the border bully. Our approach had worked! And we'd given this man a chance to do the right thing, perhaps saving some future group from similar harassment. We had no idea whether he'd acted on orders or was independently rattling his saber. But there had been at least a temporary change in his attitude. We had reached out, and he had responded positively. This was gratifying. We felt no anger, no malice. We were free.

In silence, we continued up the rich plateau of Thingri with its golden wheat fields, stone huts, and small, walled villages. The bus wound over perilous, unpaved roads inches from cliffs unprotected by guardrails. In two hours of climbing we reached the Lalung Leh Pass (17,500 feet). A fierce wind pummeled us as we stepped from the bus into the shadow of waving prayer flags. Still emotionally exhausted, but strangely exhilarated, I stood looking at the distant mountains. At that moment, my admiration for the Tibetan people was at its height. How could they maintain their tranquility and practice compassion toward their oppressors in the face of such odds?

"Hey, we made it! Long live Tibet!" shouted June. "And isn't that Everest peeking out of the clouds? Look, Lapa! Look, everyone: The top of the world!"

Meg Peterson has made two solo backpacking trips around the world, covering four continents and fourteen countries. During her travels she found romance in Nepal, viewed a sunrise from the summit of Mount Moses in the Sinai, watched a private cremation on the banks of the Ganges, and traversed the endless expanse of game reserves in Kenya. Her book, Madam, Have You Ever Really Been Happy? *was published in June 2005. She lives in Maplewood, New Jersey.*

Puja

Mother India conjures a prayer for all women.

I WALKED OUT THE FRONT DOOR OF THE HOTEL SURYA INTO the dark morning to meet Shyam and the compact car we were using to tool around India. Nothing moved on the streets of Khajuraho, save the occasional shadow of a man or a cow meandering. But the two employees from our hotel, who were required to be available at our ungodly hour of departure, stood proud and resolute beside the entrance, as if ambassadors of the new day.

The coffee-*walla* had knocked softly on the door to my room an hour before, entering with lowered eyes and his tray.

"Good morning, Madam."

"*Namaste, dost.* How are you today?"

"Just fine, Madam, thank you," he replied, as he took the white thermos of sweet, creamy Indian coffee and unmatched teacup and saucer and placed them on the low wooden table in my room.

"You go to Varanasi today, Madam?"

"Yes, sir, to see your holy river."

"Very beautiful, Madam, the Mother Ganga. Very beautiful for you to see our river. After long drive, you take bath in river, clean body and sins from life."

"Oh, really. I didn't know that. If I bathe in the river I will be absolved of my sins?"

"Yes, Madam. Mother Ganga forgive you."

"Interesting."

"You're welcome, Madam."

Now the coffee-*walla* and his associate, the luggage-*walla*, stood outside the hotel to see us off. Their hands remained in an unwavering *namaste*, in prayer position across their chests, while they bowed slightly to us in the car. The amber light from the foyer inside lit their bodies from behind like stained glass. Shyam switched on the headlights, I nodded my head to them one final time, and we drove off into the black morning.

Dawn remained elusive as we wove our way through a village on the outskirts of Khajuraho. Shyam had missed the turn he knew and slowed down to ask a man with a purple turban and giraffe eyelashes which way to go.

"This is very old village, Madam ji. I never see this part before because I always turn earlier, but now I see these buildings very old. Very beautiful buildings but very old. Very sad, because they need repair or they will not be here when your children come to visit India."

What could I say in response to my friend, Shyam, who continued to call me Madam ji, even though he could say my name perfectly and had known me for years? He was right, the buildings were disintegrating. There was nothing more to say. While Shyam maneuvered the car up the steep dirt street, calm, even when faced with unforeseen hairpin turns, rocks, and deep gouges in the road, I stared out the window at the crumbling archways and seemingly unsteady stone stairways of the old buildings. Occasional clusters of men, scarves wrapped around their heads every which way, squatted in circles around small fires in front of these historic buildings, drinking steaming cups of *chai*, warming their bodies and minds for the day ahead.

"It's so funny, Shyam. Wherever you go in the world, people love their hot morning drink, whether it's coffee or tea or hot water with lemon. It's universal."

"Yes, Madam ji, morning *chai* is very good."

"But I don't see any women at the fires. Is it just for the men?"

"No. This is not law. But women in the house. Maybe asleep or work in home for babies. Very busy Indian women, no time to relax with fire."

Since it was morning, typically the time designated for puja, or prayer, for the Hindu people, we listened to Shyam's cassette of Hindu prayer songs as we drove. Hollow, high female voices, overlaid with sitars and flutes, full of repetition, these metrical psalms of praise and gratitude felt truly ethereal to me. I leaned my head against the headrest, closed my eyes, and tried to absorb the prayers of a language I didn't speak but seemed somehow to understand.

In the Hindu tradition, the practice of puja consists not only of a personal morning ritual of homage at home, but also usually includes a walk to the temple where an offering is made at the altar of the family's deity. Like so many of the tasks of daily life in India, the puja offering at the temple is, typically, the responsibility of the women. Throughout the day, but especially in the morning hours, women can often be seen walking in small groups or alone with their small puja vases held out in front of them with both hands. It is in these small pots of silver or brass that they carry the daily offering to their deities. Since clean water is a cherished commodity in India and considered a great gift, the puja offering often consists of water laden with marigolds or rose petals or some other flower or spice.

Just moments after the young yellow dawn appeared on the horizon, we came upon a few cows snoozing in the middle of the narrow road, making it impossible for us to pass. Cows are a sacred animal to the Hindus and are never to be harmed. Shyam gave a few small taps to the horn, coaxing them out of slumber and to their feet. We chuckled to each other as these revered animals took their sweet time moving out of our way. The sky turned to lilac and then to a soft pink as we headed east towards the state of Uttar Pradesh. Low patches of fog lingered in pastures of high green grasses. The flat terrain was interrupted only occasionally by small all-white domed temples or large intricately assembled mounds of cow dung patties, which would be used as fire fuel when needed. Temples and mosques are so ubiquitous in India that I was no longer surprised to see them alone by the side of the road, or in the center of a field of crops, or perched precariously on a mountain cliff. The endless fields of yellow mustard, which had been indistinguishable only minutes before, now appeared golden and swayed slightly with the breeze as the day began to bloom.

We were in rural India now, and although we passed the occasional man on a bicycle or on foot, it was too early for the commotion and chaos that India is so famous for to appear here. There did seem to be a surprising number of women near the street, in small clusters or alone, without the usual baskets on their heads full of cow dung or greens from the fields, without the puja vases and poise that seems to accompany that walk to temple. Rather, they carried small silver or copper pots, similar but noticeably smaller than the puja vases. They seemed to be idling, not heading any particular direction. Their heads were lowered or their faces without expression. They gazed about glassy-eyed as if they were barely awake. They stood or squatted, sometimes with a cigarette in hand, as if waiting for something to arrive. But the only thing around in the gray morning light was our car.

"Shyam, why are the women standing about with those small pots? They look like the puja vases but smaller."

"Madam ji, that is for the bathroom. You know our system here, Madam ji. You use paper, we use water."

"Oh, right," I said.

And I did know the system. The people of India, and much of Asia, use water to rinse after relieving themselves, while we in the West use toilet paper. Now I also understood that these very pretty little silver pots that the women had with them, were for all intents and purposes, the same as the stout plastic pitchers, which resembled a liquid measuring cup for cooking that I saw in every bathroom in India.

As we continued on and the light lifted, I could see more clearly what was going on. I understood why the women had been waiting. They'd been waiting for our car to pass. Still, I couldn't help but wonder why they chose to squat right on the shoulder of the road instead of alone in private somewhere.

I consider myself a pretty liberated Western woman, confident with my body and the excrement that comes from it. I have no inhibition about urinating in a field under the long full skirts which I have come to depend on for privacy when traveling. But I can't imagine ever feeling comfortable enough to defecate on the side of the road—long skirt or not.

And, Indian women, in general, are a very shy and modest lot. Never showing their legs or too much skin, often averting their eyes or lowering their heads in the presence of a man. I had even become accustomed to women covering their faces with their sari scarves when they saw me, a fellow woman. I'd come to understand that being Caucasian, and Western, I was a stranger, and worthy of the extra modesty. So how was it that these same women could defecate in public for all to see?

"Shyam ji, why are the women going to the bathroom right here on the road? I know it is a human need. But why so close to the road? And why aren't there any men?"

"Madam ji, it is very hard life, the life of Indian poor woman, very hard, very sad. They take care of the kids, and work all day in fields for little money, and come home and cook, clean, take more care of kids, and husband always like jiggie jiggie at night. And then with jiggie jiggie they have more babies. Always pregnant, Indian women, always tired."

"Yes, Shyam. I see that and agree it's a very hard and grueling life. But that doesn't explain to me why they go to the bathroom here beside the road."

"Madam ji, Indian government say, we give money for people to build toilets in their homes. People don't want, they don't believe. It makes me very angry. The husbands they should build little house for family bathroom. They don't need a lot of money, they can dig a hole and put wood to stand on, they can do things for their families but they don't. So easy and they don't do. I very angry about this way."

"O.K., they don't have bathrooms in their homes. But why don't the women go into the fields, or into the woods, so they can have some privacy? Why do they go in the street?"

"Madam ji, for protection, for safety."

"Shyam, I'm sorry, I don't understand what you're saying. How can taking a shit by the side of the road with the cars and animals and everyone around, how is that safe or protected?"

"Madam ji, in India many people go to the bathroom in morning, after they wake up and have *chai* and *bidi* (hand-rolled cigarette). They need to go but it is dark. Many time, woman go to the field, to the woods for private and men see and they rape woman. They go in the street so they are safe."

"Shyam, do you mean to tell me that women are raped so

frequently when they try to go to the bathroom in private that they need to go by the side of the road?"

"Yes, Madam ji, that is what I try to tell you. Women's life here has much suffering. If they are raped, no one listen, no one care. It is better they are safe."

I could feel Shyam glancing at me as he drove, searching for some eye contact with those huge brown saucers of his. But I wasn't in the mood and stared straight ahead at the road in front of us. With his clean manicured fingers he softly ejected the cassette of prayer songs from the player and we drove on in silence.

I couldn't help but think of my white-tiled bathroom in the States with the fragrant freesia candle, the soft toilet paper, and the door that locked. I leaned my head against the headrest, closed my eyes, breathed deep into my belly and did puja for these women. I prayed that they would have more choices, more opportunities, more privilege. And when I opened my eyes, the bustling day was upon us. India was in her full regalia and the apricot sun hung in the sky.

After many years of working in book publishing helping other writers, Jennifer Leigh Rosen jumped the fence to pursue her own dream of writing. When she is not traveling around the world she can be found in San Francisco, California and Baja, Mexico with her cats, Clyde and Madeline Bea.

MICHELLE HAMILTON

* * *

Sweating in Taipei

Water, hands, bodies, talk — the fellowship of women.

"GENTLEMEN STOP" READS THE SIGN AT THE STEPS TO THE women's spa in Taipei. I smile at the odd phrase, at how things, like language, take a different shape in another culture. Still, I can't resist rewriting the expression in my head — Women Only — as my friend Ellen and I walk through the glass doors of the downtown high-rise. Cool, artificial air brushes against our sweaty skin, a welcome relief from the sticky heat of Taiwan's summer, even at ten o'clock at night.

"*Ni-hou*" — *Hello.* Three young Taiwanese women welcome us from behind a brown marble counter. They stand tall in matching pink suits with a pale purple trim that blend perfectly with the pink of their lipstick. I look down at the business card of Eliza Lady Relax Plaza and notice its pink paper and purple ink matches perfectly with the colors they wear.

One of the women watches us dig in our packs for I.D. and a credit card. Sensing we've been there before, she asks "Do you want massage?" We nod yes. She writes down our appointment time — midnight — hands us our key, and sends us downstairs. Although the city's discos and night markets are something to experience, we come seeking a different kind of nightlife, that of the sauna, the underground world of the Taiwanese housewife.

We descend the stairwell, pink carpet sinking under our feet. In the small reception area two college-aged girls sit at vanities applying the last of the evening makeup. Long, thin cigarettes hang from their lips, the tips bright with lipstick.

Two elderly women speak to us in Mandarin we don't understand, then direct us with their hands to take off our shoes. They place them in pink plastic bags and deposit them into small wooden cubicles.

In the locker room, we insert keys into pale pink lockers and unlock our escape from living where road signs confound. We undress quickly, wrap ourselves in plush towels and enter the brightly lit main room.

Taiwanese women and girls move across the spacious room from hot pool to cold pool, from sauna to a glass-walled cold room the size and temperature of a walk-in freezer. Some clutch towels to their bare chests or tuck thick black hair into plastic shower caps. Some sit on the edge of the pools massaging oil into their skin. Others gather naked at the tea dispensers, talking and laughing like high school girls meeting between classes.

A few of the older women nod hello as we walk by, their bright eyes amused by the presence of curly haired, carrot-topped Ellen and wavy, brown-haired me. We are the only foreigners at the sauna, and although I know of a few other Western women who come, I have never seen one on our visits.

"*Ni-hou*," we respond, nodding and smiling. Their eyes follow us a moment before returning to conversation.

Ellen and I walk past the traditional showers and take a seat on small plastic benches, the size found in a kindergarten room.

I prefer these seated showers, somehow it seems so appropriate, so lady-like, to sit to bathe.

The rush of running water silences the chatter at the water cooler. I catch the reflection in the mirror of the women showering behind me. One woman rapidly scours her entire body with a rough sponge, stripping her skin of the soot, dirt, and emissions that float in the city's summer heat. Another stands still, steamy hot water pours past her closed eyes and down her brown skin. I close my eyes, too, and breathe in the heat. Hot water cascades between my breasts, turning my white skin a pale pink.

"C'mon," Ellen beckons.

I follow her into the sauna. The smell of warm wood heats my nose and we take a seat on the lowest bench. Two girls who could pass for fifteen sit side by side, flipping through editions of what look like Asian versions of *Teen* or *Young Miss*. Their long black hair is wrapped genie-like in the sauna's signature pink towels and they carry on a quiet conversation without moving their eyes from the pages of the magazines.

A few women rest in what appears to be peaceful meditation and that is where the familiar sauna experience ends. Women watch the twenty-four-inch television that is built into the wall, its volume turned down to accommodate conversation. Others talk as if they haven't seen each other in years.

At home, the incessant dialogue would have frustrated me. But here the clamor is the essence of the spa. A plump woman of around forty-five enters the sauna. Shouts and waving hands fold her immediately into the conversation. It is impossible without understanding Chinese to know what the women speak of. But their laughter, smiles, and the ease of conversation give the heated room the joyful air of an Italian kitchen. Perhaps they speak of husbands and children, work and beauty, food and fortune or perhaps the two foreign women sweating with them. They occasionally look our way and we exchange smiles and I understand that the sauna is their meeting place, their barbershop, their bridge game. Here they are women, not wife or mother, daughter or child. There is something comforting about this roomful of naked women, of heat and flesh, where roles and nationalities are scrubbed off the skin and time and identity disappear in the steam.

The heat of the sauna overwhelms us well before it does the Taiwanese women. We dip in the cold pool, lounge in the hot pool, and scrub our skin red with salt in the steam room. Before long one of the staff beckons us for our massage.

Massage in Taiwan is not a private affair, but communal, like most things Chinese. Twelve tables in two rows line the living room-size space. Even at midnight every table is full. My first massage in Taiwan was painful—the force of her kneading, the surprise as she grabbed my breasts and cracked my neck. I learned later that they were perfectly willing to accommodate the less sturdy, and I do my best to convey this through sign language to my current masseuse.

It works. I lie face down, sinking into the table, the long night catching up with me. Like the sauna, the women's banter fills the room. The shrill of a cell phone breaks the flow of gossip and a distinct "*Ni-hou ma?*"—*How are you?*—is heard repeatedly as the phone is passed from woman to woman. Their conversation seeps a warm energy, the kind made by people who share long hours together.

This is one time I am thankful I do not understand the language. The music of unknown words lulls me into a half sleep. The masseuse digs deeper into my muscles; I sink deeper into the table, knots slowly dissipating.

Later, wrapped in pastel robes, Ellen and I sip tea and share a late-night bowl of noodles. The two thin girls from the sauna, their hair still wrapped in towels, sit nearby, eyes glued to the television hanging above them. Two older women exchange family photos, others flip through magazines, read, or shuffle through the café in slippers.

Before long we stuff in earplugs and enter the semi-dark sleeping room. A quick scan of the three rows of recliners reveals heads covered in curlers, eyes behind black sleeping masks, and the steady rise and fall of shoulders. The room transforms the spa into a slumber party of sorts. It is a home-away-from-home for the Taiwanese and a hotel for us, so we time our visits according to the twelve-hour limit. Peeking into the overflow area at the bunk bed-like cubicles built into the walls, we find two with no feet sticking out, nod good-night, and dive head first into the narrow beds. Lying down, I adjust my head on the pillow and fall asleep to the collective breath and dull snore of a hundred women.

Michelle Hamilton chose her college based on its study abroad program. She went to England and was quickly hooked. Her travels since have taken her to Nepal, India, and China, and across the U.S by bicycle. She's currently an editor at Backpacker *magazine.*

LYNN FERRIN

* * *

Mountain Walking

It's different in Japan, very different.

HIKERS STRUGGLING UP A STEEP MOUNTAIN TRAIL SOMETIMES taunt each other with this bittersweet fantasy: "Hey, don't give up! There's a great little saloon at the top!" Of course, it's never true—what you usually find at the summit is barren rock and wind.

So consider this: In the Japan Alps, there really are taverns on the heights. You can climb all day, up narrow paths through dripping forests and along razor-sharp aretes, and finally, at the crest, stumble into a cheery little hospice where a raven-haired barmaid dispenses mountain whiskey or beer or a steaming bowl of *soba*. Also beside the trails are amazingly comfortable mountain inns, two or three days' walk from the nearest road, where footsore wanderers can find shelter for the night. And what shelter!

Guests sleep on soft mattresses beneath thick quilts, and soak their weary sinews in hot *furos*, and dine on elaborate meals to match any hiker's appetite.

After trekking for a week on the spectacular trails of Japan

Alps National Park, I realized that the Land of the Rising Sun probably offers the most civilized mountain hiking on the planet. And so easy for a foreign visitor to do! Because shelter, bedding, and food are provided in the inns, I didn't need to schlep a large backpack and camping equipment through international airports. I took one set of warm and rugged clothes, a daypack, a few personal items, and hiking boots. I checked my suitcase and city clothes at a train station in a nearby city until my hike was over.

Generally, the hike-in huts of the Japan Alps are open from May through October—or until the first snows fly and close the trails. The huts are privately owned and operated, through a lease arrangement with the national park.

These are high, steep, difficult mountains—many topping 9,000 feet. But they cannot be called wilderness. One doesn't find solitude there; there are literally thousands of hikers— almost all of them Japanese—tramping along the trails. The Japan Alps may not be wilderness, but they also are definitely not "touristy."

I was in Japan on business, and hoped to slip away for a short vacation on the country's stony mountain paths. I heard that a group of American hikers was heading into the mountains, and arranged to join them—mostly because I don't speak or read Japanese, and they'd hired a translator.

Our party of twelve, ranging in age from twenty-six to seventy-seven, journeyed by train north to Matsumoto. There we transferred to a charming electric rattler bound for Shin-Shimashima, where we jumped on a bus for Kamikochi. The slow two-hour ride carried us into an awesome landscape of precipitous gorges, plunging waters, steaming hot springs, dark forests.

A honky-tonk scattering of souvenir shops, campgrounds, snack bars, and Japanese inns greeted us when we scrambled off the bus at Kamikochi, the main trailhead for hikers heading into the northern Alps. We raced around buying last-minute items for our trail lunches, mailing postcards, pouring over the route maps. It was mid-afternoon when, at last, we shouldered our packs and started walking up the wide valley of the Azusa River.

For the first mile or so the gentle, carefully tended trails were full of day-trippers: polite groups of businessmen in suits, impeccable women in high heels pushing baby carriages, families hauling big ice chests. Gradually, they fell behind, leaving only the serious hikers heading into the mountain keeps for a night or a week or more.

Above us, mist spiraled around the peaks; below, the braided river rippled in the late afternoon sun.

After four miles of fairly level walking, we crossed a grassy meadow and arrived at our first night's lodging, Tokusawa. I wonder if there is any other mountain "hut" like it, on any trails anywhere? After exchanging our boots for the usual slippers, we were shown to our rooms.

Tatami mats covered my floor. A thermos of hot water, tea, and cups awaited me on the table; an attendant brought a brazier of glowing charcoal, which he slid into a rack under the table. He motioned for me to sit with my feet beneath the charcoal and covered the table with a blanket for a welcome foot-warming. After donning my soft cotton *yukata*, I headed for a short scrub and a long happy soak in the steaming wooden *furo*.

In honor of the visiting Americans, Tokusawa's chef set the table with knives and forks and prepared a "Western" dinner—fresh marinated trout from Tokusawa's own pond, cream soup, pork, spaghetti, ice cream, and fruit. After supper we sat around the fire playing chess and poker and chatting with a few local hikers who spoke English.

That night as rain pattered on the wooden eaves, we slept like babies beneath the downy quilts. Next morning, in the woodsy, orderly kitchen, with its teapots hung in a row across the window, we were served a breakfast of coffee, scrambled eggs, bacon, croissants, and strawberry jam. (Perhaps I make too much of Japanese trail cuisine, but my usual backpacking fare consists of freeze-dried mystery stuff that looks and tastes like sawdust.)

All this was too good to leave. Our group decided to stay another night at Tokusawa, and spent the day nearby, exploring the jungle of birch and bamboo, of creeks that ran between carpets of moss, of wildflowers and berries. That night at dinner we used chopsticks for our exquisitely prepared Japanese sampler of sushi, tempura, *soba*, salted trout, soup, pickles, sweet grapes, and sake.

But we had come to experience the mountains of Japan, not to feed our faces, so we had to leave these sweet indulgences behind. We crept from beneath the quilts of Tokusawa to a thick rain. Outside the windows hundreds of Japanese hikers were shuffling miserably along the trail wearing ponchos and carrying umbrellas. I will not dwell upon the breakfast menu except to say that eating cornflakes with chopsticks is a precise measure of one's progress in mastering Buddhist serenity.

We started sloshing up the trail. For the first few miles we were in the mellow dripping forest beside the Asuza River. At midday we came to Yogusanso, a large inn with vending machines peddling fruit juice, crackers, beer, hot sake—and the ubiquitous Japanese pornographic magazines. The price of these things increases in direct proportion to the distance from Kamikochi. So does one's willingness to pay more for them. A few of the mountain huts are stocked by four-wheel drive, but most of the supplies come by helicopter or in great wooden packs on the backs of strong men.

After lunch we squealed across a precarious suspension bridge and began to climb a steep side canyon, out of the forest and into the low brush and black boulders. Finally we stood on a moraine at the foot of a great glacial cirque, still streaked with snow. Massive rock walls rose all around, their summits lost in the clouds. A whole city of bright blue and yellow tents spread across a field of rocks. We found our night's lodging, Karasawa, perched at the edge of the moraine. It was more rustic than Tokusawa, but still very comfortable. Guests slept in long cribs, shoulder-to-shoulder. I wondered whether, during peak summer crowds, they all roll over at once. We Americans were assigned to three cribs, four of us in each crib, which gave us plenty of elbow-and-knee room. I noticed that the Japanese guests were sleeping six or more to a crib—but then, generally, they were smaller than we were.

At dawn we were sweetly awakened by Respighi and Bach playing on Karasawa's stereo. The manager came down the aisle between the cribs, passing out *bento* lunches, each wrapped as prettily as a Christmas present in blue-and-gold paper. I wandered out to the outdoor coffee shop—where the stereo was now playing a Mozart concerto—and drank espresso as the rising sun illuminated the peaks drifting in and out of the clouds.

After a warming breakfast in Karasawa's dining room with its pot-bellied stove in the middle, we set out for the day's goal: Mt. Hotaka, at 3,190 meters the third highest in Japan—after Fujiyama and Mt. Shirane, which is only two meters higher.

The trail up the walls of the cirque was steep and slick with mist; often we had to pull ourselves up, hand-over-hand, feasting on wild blueberries and raspberries as we went. Along the way we spotted a few of the region's mountain ptarmigans. It was autumn and they were in the midst of a costume change from summer to winter plumage, half snowy-white, half speckled brown.

In a few hours we were at the top of the col, where—at no surprise to us—we found a brand new inn. It had been only a speck against the sky from Karasawa, which was now only a speck at the edge of a snowfield far below. We stopped inside for hot drinks, then finished the short climb to the peak completely enveloped in clouds, which parted only slightly to reveal more rocky pinnacles and distant snows. The trail consisted of a few slippery steel ladders and cables. We were told that the exposure is terrifying on a clear day, but since the visibility was only a few feet we had no idea how far a fall would take us. I also understood why the high trails of the Japan Alps have the reputation of being among the most difficult in the world short of technical mountaineering.

Half a dozen people were already crowded onto Hotaka's small summit, so we had to wait a moment for our own turn, then deposited the customary 100-yen notes and our business cards in the tiny rock shrine where a candle glowed. Only five of our group of twelve had made it all the way up this knee-killing route. It was sad to think of the view we might have enjoyed had the day been clear.

We descended and slept one more night at Karasawa. Sitting around our cribs late that evening, we nursed our sore feet, joked with the rows of Japanese hikers in the cribs across the aisle from us, and drank a powerful white liqueur which, the manager said, was a kind of vodka made from noodles.

After a hard night's sleep and a breakfast of seaweed, salted salmon, and pickled plums, we scrambled back down the glacial canyon and headed for another inn below Mount Yari. Yari is ten meters lower than Hotaka, but far more dramatic—a sharp spear of gunmetal-gray rock stabbing at the sky. High on the ridge near Yari there's a mountain hut, which, they say, can sleep 1,000 hikers—maybe 2,000 if they're willing to roll over at the same time.

However, we stayed low in the wooded canyon at an inn called Yarisawa, although we walked up high enough for some fine views of Yari in the setting sun. Yarisawa, like Karasawa, had cribs for sleeping—and hot *furos*, outstanding mountain photographs on the walls, shaky wooden platform clogs to wear in the toilets, and color television. After dinner we watched sumo wrestling and Samurai movies until fatigue drove us to the cribs.

One man in our group, having failed to bag Hotaka, set off for Yari in the morning. He made the summit in about four hours of hard climbing, and reported more ladders and cables and a reward of stunning views of ridge after ridge running off to the west, and deep, narrow river valleys below.

The breakfast fare at Yarisawa got the rest of us moving quickly: pickles, cold raw eggs, and chili peppers coated with sinus-blasting mustard. We longed for Tokusawa's croissants and coffee; everyone was on the trail early, double-timing back down the river valleys, stopping briefly at the vending machines of Yogusanso—for the hot sake, not the pornographic magazines.

We spent one more wonderful night at Tokusawa, our sixth in a trailside inn. We had one more gourmet dinner, one more long soak in the hot *furos*, one more mountain night beneath the quilts. Next morning it took us only two hours to walk back through the birch forests to Kamikochi, and roads and buses. We returned to Tokyo strong and healthy as a million yen.

Lynn Ferrin has published more than fifteen hundred travel articles and served thirty-seven years at VIA *magazine (formally* Motorland*), including seven years as the magazine's editor-in-chief. She currently lives in San Francisco.*

PAMELA LOGAN

✦ ✦ ✦

Dancing with
the Conqueror

Biking China's frontiers provides a memorable encounter.

I HAD AN APPOINTMENT WITH THE KHAN.

No, not just any Khan, but the Khan, Khan of Khans. The one who led his Golden Horde out of the steppe, the one who stomped over passes, romped over deserts, and flew like a firestorm across central Asia all the way to eastern Europe. The Khan who built one of the greatest empires the world has ever seen. The Great Khan. Genghis Khan.

That Khan.

I and a few thousand other pilgrims were slowly converging on Ejin Horo Banner, whose name means "enclosure of the Emperor" in Mongolian. In the past, worshippers trekked to this spot on the back of sturdy Mongol horses. Times have changed and nowadays they use minibuses, Land Cruisers, and Beijing Jeeps.

All except me. I was coming by mountain bike.

O.K., so I was slightly demented to be crossing Inner Mongolia on a mountain bike in March. But I had biked in China before—mostly in the country's wide-open west—and was therefore in practice. This foray into Inner Mongolia was part of my long-term and distinctly unofficial project to explore China's exotic frontiers. In between my responsibilities as Director of Research for the Hong Kong-based China Exploration & Research Society, I had managed to log more than six hundred miles in the provinces of Yunnan, Sichuan, Qinghai, and Xinjiang. Now I had a well-seasoned bike and yen to get even farther off the beaten track. Guidebooks had neglected Inner Mongolia so much that I knew it was a place with possibilities.

My destination was Genghis Khan's "mausoleum"—although almost no one believes his remains are really there. No matter. It's still a monument to their hero, and Mongolians come regardless. On the 23rd day of the third lunar month they come: in business suits and track suits, in lama's skirts and robes of azure silk. They carry wine to drink in the Khan's honor and slaughtered sheep to place on the altar before his crypt. Some bring nothing at all, but still they come.

The Great Sacrifice is held in spring, and spring is a miserable season on the Gobi. I had expected cold but didn't consider wind, and certainly didn't figure on blinding sandstorms dogging my path all along the way. Luckily, I had plenty of time, and the few days of good weather were just enough.

What I was learning had turned upside down everything I expected of Mongolians. I expected to find a stern, exacting people—men in silent communion with the limitless steppe on which they live, women rearing their children in the image of their warrior forefathers. What I got was completely different.

"You must drink the wine," one of my new friends whispered to me at my first Mongolian party, "otherwise he'll keep singing all night!" We were in a yurt—one of those round, felt-covered tents that are the traditional dwelling of nomadic tribes across Central Asia. Nowadays they are rare in Inner

Mongolia, but once they were a ubiquitous sight. This particular yurt was set on a sidewalk in the capital of Otog Banner where it functioned as a pub for local Mongolians.

The yurt's owner was standing before me, his outstretched hands holding a blue silk scarf and a bowl of clear liquid. He had just finished a loud and hearty stanza of traditional song. Lesson One: Mongolians love to sing, and to them, song and drink are inseparable.

I took the bowl in my hands, steeled myself, and poured cool liquid lava into my belly. "Wine" it certainly was not; from its industrial-strength bouquet and its 160-proof kick I guessed it must be *baijiu*—Chinese whiskey. I returned the bowl, it was refilled, and the singing-drinking exchange moved on to another pair of guests.

After a few rounds, the scarf and bowl came around to me. "Sing an American song!" they begged.

Let me tell you something about Mongolians: You can't— you just can't!—say no to these people. It doesn't work. They won't hear you. They believe that, more important than anything else including God, King, and Country, it's their mission on earth to make sure you have a good time. Besides, Mongolians won't believe that such a wretched, pitiable human being exists as one who can't sing, for Mongolians are born belting out tunes over the wide-open spaces of the steppe. I would have to show them that Americans are different.

I picked a blues song, thinking that its soulful strains would carry across the language and culture gap. As I opened my mouth I saw a ring of happy, anticipatory faces. Then it came: "Swing low, sweet chariot..." I croaked, and the faces suddenly fell. In my hands was the whisky-filled bowl, offered to the man sitting opposite. He snatched it from me and downed the booze in one swig. I closed my mouth, to everyone's obvious relief, and handed the bowl and scarf to the woman sitting next to me.

That night I began an informal research project into Methods for Alcohol Avoidance at Mongolian Parties. Being female helps, but it's not enough. One trick is to wait until their attention is elsewhere, then jiggle the bowl so that the contents slosh out. Pleas of a sick stomach work for one or two rounds, as do requests for beer instead of whiskey. But it's not easy.

The next morning, feeling a little wobbly, I pedaled out of there and on to my next adventure.

The road north from Otog Town is rough—little more than gravel sprinkled haphazardly over the sand of the Gobi. It passes through the heart of the Ordos, which is a league (prefecture) of Inner Mongolia. The Ordos is hemmed by the Great Wall to the south and the Yellow River to the north; girt by such durable geographic boundaries, the Ordos has developed its own distinct brand of Mongolian culture.

During most of its long history, the Ordos has had the bad luck of being a fertile and strategic buffer between two bristling empires. For 2,000 years, Mongolians and Chinese politely took turns overrunning it. By the early twentieth century the Chinese had won, but incessant warring and a weak central government had taken their toll. The Ordos was a wretched, bandit-infested land wrung dry by rapacious feudal princes and corrupt, parasitic lamas.

That's all changed now. Since Mao Zedong's communists took over in 1949, the Ordos has been cleaned up. Bandits and warlords are gone, and lamas (who have only recently reappeared on the scene after a long period of repression) concern themselves only with religion. Mongolians and Chinese don't always love each other, but they manage to live peacefully side by side, and intermarriage is common.

Before I came to the Ordos, I blithely imagined that society here is divided into two neat halves: settled Chinese and nomadic Mongolians. But it isn't that simple. Lesson Two: Beware of ethnic generalizations in the Ordos. Nomadism is virtually extinct; everyone lives in permanent houses now; moreover in the last few decades many Mongolians have become educated, learned professionals, and become city-dwellers.

In the countryside, choice of livelihood is driven not by race, but by economics. Long ago many Chinese settled here hoping to put the steppe under the plow, but poor soil has made agriculture a dicey proposition. It's not uncommon, therefore, to find Chinese living as herdsmen just like their Mongolian neighbors. Influence works both ways, and some Mongolians have taken up farming.

The ecosystem of the Ordos is fragile and changing. Archaeological evidence shows that the Ordos was once much wetter and warmer than it is now, and its inhabitants may well have been among the first farmers in Asia. But around 1500 B.C. the land turned dry, becoming what Mongols call classic "*gobi*"—arid, sparsely vegetated, gravelly land that is useless for agriculture but good for grazing sheep, goats, horses, and camels.

Lately the Ordos' population has begun to outstrip the land's meager resources. Despite the truckloads of fertilizer that go into the Ordos every year, its soil is dying. And even where no plow has ever touched, overgrazing is destroying once-verdant pastures. Now the Ordos is on the verge of total desertification. The government is well aware of this problem; widespread tree-planting has reduced the fierce winds, slowing movement of sand dunes that threaten to bury what little useful pasture that remains. Yet these non-native trees bring their own problems, and no one is sure what the long-term consequences will be. With a rising population and a dropping water table, the Ordos has difficult days ahead.

Desert is what I found under my tires as I rode north across

Otog Banner on an unpaved track. A steady headwind battered me, and sometimes I had to dismount to push my bike through sand dunes that had drifted across the road. But I didn't mind. The day was fine, the distance not far, and a slower pace gave me more time to enjoy the desert.

By now, after more than a week in Inner Mongolia, I had met a lot of Mongolians, but I didn't start to feel like a Mongol until I was crossing the Gobi's vast empty spaces. Riding a horse is undoubtedly best, but pedaling a bike is pretty good. In springtime the Gobi Desert is an endless plain of sand sprouting with withered grass and leafless bushes as far as the eyes can see. No wonder Mongolians have such sharp eyes; everything in their world is far: a runaway horse, a grazing camel, a house perched on an ever-so-gentle rise, clouds dancing over the horizon. As time went on I came to sense subtle changes in the desert: its slope and texture, its faded green and brown pastels. A greener spot means underground water and this, to a herdsman, is good.

Halfway along, I came to a crossroads where a highway maintenance station was built in the middle of nothing. The Chinese who inhabited it invited me inside for lunch. While I sat eating their humble fare of stewed mutton and rice, outside the wind suddenly increased, and the sky went black.

"*Guafeng*," muttered one of the men as he stood before the window. Lesson Three is the meaning of this all-important word: icy winds screeching from the north, lacerating airborne sand, and visibility shrinking to nothing. I settled down for a long siege.

Before long a lonesome wail surrounded the brick house, which was stoutly built with a thick windowless wall facing Siberia. Gradually the keening grew into a dull, surging roar, as if ocean waves and not mere air were threatening to hammer the house to dust. Outside, grit flew and trees flailed. I was glad

to be indoors, and that kindness to travelers is an enduring
tradition on the Gobi.

After a couple of hours the storm unexpectedly died down.
Rested now, and charged with new energy, I set out with my
bike again. After three hours of wallowing on the sandy road,
at last I reached a small town huddled in the lee of a sandstone
hill. As I pedaled into the outskirts, Buddhist monks in
flowing crimson robes came out to greet me.

After 1949, monks almost disappeared in Inner Mongolia,
but since the 1980s, when China's government decided to tolerate religion, Buddhism has been making a minor comeback.
The cities hold few believers, but in the hinterland there are
enough to support a few scattered monasteries. Xin Zhao,
where I had just arrived, had about twenty monks, most of
them old men. They were hard at work reviving their ancient
traditions—virtually identical to those of Tibet—here in this
lonely, windswept corner of desert.

As an honored (if unexpected) guest, I was put up in a room
on the monastery grounds and given all the tea, millet, cheese,
and noodles I could eat. By day I went to the temple—a
simple brick building erected to replace the original destroyed
during the Cultural Revolution—to listen to the monks
chant. I studied the religious paintings and books stored in
the monastery, so familiar to me from travels on the Tibetan
plateau. From villagers I learned fragments of Ordos Mongolian,
and worked on my Chinese, which virtually everyone there
knew. When the sandstorms eased I went for walks in
the hills.

At Xin Zhao I learned to eat Mongolian-style: pocket knife
in one hand, a joint of sheep in the other, mutton-fat lubricat-
ing my fingers and lips as I quickly reduced the joint to dry
bones. This simple ritual made me feel part of the numberless
nomadic tribes that have for millennia wandered Central Asia.

At Xin Zhao, time seemed to stand still, and before I knew it nearly a week had passed. The Spring Sacrifice of Genghis Khan was now fast approaching, and I hurried back on the road.

First traveling to the Ordos capital of Dongsheng, I then went south to Ejin Horo Banner, pedaling in the tracks of countless pilgrims. It was one of the Ordos' better roads, paved to accommodate tourists and others going to pay their respects to the Great Khan. Groves of hand-planted trees marked the borders of fields, for in the eastern Ordos many pastures have been given over to farming. After twenty-seven miles I knew I was getting close. Then, through a grove of willows, I spotted a high brick wall, and beyond it a triumphal blue-and-yellow dome rising from the summit of a hill: Genghis's great monument.

Legend has it that the Khan himself chose this spot to be his eternal home. They say that one day he was riding through the Ordos, accompanied by a contingent of mounted warriors, when he happened into a valley of extraordinary beauty. The Great Khan declared that it would be his final resting place, but when death actually came in summer of the year 1227, he was in the middle of a military campaign against the rebellious Tanguts in far-off northwest China. His lieutenants decided that the Khan's burial place and even his death itself must be a state secret. Accordingly, as the bearers carried his corpse in procession to a burial ground somewhere in northern Mongolia, they slew every living creature they met upon the road. The Khan was buried in a carefully concealed grave, which to this day lies undiscovered.

Sometime later, at Ejin Horo a cenotaph was erected in the Khan's honor, and the Seven Banners of the Ordos charged with the responsibility for its care. Originally the monument consisted of several great tents housing a crypt and assorted relics—bows, silver-plated saddles, swords—said to belong to the Khan. In 1955 the government replaced the tents with three permanent structures: domes, decorated in Mongolian style. The interior has a gallery of huge murals that tell Genghis Khan's life story. In the climactic panel the burly, square-jawed conqueror appears sitting on a high throne, surrounded by representatives of all his conquered peoples; their faces span the rainbow that is Eurasia. Part museum and part shrine, the complex at Ejin Horo is an enduring place of worship for Mongolians.

The tiny town was buzzing with activity when I arrived. As if emerging from a long winter's hibernation, everyone was outside busily sweeping, polishing, and cleaning. The guest-house windows were being shined to perfection by house-keepers garbed in brilliant robes. And bus-loads of guests were arriving every hour. That night I was visited by a smiling trio of Mongols, emissaries of a group of teachers from Wushen Banner who were staying next door. They asked, would I like to come with them to a dance? At their words my head was filled with visions of colorful ethnic twirls and flourishes, an authentic Mongolian celebration. My answer was: Of course!

The teachers had a mini-bus to take us to the venue, which was outside the town. We pulled up to a building, and when I spotted a sign with the word "karaoke," suddenly my heart fell. So much for traditional ethnic dance, I thought. Inside the place was a twirling reflecting ball hanging from the ceiling, colored lights, and an enormous battered boombox. Someone started a tape, and the schmaltzified strains of "Thus Spake Zarathustra" blared out.

Couples formed and began two-stepping in time to the music, which briskly evolved into a John Phillips Sousa march. Soon the floor was full of shuffling pairs. A jazzed-up "Auld Lang Syne" came on, followed by "The Blue Danube." Then Otelai asked me to dance.

He was short and barrel-chested, strong as a bull, dressed in jeans and a much-worn denim jacket. He had untidy, razor-cut hair and a square face that seemed oddly familiar. "I'm called Otelai," he shouted into my ear in hoarse Chinese, afterwards saying no more.

The music came faster, and Otelai's feet sped up. Striding in perfect time to the music as he whirled me around the room, he made it impossible for me to miss a step for he was practically lifting me off the floor. Out of the corner of my eye I saw the teachers' prim, disdainful glances at the boorish usurper who was monopolizing their honored guest. He wasn't one of them, I realized. But who was he?

The music stopped, and Otelai went off to grab a slug of beer. But before I had even caught my breath he was back again, the next dance was starting, and he was begging for another turn. Without waiting for an answer, he took my hand; we were off and flying again.

Faster the music came, and the wild Mongolian dervish was spinning me with ever greater speed and abandon. Soon we were colliding with other couples and bumping into furniture. In the middle of the blur, I heard his voice in my ear: "Please excuse the Ordos—we're so poor and undeveloped."

I said, "That doesn't matter. You are still good people." At this his grip tightened and his hand became warmer. At 10:30 the party ended, and Otelai disappeared as mysteriously as he had come. The teachers and I piled back into the mini-bus and returned to our guest house at the Genghis Khan Monument.

The following day was the Great Spring Sacrifice. Each of the Seven Banners of the Ordos sent representatives to present sacrifices at the shrine of Genghis, and hundreds of ordinary people made their own small offerings. All day long, parties of reverent Mongolians were carrying sheep carcasses, silk scarves, brick tea, milk, and bottled liquor to give to their Khan.

Kneeling, they sipped sacred wine and repeated the incantations of a tall, dour-faced priest. I'll never forget the solemn faces of a people who, even seven hundred years later, still worship their ancestral hero.

And I'll never forget when the ghost of Genghis Khan asked me to dance.

Pamela Logan received her doctorate in aerospace science from Stanford University before changing career paths. An interest in martial arts and photography led her to Tibet and resulted in her first book, Among Warriors: A Martial Artist in Tibet. *Returning to Tibet and taking an interest in ancient monasteries, she began leading international expeditions and established the Kham Aid Foundation to support monastery conservation work. She subsequently wrote* Tibetan Rescue: The Extraordinary Quest to Save the Sacred Art Treasures of Tibet. *Her life and work are chronicled at www.alumni.caltech.edu/~pamlogan/.index.html.*

$\star^{\star}\star$

Passing through Bandit Territory

A Nigerian-Nordic-American learns
new things about being a chameleon.

I AM ON A TRAIN IN SOUTHERN THAILAND HEADED NORTH UP
the Malay Peninsula. The train, windows shut tight against the
black night air, rattles from side to side. Outside, thick vegetation crowds a landscape so different from the mountains of the
north where I have spent two years. If I squint hard, I can make
out rubber trees, dark tendrils reaching to the ground, bright
red flowers like flecks of blood on a shadowy body, shuttered
houses on stilts. Each stop seems ominously static, like the set
of *Swiss Family Robinson* might look once movie production
has shut down.

Southern Thais say two things to me. The first is phrased
as query, after a sharp glance at my sarong and local sandals:
"You. Malay?"

"No, American," I usually admit, reluctantly owning up to
all that it implies. Unless I'm negotiating for budget accommodations, in which case I give myself leeway to claim my
father's nationality: "Nigerian."

"You could be Malay," they insist, eager to explain that there is an indigenous group on the peninsula with Negroid features, light brown skin and curly hair—just like mine! With my smooth Thai, they assure me, I could almost "pass."

These earnest ethnic Chinese and Thai and Lao encouraging me—a Nigerian-Nordic-American girl—to pass for Malay, make me smile. The idea of passing has long intrigued me, my child's fancy piqued by accounts of light-skinned blacks who left home and became white, trading all ties to self and family for freedom, something I could understand, or wealth, something I could not. The only biracial member of my family, I devoured tales of Tragic Mulattas who married white men then waited in horror to see how dark the children would turn out.

For me, with my brown skin and dark curls and round nose, passing in its most commonly used sense—for white—was out of the question. As if to underscore the point, I'd been born to a Nordic-American mother whose family of tall blondes embodied American ideals more than most Americans. While it didn't bother me not to look like them, it was frustrating not even being able to pass for what I actually was. I was fascinated by those mixed-race children with golden skin and wild sheaves of hair like straw. Delicate, exotic birds, they clung to their white mothers in public, as if their blue and green and hazel eyes that passed through and over me, refusing to see the world staring at them, were indeed transparent. Unlike them, I looked like every other brown girl, my split heritage hidden from the naked eye.

I worried. How, then, would my tribespeople, the other Nigerian-Nordic-Americans, recognize and come to claim me?

What I wanted most to be recognized as was Nigerian, a foreign identity I imagined might account for my perpetual feelings of misplacement. In college, I studied other African students—their dark skin firm as tree trunks, their bodies so strong they nearly burst out of their flimsy European clothes—and gave up. There was no imitating the deliberate roll of the girls' hips, the way the boys threw back their heads and laughed, white teeth flashing. They were too confident to have come from any country I knew. And so I passed for African American, a dynamic which carrying no privilege, was not even considered passing. I was just another insecure brown girl on the unwelcome shores of America.

The second thing locals on the Malay Peninsula say is: "Be careful. Armed bandits."

Southern Thailand is notorious for gun-toting robbers and smugglers who roam in bold bands, sometimes posing as shaven, saffron-clad monks, oftentimes murdering their victims. The Bangkok papers teem with sensational reports of gangs attacking long-distance buses then slinking into jungle lairs or melting over the border to Malaysia. It is whispered that some villages are virtually owned by bandit leaders, who conscript young men into service like the drug warlords of the north. Popular books and movies, on the other hand, claim bandits find easy followings, due to Robin Hood-like tendencies to steal from the landed and give to the poor.

So far I've been lucky. A woman—and *farang* (foreigner) at that—traveling solo with her wealth in a single bag is a laughably easy mark. When queried about the existence and location of my Protective Male, I reply that I am a serious student on *thudong* (pilgrimage) and have only recently stopped being a Buddhist nun. No men for me!

"*Buad maechi?*" the Thai exclaim in disbelief, and I nod, yes, I did indeed ordain. My close cap of curls, just now recovering from the razor, supports this wild claim. All interest in my recalcitrant Protective Male now lost to the desire to make merit for their karma, they confide which guesthouses are not in league with bandits, which towns to avoid. And except for once hearing gunshots during dinner near the Malaysian border and having to shutter the kerosene lamps and lie with faces pressed to the floorboards for the rest of the evening, nothing untoward has happened.

Staring out the train window at the murky, abandoned streets, I decide that good karma and luck may not be enough this time. It occurs to me that the Thai's two discussion points are somehow enmeshed to my advantage, that I can best *be careful* of armed robbers by *passing* as Malay. Many of the bandits are rumored to be ethnic Malays, members of the Muslim separatist movement fighting against Thai Buddhist government. The less foreign I am, I try to reassure myself, the greater the likelihood that I will be passed over when choices are made to rape, rob, and kill.

I stand up and stagger through the rocking train, keeping my movements muted and tight, resolving to be less forthcoming in my conversation. In the north, no matter how Thai I acted, I was always too big, too brown, my body movements too unrestrained. There was never any possibility of melting into the scenery. Now, if viewed at a distance, my very brownness might save me.

In the dining car, three men in the snowy shirtsleeves and dress slacks of Thai businessmen blow my cover. First they send the waiter to my table to ask if I speak English; then they insist on buying me dinner. They look to be in their mid-twenties, which means thirty-something, and are on a slow, steady path to drunkenness, having chosen pricey Singha beer rather than cheap Mekong whiskey. Everything about them, from their pinkening faces and expansive gestures, to their courtly invitations of "Please to join us," seems more intent on impressing each other than me.

I accept.

Their questions, phrased in excellent English, are the usual suspects: *Where do you come from? How do you like Thailand? Where is your husband? Can you eat Thai food?*

I reply in English, with a few Thai words dropped in, pretending to speak far less than I actually do. This is Plan B: if unable to pass as Malay, always make sure your opponent underestimates you.

They crow with delight to hear my simple Thai, and when I cover my rice with tiny green heaps of chilies, there is much giggling and nudging. "Look, look," they tell each other, squirming with delight. "The *farang* eats Thai chilies!"

I begin to doubt the likelihood of them being hustlers. Still, I shake my head when they ask if I drink Singha and keep to tiny, chilled bottles of orange Fanta.

They order another round and tick off a list of beautiful beach islands near the Gulf, places like Phuket, Haad Yai, Koh Samui, the so-called James Bond Island, all of which will later be immortalized in big budget movies, blonde starlets spilling onto the sand like oil slicks.

I explain that I'm not on vacation. I'm on a pilgrimage in search of famous nuns.

In my pocket is my most valuable possession, next to my passport: a list of nuns and temples. Next to each woman or *wat* (temple), my teacher has scribbled the name of the province in which she or it is located or, if I'm lucky, the town. Nothing more.

Imagining myself a black female Paul Theroux, I will traverse Southeast Asia from Malaysia all the way up to Burma, throwing myself off the train wherever I hear of someone or someplace I should see. The words "I've heard of some nuns living near…" are enough to start me fumbling for my bag, heading for the exit.

"Let me see," the youngest and best-dressed businessman

insists, holding out his hand. It occurs to me that this might be his promotion celebration or that he could be the CEO's son who has just landed his first big deal. He studies the list, his eyes tiny slits of slate in a lobster-red face. I feel drunk just looking at him.

"Wait a minute," he says, his whiskey-softened shoulders tightening in alarm. He jabs a manicured finger at the very next stop on my list. "You can't go there! Petchaburi is owned by bandits!"

The train jolts around a corner, throwing my heart against my rib cage. I am scheduled to disembark in Petchaburi tonight. The town is crucial to my pilgrimage; one of the only centers for nuns is rumored to be nearby.

I shrug, feigning indifference. "*Mai pen rai,*" I say, invoking Thailand's most commonly used phrase. *Never mind. It's O.K. No problem.*

"No, no," he insists, his eyes sharpening with increasing sobriety. "The train gets in at three in the morning. They know who arrives, where they stay!"

He whips around to his friends and blurts a flurry of southern dialect. Though most of the words are familiar, I assume a blank expression, heart still racing.

"What should she do?" one of the men asks. "*Mai dii leuy.*" *It's not good.*

"She shouldn't go alone," he replies. "They kidnap visitors and plantation workers to extort money."

"Why doesn't she get off at your stop?" the third suggests.

"Yes," my would-be savior agrees, turning his palms to face upward, a gesture I think might be safe to interpret as sincere. "My town is larger and more secure. I can make sure she gets to a guesthouse. In the morning I can come with my car to drive her to *samnak maechi.*" *The nun center.*

"*Dii lao,*" the second man counsels. *Good enough.*

It is indeed a good plan. I decide to accept. I know that to ask a Thai for help, even directions, is to embark on an extended relationship in which his responsibility will not end until I have achieved my goal or safely reached my destination.

The first businessman, face red above his pristine white linen shirt, turns back to me and proposes his solution, speaking careful, clear English. "You should not get off at Petchaburi, which is the next stop," he cautions. "You should get off at Ratchaburi, the following stop, where I live." He explains why.

I look skeptical for a few minutes before making a show of allowing myself to be convinced.

The bill is then settled, a ritual involving a drunken race to unzip their clutch wallets of Italian leather, plus shouted claims and counter-claims of being the eldest and thus responsible for paying. Each tosses red and tan bills onto an increasing mound on the table.

I thank all three, placing my hands together in a steeple and bringing them to my forehead in a traditional *wai*. This delights them immensely, though their drunken attempts to return the gesture look more Three Stooges-like than Thai. Afterward, I head back towards second-class, while they exit out the front of the dining car, to first-class, fresh bottles of Singha clinking in their hands.

"See you in a few hours," the first businessman says. "Remember not to get off at Petchaburi—wait for Ratchaburi!" We agree to meet on the platform.

Back at my seat, I find that a family, a tiny mother with three children, has joined me. Trying to keep my head respectfully below the mother's, I duck into my window seat, diagonally across from hers. Once seated, I nod and smile. The broad planes of her face twitch a moment, as if processing the infor-mation that she has inadvertently installed her family next to something strange, be it Malay or *farang*, then smooth into determined pleasantness. The two younger children freeze in mid-gesture, saucer-eyed and speechless.

The eldest child, a boy of about ten, has ended up in the seat next to mine. Spine rigid as a dancer's, he perches at the absolute edge; one more inch forward, and he would be levitating in air. He makes a fluttering gesture with his hand, an unspoken plea. His mother snaps a single syllable in southern dialect, its meaning unmistakable: *Stay!*

Keeping his head perfectly still, the boy monitors me out the corners of his eyes, pupils rotating in their sockets as if he were performing *khon*, a Thai masked dance based on the Ramayana. He is Hanuman, the Monkey General, terrifying the demon army with his jerky movements and wildly spinning eyeballs.

Grinning to myself, I fall into that half-waking state of train travel. My limbs loosen and follow the jarring rhythm. Outside an epic battle rages, blue-faced demons pitted against Lord Rama and the monkey soldiers, little Hanuman poker-straight at my side.

When the conductor comes through the car, calling Petchaburi, my original destination, I consider jumping up and dashing for the exit. *Why have you allowed your plan to be modified?* I reprimand myself. *What if the businessman, now drunk, has forgotten our agreement? Or what if he was just talking? What if there are no armed robbers?*

I press my nose to the cold glass and peer out. The platform looks empty, though it's too dark to be sure. *What does a bandit-owned town look like?* I wonder. I imagine clusters of men with machine guns on every corner. Will they be dressed in dark blue farmers' shirts with red headbands and sashes like the opium smugglers of the north? Or in snug polyester pants with flared legs and mirrored sunglasses, like the blood vendetta gangsters in Bollywood movies? I imagine a banner strung across the train station: *Welcome to Bandit Territory!* spelled out in six-inch letters.

I decide to get off the train. Stick to my original plan. Rely on myself. I lean forward to grab the knapsack under my seat.

Just then Hanuman nods off, his head dropping face-first into the crook of my elbow. He is warm as a furnace, his soft cheeks like sun-ripened peaches against my skin.

Startled, I bolt upright and jerk my arm away. The stubble of his shaven head scrapes along the tender flesh of my inner arm. He squirms into fetal position, his small, round head falling into my lap like a gift.

Across the aisle, his family dozes, piled atop one another, the younger children's mouths half-open like tiny, budding flowers. I rest my hand lightly on the shoulder of the sleeping boy. The train hurtles through bandit territory.

An hour later we reach Ratchaburi, my new destination. Reluctantly, I lift the boy from my lap. His eyes flutter open for a split second, momentarily wild, and then close, the lids settling into smiling gold crescents. I drape him over both seats, and then grab my knapsack and sprint to the end of the car.

The conductor watches as I disembark and scour the length of the train in both directions. "*Khon oen?*" he asks. *Someone else?*

I nod.

A minute later he jerks his chin at me—"Malay?"

I nod.

We wait some more. The station is locked and dark. No banner, which is good. Except for a *samloh* driver asleep in the back of his three-wheeled rickshaw, the platform is empty.

Finally, the train conductor shrugs. "Sure this is the right stop?"

I wonder if I got them mixed up and was supposed to have gotten off at Petchaburi, the first stop. "Did a man get off at the last stop?" I ask.

He shakes his head, the gold braid on his cap glinting in the light from the train doorway. "No one likes to get off at these stops at night."

This is why he has kept the train waiting.

I stare open-mouthed, just now beginning to comprehend the size of his concern, of my stupidity. I know nothing about this town, other than it is an hour north of my original destination, closer to Bangkok, and therefore supposedly larger and safer. For all I know, this is the heart of bandit territory, and the businessman gets a commission on all *farang* women he lures here.

The train begins to snort and strain, like an animal in restraint, and the conductor hops onto the metal step. "*Glap maa?*" he offers. *Do you want to get back on?*

I shake my head. In the *wat* they taught us to confront the very things that terrify us. Or perhaps I am simply paralyzed with indecision.

With a great squeal, the train pulls away. "Good luck," the conductor calls. "Be careful!"

I hoist my knapsack to my shoulder and turn to find the *samloh* driver sitting up regarding me.

"*Samloh?*" he inquires.

I nod briskly and scramble into the back. "Take me to the Chinese hotel," I bark. "I'm late."

As the driver begins to pilot the *samloh* through the abandoned streets in that slow, standing pedal that resembles slow-motion running, I pray that the stereotype about *samloh* drivers being drug pushers, pimps, or bandit informants is greatly exaggerated. I also pray that there *is* a Chinese hotel.

Though the town doesn't seem as large as promised, the center resembles any other Thai town at night—dark and shuttered, with metal grates pulled down over shop entrances, crushed glass atop stucco gates, and decorative grilles covering the windows of upstairs apartments. These are standard security measures, as common as the high sidewalks to protect against flooding, so I tell myself there is no reason to read them as ominous.

I think about Maechi Roongdüan, the head nun at my *wat*. It was she who inspired me to make this pilgrimage. When she was in her late twenties, not much older than I, she spent three months walking from one end of Thailand to the other with only an umbrella, a mosquito net, an alms bowl, and the robes on her back. She reached the Malay Peninsula during rubber season, which meant that the villagers worked at night stripping trees by candlelight and slept during the day, when alms rounds happen. As a result, she went for days without food and had to meditate to overcome hunger pangs. Often, alone in empty fields, the stench of rubber heavy in the dark air, she came out of meditation to find cobras with their heads in her lap.

"Perhaps drawn by my body heat," she'd marveled to me, and I had instead marveled at her and her fierce determination to love all creatures, no matter the cost.

To my amazement, the *samloh* driver deposits me at what is indeed a Chinese hotel, a modest gray stone building in the center of town. I pay him, tipping just enough to suggest gratitude but not wealth, before thrusting my hand through the iron gate and ringing the bell.

The ubiquitous old Chinese watchman in white undershirt, drawstring pajama bottoms and slippers shuffles across the courtyard with a lantern and heavy ring of keys. He shows me to a room, clean and Spartan, and points out the shower room. We exchange not a single word.

Once inside the stone shower walls, I ladle cool water from a giant jar over my body, shaking a bit in the chill air, allowing myself a few tears of relief under the camouflage of water. For a short time in this tiny, gray space, I am me. Not moving. Not negotiating. Not passing into any particular shape.

I have just returned to my room when the watchman knocks on the door and announces that someone has come for me.

My heart thuds. This is it. The *samloh* driver has sold me out!

"No visitors," I cry, eyeing the flimsy bolt. "It's too late, and I'm a respectable girl."

"No, no, it's me," a familiar voice protests, and I crack the door to find the businessman from the train standing in the hallway. He is red as ever, his boyish face sheepish. "May I come in?"

"Only for a minute," I say, "I must sleep."

He enters the room and plops heavily on the bed.

Alarmed, I leave the door open wide and stand between it and him. "What happened to you?"

"I fell asleep," he says, rubbing his puffy eyes, "and missed our stop. I had to get off at the next town and find a taxi to bring me back to Ratchaburi. It was difficult at this hour. Then I had to get to this hotel."

"How did you know where I was?"

He chuckles. "How many *farang* disembark in the middle of the night? I went to the train station and asked the *samloh* driver. He brought me here."

I join his laughter, though it occurs to me that my initial assumption was correct and the driver did indeed sell me out, albeit to this bumbling businessman instead of a bandit king.

"How did you know about this place?" he asks.

It is my turn to chuckle. "I didn't! I knew this wasn't a tourist town, so if there were a hotel, it would be a 'traveler's hotel' for traders. I just guessed that ethnic Chinese would run it. I said, 'Take me to the Chinese hotel' and it worked."

He roars. "That's very clever. You're quite resourceful!" He shakes his head. "Here I was supposed to protect you, but you did fine without me."

I duck my head modestly.

When he expresses some interest in more drink, I tell him it's time to go. He stands up, shoulders slumping in exhaustion, his fine linen wilting like a warm carnation, and says he'll be back with his car at eleven to take me to the nun center.

"I will make it up to you," he vows. "Eleven it is!"

At half-past noon the following afternoon I consider my options. Who knows how far the nun center is and how long it will take me to find it? I need to budget time to travel back to Petchaburi, time to find the center, time to meet the nuns and see the place, time to return here to Ratchaburi. I want to be back on the train this evening and get the hell out of bandit territory before dark.

The Chinese hotel owner confirms that there is indeed an evening train and tells me where the marketplace is. He's never heard of a nun center in this town or the next, however.

"If a man comes," I tell him, "please explain that I had to go but will be back for the evening train."

The walk through town skirts new territory. I am used to two extremes, either tourist metropolises like Chiang Mai and Bangkok that teem with expatriates and English-language signs or small, traditional villages, where everyone turns out on the dirt path to greet the *farang*. I have never before negotiated a mid-sized city filled with ethnic Chinese, Thai, Lao, Indian, and Malay. I feel like an extra who didn't get the script.

At the market I wait beneath the sign for *tuk-tuk* going to Petchaburi. Several Nissan pickups pass by, the narrow, padded benches in back already crowded with passengers. Finally a newer Nissan pulls up and parks. The driver gets out and heads into the market. A pretty young woman remains behind in the passenger's seat.

I approach and lean in though the open window. "Are you

going to Petchaburi?" I ask. "I'm looking for this center—" I proffer the piece of paper. "I think it's on the road between here and Petchaburi, somewhere in the country."

She squints at the paper, frowning. "I'm not sure," she says, "I'll have to ask him."

The driver returns with a giant burlap bag of rice draped over his shoulder. He staggers to the back and tosses it in, then joins us, slapping his palms together. He has the same face as the girl and looks a bit older, in his early-twenties. "*Arai na?*" he asks us. *What is it?*

"Can we take her to this place?" the girl asks. "It's a *wat.*"

He gives me a quick once-over. "A temple?"

"Well, a nun center, really," I explain.

The three of us study my teacher's list of names and provinces. I know what they must be thinking. Thai *wat* are cursed with long, flowery names that no one uses. In common parlance, they are known by descriptive nicknames: Marble Temple, Temple of Golden Caves, Temple of the Emerald Buddha, Temple of the Reclining Buddha, Temple of the Ceylonese Buddha. If you don't know its nickname or address, a *wat* is nearly impossible to find.

"Get in." The driver motions for the girl to slide over.

"Oh no," I protest, "I can get in the back."

"No, no," both insist, and so I squeeze into the front. We start off immediately, without waiting to load more passengers.

Worried that I've allowed my fat *farang* itinerary to supercede everyone else's, I glance back to check on the others through the small window in the cab. The pickup bed is empty, save for the bag of rice. There are no vinyl benches, no intricate grillwork on the canopy, no passengers.

This is not a *tuk-tuk.*

I whip around to regard my companions. The young man drives hunched over, conferring softly with the girl.

Then it dawns on me. They are brother and sister come to market to do shopping, not pick up fares. I have just commandeered the private car of some family out doing errands.

"*Khaw thôod!*" I cry. *Excuse me!* "I thought you were a *tuk-tuk*! I am so ashamed! Please," I beg, fumbling for the door handle, "you don't have to take me."

"No, no," they assure me. "*Mai pen rai!*" *Never mind. No problem.* For the next hour I cringe against the door of the cab, trying to make myself as small as possible, as if the size of my gall could somehow shrink with my body, while my shy hosts motor around town, silently intent on their task, asking none of the usual, eager questions.

At each bend in the muddy, rutted roads, the brother disembarks and asks for directions from befuddled monks and laypeople. At each wrong temple, we are directed to another, equally wrong.

Finally an old woman sends us to the long-distance bus park, where a driver in a silky disco shirt and wraparound sunglasses assures us that yes, he passes by the road to the nun center.

As they hand me over, my hosts apologize for abandoning me before my destination has been reached. They would like to take me to the center themselves, the sister explains, a crease appearing between her perfect brows, but their mother expected them home an hour ago. Can I possibly forgive them?

They lean forward, twin faces rosy with sudden boldness and affection, looking for all the world as if we have spent a lovely afternoon together.

"Are you Malay?" the brother blurs out, finally daring to ask something of me, of this interaction.

"No, American," I say, for once happy to be so, eager to give them a story for their mother that's a fair exchange for their generosity. "I used to be a nun in the north, and now I'm on pilgrimage. You've helped so much."

Their eyes widen, and we all grin. I entered their truck under misapprehension and they invited me under a misapprehension of their own, and all this time we've been sitting side by side, mistaking each other for someone easier to imagine. Passing.

"Goodbye!" the sister calls out the window. "Good luck!" her brother adds. Both wave. "We'll miss you."

When I return to the Chinese hotel that evening, after the bus ride into the countryside and the three-kilometer hike down a dirt road, after my tour of the nun center and my afternoon spent talking with the head nun, after a catching a ride back to Ratchaburi with some local farmers, I find the businessman from the train waiting in the lobby.

He looks forlorn yet dapper in fresh linen and glossy leather sandals.

"I overslept again," he wails, standing at my approach. "It took me forever to get home last night — the *samloh* driver didn't wait outside — so I was completely exhausted." He blushes and hangs his head. "I got here at one."

I make a flowery apology for not waiting and explain that everything worked out. Ten kilometers outside of town, the long-distance bus had stopped alongside a lonely stretch of rice paddies, hectares and hectares of emerald and gold fields broken only by the occasional, morose-looking water buffalo. The afternoon sun beat down, hotter than I was used to in the north.

"Here?" I'd asked the driver. "This is the nun center?"

He'd shrugged, eyes camouflaged behind the sunglasses gripping his face, and pointed to a dirt path bisecting the road. "There are nuns down there," he'd said. "I hear."

Fair enough. I'd thanked him. "*Khob khun kha.*"

The bus lumbered away, and I'd started down the path, trying not to think about how I'd get back to town. After all,

I'd made it the entire length of Southeast Asia with no plan.

After reporting on the success of my visit to the businessman, I collect my bag from the old Chinese watchman, who startles me with a flash of betel-stained teeth, and ask the businessman to do me the great favor of seeing me to the train.

Perking up a bit, he ushers me to a sparkling cream Mercedes. As he holds open the passenger door, he shakes his head. "You're a woman alone," he marvels, "a poor student, a *farang*. Imagine!" He pauses, as if pondering this triple source of my supposed isolation before concluding, "But you don't need any help."

And though it isn't quite true, I smile modestly, once again accepting the compliment, momentarily relishing what it is to be Malay.

Faith Adiele, a graduate of Harvard Collage and the Iowa Writers' Workshop, is assistant professor of English at the University of Pittsburgh. This story is excerpted from her book Meeting Faith: The Forest Journals of a Black Buddhist Nun. *She lives in Pittsburgh, Pennsylvania.*

CAROLE JACOBS

⋆ ⁕ ⋆

On a Wing and a Prayer

Nature will ensure that you go at the right pace.

ON AN OVERCAST MORNING, THE AIR IS HEAVY WITH RAIN.
The Himalayas, which on clear days loom over the valley
like shimmering sentinels, are now obscured by dark
clouds. Thunder echoes against distant foothills, and a bolt of
lightening strikes close. Our guide clutches her prayer beads
and shakes her head. "It's not a good day for flying," she says.

We had risen at dawn today in hopes of catching a flight to
the tiny village of Lukla, at 9,275 feet, the start of the winding
trail to Mount Everest.

Even in good weather, it is a precarious flight through
narrow valleys and gorges up a precipitous mountain staircase.
With no ground control, pilots must fly by land vision, which
means the only "good" day for flying is a perfectly clear day. In
early spring, such days can be few and far between. Worse, only
four of nine planes servicing Lukla are working.

I glance at my traveling companions and almost read
their minds.

Last night had held such promise. It had been a soft, starry night; hopeful the clearing would hold, we hailed a cab for a celebratory last supper, clattering down into a brainlike maze where candles burned in hundreds of shantytown windows. As we approached the riverside burial ground, a blue flame flickered above a funeral pyre, illuminating a pair of charred feet. I covered my eyes and shuddered: We had stayed too long at the fair. After a week of dust, crowds, fumes, and stench, we were all ready to trade the cacophony of Kathmandu for the tinkling of a distant waterfall.

Not that Kathmandu isn't worth a visit. At once modern and medieval, the bustling capital of Nepal is relentlessly fascinating. Like Alice going through the looking glass, I'd tumbled into a labyrinth lost in space and time where every turn delivers the unexpected. Bells chime from hillside temples where monkeys roam; barefoot farmers carry huge baskets of cabbages to market on shoulder poles. In twisted alleyways crammed with shops one can buy, why, anything at all: lopsided yak wool mittens and sweaters, Buddha masks, embroidered knapsacks with peekaboo mirrors, Tibetan knives with huge curved blades, even Chiclets chewing gum. Icons grin and groan from ancient temples, children peer from darkened windows, and through a succession of open doorways I see two girls in silk saris sitting in a darkened courtyard, picking nits out of each others' hair. To those back home I write, "You can't imagine."

Down a dusty lane, the Mad Hatter's watch had stopped in the 1960s. It seems everyone sports blue jeans, sandals, a backpack; the Western women in long, flowing skirts in deference to Nepali custom. Narrow streets are jam-packed with bookstores, backpackers' shops and cafés with names disorienting in their familiarity, like Alice's Restaurant and Pumpernickle's, where trekkers pore over guidebooks and scribble furiously in their journals.

Now, for the third morning in a row, we rise to a gloomy dawn and head to the domestic airport.

Our guide, Cynthia, who has lived in Nepal off and on for six years and speaks the language, corners an airport official in hopes of pulling some strings in the cat's cradle of Nepali bureaucracy.

An hour later she comes rushing toward us, her long red braid flying. "Let's go! We're on! Hurry!"

We stare at her dumbly and follow her to the departure lounge, where we wait another hour before we're escorted to the runway and waved toward a small plane. As I crouch low to enter, I hear droning behind me: *Om mani padme hum!* (Oh lotus-seated god of the celestial jewel!) Apparently, I'm not the only one who's nervous.

Norm, a lawyer and pilot from Los Angeles who spent a year in an aerobics class to train for the trek, takes a seat by the cockpit to keep watch; Cynthia collapses in her seat and draws out her prayer beads. Doug, a philosophy professor, and his sidekick, Donna, a newspaper reporter, embrace. As we lift off, I look down on the airport and say a silent prayer. I'm glad we're on our way.

Meanwhile, in Lukla, the Sherpa guides are waiting to take us into their homes and hearts. The Sherpas emigrated to this mountainous region from Tibet 400 years ago and still practice an ancient form of Buddhism. In the past century, famous mountaineers discovered in these gentle, fun-loving people a natural aptitude for guiding. For the next week they would lead us from one small village to the next and finally to the remains of the Thyangboche Monastery at 13,000 feet, perched on a panoramic ledge in the shadow of Mount Everest. We would stay in the guides' homes and learn firsthand about their way of life.

Out the left window of the plane, snowcapped peaks form

a wall; to the right, the countryside rises in steplike terraces to hazy foothills blued by mist and distance. The plane turns right into a narrow gorge lined by a turbulent river, where cliffs and valleys intersect at unearthly angles. We follow it to a sheer ledge outcropping.

As the plane noses toward the ledge, my stomach flip-flops. It is the Lukla runway, a strip barely longer than a football field that bulldozes through town like Main Street. The plane touches down with tentative wheels, wobbles along the runway, then shudders to a stop. As the pilot pries open the squeaky door, we leap out to freedom, blinding light, and a landscape from Oz, where emerald foothills soar above a storybook village of weather-beaten chalets.

Puffy clouds play peekaboo with distant, snow-covered peaks and far below roars a river churning with glacial silt, racing through a gorge laced together with threadlike suspension footbridges. Before we can pick up our luggage, our guides materialize—a ragtag band of hearty souls wearing secondhand clothing donated by trekkers and accompanied by yaks, each wearing a bell.

The guides hug Cynthia, an old friend, greet us shyly with the traditional Nepali *namaste* ("The divine in me salutes the divine in you"), then hoist our fifty-pound bags on their shoulders two and three at a time. They lash them to the yaks, along with a week's supply of food, tents, pots and pans, even a kitchen table. Then with a flick of a stick against the yaks' backs, we're off. Despite their bulk, the yaks step along lightly like cartoon ballerinas.

The trail we're on is the major thoroughfare from Lukla to all villages and peaks north, a human highway of loadbearing Sherpas. Small boys trudge past us with eight-foot beams strapped to their shoulders; young girls balance gigantic baskets on their heads; old women lug crates of produce.

About a half-mile down the trail, Newang, a Sherpa with an impressive command of English, comes up from behind and puts a gentle hand on my shoulder.

"It is not good to walk so fast," he says.

"The mountains will wait."

Trekking: The word conjures up visions of trudging up steep, rugged trails with sixty-pound packs strapped to the back. But little of Nepal is wilderness, even though it houses the world's highest mountains and several national parks; in the fourth-poorest country in the world, every acre of arable land is farmed. The remaining forests are felled for firewood. The high country, full of moonscapes bald from deforestation, is used for hunting and grazing. We would hike from village to village with guardian angels who insisted we laydown our burdens (five-pound day packs) and partake of tea at every available tea shop. "At this rate," quipped Norm, still on LA. time, "we'll get there in about three years."

The Sherpas live close to their gods.

Around every bend is evidence of their devotion: god statues; stupa shrines; boulders carved with religious symbols, called *mani*. Tattered prayer flags flutter from rooftops and from the swaying suspension bridges we gingerly cross.

After hiking an hour, we stop at a tea shop bearing a hand-lettered sign which lists the menu and the suggestion to "Find Your Self." Doug, our resident philosopher, muses over the phrase's meaning for a moment, still warming up. By the end of the week he'd be debating life, death, Jesus, and George Bush, not necessarily in that order.

The Sherpas are warming up, too. At the next tea shop, they tell us a story about the head of yeti, the sole remains of the legendary Abominable Snowman.

In 1954, large, humanlike footsteps were seen in the snow

near Mount Everest. Expeditions were made in search of the elusive beast but all that surfaced was a domelike scalp, which to this day resides in the Khumjung Monastery, near the high point of our trek. Experts pronounced the scalp a fake, but the Sherpas said we should decide for ourselves. We would be able to do that if we were lucky and the monk was home in Khumjung.

As we hike up a hill to our first night's campsite, we're amazed to find the Sherpas have already erected a small tent city, including a toilet tent and dining tent. A fire blazes in the shack where they're cooking dinner. On seeing us approach, the guides carry out pans of hot water and place one at each of our tents. "Hey!" says Norm. "Room service!"

By the time we finish cleaning up, dinner is ready, a four-course meal of soup, chicken-rice casserole, bread, several vegetable dishes, and pudding and tea for dessert. After dinner we roll into our tents and fall asleep to the sounds of the Sherpas singing as they wash dishes. Tomorrow we'll awaken to a tinkling bell and another pan of hot water by our tent.

Sophie, a Utah widow with two months' worth of Handi Wipes in tow, scolds me about drinking from dirty cups. Newang repeats his suggestion that I slow down. Do I listen? Nah!

Invigorated by the brisk mountain air and fueled by a hefty breakfast of oatmeal and pancakes, I scamper up the steep, 2,000-foot rise to the next village like a mountain goat and leave the guides and yaks in the dust. For an hour I'm on top of the world, with the views to prove it. By the time the rest of the group arrives in Namche Bazaar, I'm flat on my back with altitude sickness. So, apparently, is Norm, who becomes so weak en route to Namche he has to hike back down, and out of our lives.

A day later, I'm still flat on my back while my companions

romp about the bustling cliffside streets of Namche, an amphitheatre carved in a rugged hillside, soaring peaks forming a glistening backdrop.

Doug and Donna have problems with altitude sickness but recover fairly quickly. They hike the town's steep trails to a museum and monastery, and bargain in the open-air bazaar. Sophie gets a private viewing of the Namche yeti head which, to distinguish from the "real" thing coming up in the next village, Donna dubs the "son of yeti head." When another day passes and it becomes clear that I'm not going to recover without going down to acclimate before coming back up slowly, the group and I part company—temporarily, we hope.

As they ascend to Thyangboche Monastery at 13,000 feet, with views of Mount Everest and her sister peaks towering 21,000 to 29,028 feet, my hiking buddy Newang and I descend 3,000 feet to a small village. This time he doesn't have to tell me to slow down; I'm so weak I nearly crawl. Normally bilingually loquacious, Newang is silent as a monk. I think he's praying for me.

I feel better as morning dawns, so we idle back up to the Khumbu Lodge in Namche, a popular hiker's hangout with hot showers, a restaurant, and panoramic views. Here I sleep in the same suite as former president Jimmy Carter. His mountain vigor is legendary; rumor has it his Secret Service escorts fell like flies.

After another day's rest, Newang and I climb up to Khumjung on back trails to the four-star Mount Everest View Hotel. At 13,000 feet, it is the highest hotel in the world, with its own airstrip and direct forty-five-minute flights from Kathmandu. Every room has a private view of the mountain, which is a good thing.

Because it is nearly impossible to acclimatize to such a high altitude within the space of a forty-five-minute flight, many guests spend most of their time in bed recovering from altitude sickness.

Newang pores over the fancy menu, written in English-as-the-Japanese-speak-it, learning a few new words along the way. We order tea and drink it quickly, not wanting to stay too long: at well over $100 a night, it's a pricey place for a relapse.

As we hike down a snowy back trail to Khumjung, the group spots us and cheers us on. It's good to see them again; in ten days we have come to know and count on each other. Tomorrow we will begin what should be a less eventful descent. But not before making one last stop.

The monk just happens to be home at the Khumjung Monastery. With great flourish, he brings out a box, unlocks it, and withdraws what looks to be a coconut with rock musician's hair. He holds it up briefly before hurrying it back into its box. Then he demands an exorbitant fee.

"Oh, come on," says Doug, digging into his pocket. "You don't really believe that's the head of yeti now, do you?" The monk starts, as if he has been slapped.

Donna mutters something under her breath: "That's a bunch of bunk."

"Bunk...what does that mean, bunk?" Newang asks as we walk back to the lodge to pack up. When Donna explains, he explodes with laughter, as if it's the funniest thing he's ever heard. Safely back in Lukla two nights later, we sit around the farewell dinner table discussing the Sherpas. They are the most polite, good-natured, and even-tempered people we've ever met. If we had come between them and their gods, they had never let on.

They are so much more civilized than we are that we fear our stumblings, grumblings, and wisecracks have offended them. When we ask if this is so, they smile and say of course not, although we frequently surprised them.

"In a good way?" I ask hopefully.

They gaze at us for a long moment, apparently searching for a polite way to explain.

Another minute passes; they are obviously thinking very hard. Then Newang breaks the ice. "We learned many surprising things from you," he says, laughing. "But the best was 'bunk'!"

For me, the lesson to learn from Nepal is a lesson for life: Don't walk so fast. The mountains will wait.

Carole Jacobs is an award-winning freelance writer, editor, and author who lives in Kennedy Meadows, California with her husband, Thomas. A senior editor at Shape *magazine for eighteen years and the founder of its travel section, she currently serves as fitness travel editor for* Travelgirl *magazine, travel editor for M.D. Publishing in Charlotte, North Carolina, and is a longtime contributing editor, writer, and columnist for Vacations Publications, Inc., publisher of* Vacations, Travel 50 and Beyond, *and* Where to Retire *magazines. Her books include* Fat, Free and Fit *and* The Most Scenic Drives in North America.

KATHERINE L. CLARK

✦

Madame Fung

The hidden treasures of China are in the people.

> *If there is righteousness in the heart,*
> *There will be beauty in the character;*
> *If there be beauty in the character,*
> *There will be harmony in the home;*
> *If there be harmony in the home,*
> *There will be order in the nation;*
> *If there be order in the nation,*
> *There will be peace in the world.*
> *— Confucius*

I CAN STILL REMEMBER THE DAY WE MET PASSING EACH OTHER along the pink granite walkway of the campus mall. Madame Fung introduces herself and allows her delicate fingers to rest in mine like a soft sycamore leaf crooking its tiny ribs. Still attractive in her sixties, she is born of that vanishing breed of genteel Chinese who learned French and English from Catholic nuns in Beijing before the knowledge of a Western tongue was considered treason. The epitome of old-world charm and steely grace—her smile, half-mocking half-curious, transmits a light from the depth of her eyes that probes me like a beam of radar.

133

A feeling washes over me of being discovered by a wild creature who has come upon an alien form of life, oddly familiar; no Western woman could have disarmed me so discreetly. Madame Fung's face is like an extraordinary visage of the Great Mother with surprising Oriental eyes and raven hair, so different from my own. Nudging me a bit to see what foreign fish she'd found, she cocks her head to the edge of her mandarin collar and queries me as to how I like China.

"The students here are wonderful," I answer honestly, for at that point I have been teaching English nearly four months.

Nodding with approval, she inquires how many students I have in the Department of International Business.

"One hundred sixteen," I tell her, but I sense she already has the answer. As is true of refined Oriental women and southern belles, Madame Fung gives an impression of naiveté when the opposite is true. I'm told she advises postgraduates in the Accounting Department and does not teach Mandarin to foreigners; but something about her smile emboldens me, and in February I find the courage to call and ask if she will be my tutor.

If Madame Fung is insulted by my call or unorthodox request, she does not let on; and when I explain that I do not want to learn Sichuan dialect on the streets and that I assume her pronunciation is closer to the standard Beijing accent, she agrees. Later, we laugh about this when she admits that Sichuan slang hurts her ears, too, and that growing up in Shanghai causes her to feel nearly as much an outsider in Chengdu as I do.

Her campus apartment is located among the units for retired workers, a five-minute walk from the guest hotel. Passing by administrative offices and a nursery school along the way, I might say hello to one of my students riding by, but the deeper into her neighborhood I go, the less often I am recognized or hear the sounds of English.

We agree to meet on Sunday afternoons at two, following the usual nap hour, but my knocking on the metal door must wake her at times, because I hear a furious rattle of bolts and chains as she undoes the locks and flings it open. There will be the university's most esteemed professor with her black wig slipped askew greeting me with giggles, "Qing jin; Qing jin! Come in! It is laundry day, please excuse the mess."

The place, however, is immaculate, smelling fresh as rain from the wet clothes the maid has dried in the living room. Her favorite flowers, sword lilies (gladioli), stand in a tall vase on the bookcase, and the tile floor is swept clean. As she talks from the kitchen preparing tea, I wait on her living room sofa that is covered in faded, flowered bed sheets, and gaze about the room at the mementos of her career—academic plaques and photographs of her with students in Melbourne, Paris, and North Carolina. Inside a china cupboard next to the piano, are dozens of gifts from universities and foreign businesses, still in original wrappings. And, along one whole wall looking like a row of medals, are graduation portraits of her four handsome daughters, posed with master's degree or doctoral diplomas in their hands. Now, all but the youngest girl are married and working in the U.S., while Madame Fung and her husband survive modestly in Chengdu.

Women work to the bone for their families in China, and because Madame has no sons, she has been at a cultural disadvantage. About this time I, also, begin to notice how mothers use their children's success as a means of competition.

"You must be so proud of them!" I comment, looking at her daughters' portraits and thinking of my own two girls in Ohio, just starting college.

"Yes," of course, she replies as though it were nothing; then admits to me later that her daughters resented her career when they were young, and it was their father who was the "kind one," the one who cooked meals while she stayed up late working. Why is it that even the most dedicated mothers are blamed for a child's discontent? Even if there is no one around to point a finger at her, a woman will do it to herself. Considering how meticulously Grace instructs me in Mandarin, I can imagine how severe she was with the girls. Only now are they old enough to value her profession and see their mother as that rarest of Chinese women who achieved recognition based purely on merit. Certainly, she had no choice but to rely on her husband's help at home.

Even now it is obvious her husband adores her. Stoop-shouldered and gray, he wanders into the living room from time to time and pours our tea and smiles tenderly from one to the other as if to say that he approves of my coming there to listen to her talk. Both of us know it pleases her to converse in English with an American, yet in Madame's growing fondness of me there is still a missionary's zeal to instruct.

A teacher teaching a teacher is like a doctor caring for a medical colleague, both need to exhibit the right degree of expertise and respectful insistence while enabling the other to play the part of humble protégée. Feeling outranked by Madame Fung in every department, it is easy to set aside my ego at the door and accept her as a taskmaster with my best interest at heart. Despite her age, there are those piercing eyes and the ability to read fine print in a Chinese dictionary without the benefit of glasses. In her grip, I am an adolescent chick pressed firmly beneath the wing of a matronly falcon who carries me until I can carry myself.

Launching each Mandarin lesson with a dialogue using commonplace phrases I ask her to teach me, Madame adds new vocabulary words and drills me as long as my brain can bear it and I have to slow her down by asking a question. I am curious to know, for instance, the derivation of a word or a phrase, and before long she pauses to think of illustrations that drop from her lips like pearls.

She explains, for instance, that *shangshan xiaxiang* is interpreted as, "going to the countryside," not in the sense of having a picnic, but in the context of being ordered there by the communists during the Cultural Revolution. She recalls that by the time the Revolution was underway in the 1960s she was a married woman with four children who was forced to give up her job as an international accountant and work on an assembly line in Beijing. Her husband, a former businessman, was assigned to labor in a steel mill, and the older girls, who should have been in school, were *shangshan xiaxiang,* dispatched to work on farms and grow vegetables, while the youngest daughter lived with grandparents in the country.

I try to imagine my own mother's reaction if her four children had been separated and sent away in the 1960s. How would an American woman have responded? Yet, isn't it ironic that, during that time, a struggling nation of Chinese was telling their children to clean their rice bowls because people in America were starving? Why did communists living on the other side of the world despise us so much that they imprisoned the brightest members of their own society for adopting Western ways? How can those intellectuals accept their fate and not be bitter? It is both a mystery and a national secret that is hidden in plain view of outsiders; like Nazi concentration camps or Salem witch trials, Chinese history is both fascinating and horrible.

I would like to think that in the 1960s my mother would have been brave enough to shield us from such indignities. Witch hunts, wars, and religious persecutions were, to our middle-class way of thinking, atrocities that happened to someone else "over there" or to us "a long time ago." Why, my mother would have rounded up a neighborhood posse to fight the Red Guards and protect us and our belongings with her life. At least, I'd like to think she would have, and that neither my brothers nor I would have turned her in to the authorities for trying. In modern times such events seem unlikely. But in China, it is different.

For one thing, Confucian ideology does not begin with the notion of human rights, but the concept of individual responsibility. A sense of righteousness that fosters "beauty in the character and harmony in the home" emanates from an inner sense of duty to one's family and is not the equivalent to the Western definition of righteousness, based on religious beliefs. Chinese tradition extends the idea of filial piety to include rulers who are scholars, trained like philosopher kings, to be free of violence and behave courteously towards others, even enemies. But what if, heaven forbid, sons disagree with fathers and fathers with rulers? This is what happened during the Cultural Revolution on a grand scale, and the result was chaos.

Because I am a lazy student when it comes to practicing my Mandarin lessons, I spend the better part of my time with Madame teasing memories out of her heart. Like many Americans at the end of the twentieth century, I am lulled by prosperity into a state of ease, and I feel drawn to her voice of experience without understanding the need for it. When she asks why I've come to China, I find it difficult to answer her as well as other resident faculty who, even after spending time abroad, seem unaware that instructors from non-communist countries do not belong to cadres, units, and teaching institutions. Madame is puzzled by my independence regarding work, but understands my reasons for choosing China as the place to teach.

Whereas her father was a renowned professor of Chinese literature in Shanghai, my parents were collectors of Asian art and decorated our home with rosewood carvings, Oriental carpets, cloisonné vases, and silk embroidery. My fascination with China was an easy progression from tangible possessions to a degree in Eastern philosophy, just as her interest in the West was the result of reading books in her father's library and meeting foreign teachers. Uncharacteristically immodest, Madame reveals one day that she was a child prodigy on the piano. Her father refused her wish to join the opera, however, and insisted that his only daughter study mathematics. As a result, he sent her to a boarding school in Beijing, where in the 1950s she learned French and English and fell in love with the son of a family friend.

A period in the People's Republic of China known as the Hundred Flowers, the 1950s was a time when artists and scientists were watched for signs of collaboration with Chiang Kai-shek's Kuomintang. Early on, Chairman Mao encouraged the "flowers to bloom" and express their opinions freely, but later, he changed his mind and arrested more than thirty thousand intellectuals, sending them to labor camps where they were forced to write self-critical biographies. It was during this stage that Madame Fung's fiancé escaped to Formosa with his family, and he saw her for the last time.

"We wrote for decades," she tells me with tears in her eyes. "Friends carried letters for us on the boats between Formosa and the mainland, but when the Revolution was over he stayed."

Meanwhile, agricultural communes on the mainland started to fail, and city people starved on cupfuls of rice and an egg once a week, if they were lucky. Smiling as she explains, I have difficulty picturing Madame Fung in Beijing stitching shoes from scraps of cloth and carefully gluing the cardboard soles by hand while thinking of him on Formosa—the man she'd loved, now married to someone else, the man who is free, yet not free to cross the China Sea for her.

And then there was the piano, as rare to see in China as a brass band. With students going mad under Chairman Mao's orders to rid the country of old thinking, old culture, old customs, and old habits, they attacked educated persons with "bad class" backgrounds, including parents and teachers. Confucian ideals were turned upside down, and Grace's family fell to society's lowest level. To save their lives she had to destroy the evidence of her family's heritage: the painted scrolls, antique furniture, leather-bound books all had to be burned. Nothing could be left as a visible reminder of her life in Shanghai, except the piano. But why, I wonder, after so many other fine instruments were destroyed as symbols of Western decadence, had she been allowed to keep hers?

In 1976, following major earthquakes in China, Chairman Mao died, and three years later Madame was reassigned to teach accounting in Chengdu. The capital city was a frontier town, having recently opened to the outside world as the result of new railroad lines connecting it with Baoji, Chongching, and Kunming. Coming alone on the train, Madame left behind her husband and youngest daughter in Beijing and sent the older ones, who had won academic scholarships, to universities in the U.S. Even if it was not *shangshan xiaxiang* in the sense she toiled in the cornfields, the backwaters of Chengdu were for Madame Fung a form of Siberian exile and, possibly, her long delayed punishment for owning a piano.

"When I arrived eighteen years ago," she says, "the President of the university was very kind. I was given the best treatment of anyone here because they needed me. All the same, I do not like the harsh sound of the Sichuan dialect or the boniness of the river fish."

What kept her alive, she says, was working with students and her love of music. "My husband and I both enjoy singing. Now that he is retired and we are living together for the first time in many years, he belongs to a choir in the Christian church downtown and sings every Sunday. What is my favorite song? That is easy, 'Amazing Grace.'"

Even though my Mandarin is slow to improve, what I learn from Madame is an appreciation for the oral and written formation of words and the nuances and layers of meaning. She enlightens me as to the extensive use of puns and satire and the subtleties of tone. It's no wonder the Chinese have such difficulty recognizing Mandarin coming from the mouths of foreigners! How barbaric we must sound to their ears; how crude we appear in manner.

Among my students in the classroom, I have discovered that words can make the difference between a friend and a foe, and that invisibly linked to the English language are cultural implications I cannot easily discuss in China. Words like "privacy" and "human rights" do not translate well. Speech, I find, is not a mechanical combination of symbols and sounds that can be simulated by a computer, but a living force that binds people or separates them on an almost cellular level. Words shape our view of the world, set the cadence of our body language, and reveal to others our very soul and emotions. Knowing the right words to say is not enough in a country like England, France, or China where language students soon discover that accent and articulation are supreme indicators of cultural sophistication.

On the morning of my departure from the university in June, Madame insists on seeing me off from the hotel lobby. Having refused all along to accept compensation for my Mandarin lessons, I hope to give her a special gift that will be useful and not sit in a box among the others in the cupboard. Because it is the custom to not open a present in front of the person who gives it to you, I do not learn until weeks later (by e-mail) that every night she and her husband fall asleep listening to the CD I have given her of a Southern Baptist choir singing "Amazing Grace."

I can just imagine the two of them ducking under the covers at night, the volume on the computer turned low so as not to reveal their secret love of Christian music to the neighbors. Not that they really care anymore about other people's opinions—they have witnessed enough terror in their lives to keep such matters in perspective—but, because it gives them a sense of peace.

Still, I am curious about the piano, and before leaving Chengdu I ask a colleague, Frederic, who first met Madame Fung in Paris, "How do you think she managed to avoid denunciation in the early days of the Revolution when there was random imprisonment of so many intellectuals? Her father's reputation, her skill in foreign languages, her piano sitting in full view; any one might have been used as an excuse to arrest her and force a confession that she was loyal to the Imperialists."

"I don't know," he said. "What I mean is that I very much respect Madame Fung, and I don't ask or want to know these things about her. They say that people stayed alive by reporting things to the police; they told lies about their neighbors to keep themselves from prison. But, if she acted in that way, it was not her fault." Some believe that no one is a pure victim and we are complicit with the things that happen to us. If this is true, then how far should one go to try and change events; when is it wise to accept misfortune and not resist it?

Frederic and I both agree that Madame Fung is a treasure kept too long hidden in Chengdu. For as much as Americans admire charity, the Chinese venerate sacrifice; and what more could she have given? To me, she exemplifies the finest characteristics of Chinese culture: modesty and persistence in the face of danger. She endured the Cultural Revolution, and out of it, her four daughters thrived. Yet, ironically, as her teaching days dwindle towards full retirement, the need for her expertise in China only increases. But who will listen to her now—an old woman, born of the elite, whose ethics have fallen from favor? It is dismaying to realize that when the last of her generation dies, there will be no one left to remember the days before Chairman Mao.

Katherine Clark is an English as a Second Language instructor at Portland Community College in Oregon. In 1997, she left her husband and three teenage children in Ohio to spend ten months teaching at the Southwest University of Finance and Economics in Sichuan Province.

✦ ✦ ✦

Tibetan Bargain
with a Twist

She didn't know what she was haggling for.

"PLEASE! PLEASE!" THE TIBETAN WOMAN PLEADED, HER YOUNG son trailing behind her. She approached me in the ancient market of Lhasa, the capital of Tibet, holding an orange beaded necklace that hung around her neck, smiling sweetly as she implored me to buy it.

But I didn't want orange beads. I was on an extended solo trip through Asia and, wanting to travel as long as possible, had to be judicious with my spending.

"No, thank you," I said.

"Please!" she said. It must have been the only word she knew in English.

"No. *Tu-jay-chay.*" It was the only word I knew in Tibetan. "Thank you."

"Please!"

China had opened Tibet for independent travel only three months before so my Western face was a novelty. Or maybe she sensed that I love unusual jewelry.

"Please!"

She was insistent yet endearing with her lovely smile and that mischievous twinkle in the eye that is unique to Tibetans. Red and brown yarn twisted through long black hair piled onto her head, and in front a few strands threaded through four small turquoise beads. A rough black sash with pockets hung over her pink-striped blouse and gray skirt, and a small pouch secured with string peeked out above it. Her son, who was about nine, stood silently at her side, a threadbare brown jacket over his red shirt and an unsure look on the face peering below the brim of his gray cap.

Again I said, "No," to beads—but I pointed to the bracelets on her wrist.

She removed one: a strip of twisted brass, twisted again with copper and silver, and shaped into a rustic cuff.

"One yuan," I said, holding up my index finger. It was a ridiculously small sum. About 50 U.S. cents.

"Oh!" She was shocked. Or she feigned shock. I saw that twinkle in her eye. She held up ten fingers, no, ten again—twenty.

"Twenty yuan?!" I stepped back. That was ten bucks—a fortune in backpacker travel money. "Oh, no, no!" I said. "Two yuan," two fingers.

She pretended to be horrified. Then she indicated "Eighteen yuan."

This dance continued, each of us alternately pretending to be offended at the other's offer and tendering a new price. We grinned, laughed, and settled on six yuan.

That was fun, and I loved the bracelet. I pointed to another and off came the twisted brass, copper, and silver design, smoothed into one solid piece. We repeated our game, faster this time and with fewer dramatics and even more smiles, our eyes meeting with laughter, but we got to the same price, six yuan.

Next I bought a silver ring. Our opening offers were not so

far apart this time, and we completed our transaction quickly.

Behind us, Lhasa's denizens, nomads, and worshipers from across Tibet ambled around the "Old Town" section of Lhasa—the Barkor, the maze of dirt alleys twisting among 700-year-old stone buildings encircling the most important Buddhist temple in Tibet, the Jokhang. Many Tibetans twirled brass prayer wheels, small cylinders revolving on a shaft, each spin offering a prayer for compassion. For more than thirteen centuries Tibetan pilgrims have reverently circled the Jokhang Temple, always clockwise, always with the temple off their right shoulder, each half-mile circuit a prayer.

I gestured toward the procession, and my new Tibetan friend, her son, and I joined the throng. We strolled through the alleys, smiling, laughing, and surveying bells, prayer flags, saddle blankets for yaks, and hand-loomed fabric in stripes of fuchsia, ocher, indigo, and emerald.

Pilgrims stretched out full body-length on the dirt road, marked where their extended hands touched, stood up, moved their feet to where their hands were, and repeated the process as they circled the temple and the Barkor. Some used the same grueling technique to circumambulate Mt. Kailash, the holiest mountain in Tibet—a distance of thirty-three miles. We looked at each other and nodded with respect toward the pilgrims.

Her son's eyes, wide-open, followed a man who whirled a paper cone around the inside edge of a circular metal pan, accumulating white spun sugar with each twist. I bought cotton candy for the three of us, and the boy beamed.

I photographed my friend with her arm around her son, and I asked someone else to take a photo of the three of us in the square in front of the Jokhang.

My friend led us toward the Jokhang, past a dozen Tibetans prostrating themselves at its entrance, and into its candle-lit darkness with the pungent odor of burning yak butter, the rancid aroma that permeates Tibetan temples, blended with juniper incense. For two hours we silently turned dozens of prayer wheels, again and again. We were the energy source spinning golden cylinders engraved with prayers and sending those prayers to the heavens. So many wheels, so many prayers....

Rejoining the circuit, we stopped at a Tibetan merchant's table. The merchant spoke English. He had left Tibet as a child many years before, and now that China had opened the border with Nepal, he returned as a businessman.

"Your friend's name is Gele," he said. "She has a sixteen-year-old daughter, who is on a pilgrimage to Mt. Kailash. Gele is a recent widow, and she's trying to move from Chamdo in eastern Tibet to Kathmandu in Nepal." She had traversed half of her 1,000-mile voyage. I said I was impressed.

Gele reached into her pouch and brought out a one-inch, camel-shaped brass pendant. Its plain surface was worn smooth, and a hand-braided string looped through a hole in its center. "She said this was made by the gods and dropped from the sky," the shopkeeper said. "I can tell it is very old."

The magical story intrigued me—I bought the amulet for a few yuan, a price I thought was too low, but she wouldn't go higher.

"She says you've helped her a great deal on this journey because you've bought so much of her jewelry, and now she has money to travel." I asked him to tell her how much I treasured her jewelry.

He said she wanted to meet the next day so I asked where and at what time. He said not to worry. "She will find you. These people are very clever."

She did find me. Again we circumambulated the Barkor three or four times.

I pointed to her squared-off brass ring with a small turquoise stone in the center. She took it off. It was rustic with rough edges—sturdy with geometric patterns engraved around the stone. And I wanted to help her with her trek— although the distances were shorter, her travels were more monumental than mine. If I had to cut my trip short by a few days, I would survive. It was she who was beginning a new life, or who would be if she could get herself and her son to Nepal. I would offer her earlier starting price.

I held up ten, then ten-again fingers. "Twenty yuan," I said. She shook her head. No, no, no. She held up one finger.

"What?" I asked. I held up one finger. "One yuan?"

She nodded.

"Oh, no, no," I said, shaking my head. "Twenty! Twenty yuan!" Ten-plus-ten fingers.

One finger.

Twenty fingers.

I held out twenty one-yuan bills. She took one. I gave her the others. She pushed them away.

"No!" I said. "You must take more!" We laughed. But she wouldn't take more. In bargaining throughout the world I'd never encountered such a thing—she was refusing my higher price. Surely she could use the money. But she had enough for her needs. I was stunned—I could only look at her and smile in amazement.

We walked again, watching the pilgrims, smelling the juniper incense, hearing the prayer wheels spin. Then Gele *gave* me her last bracelet....

April Orcutt has made extensive solo trips through rural Asia, Europe, New Zealand, and the U.S., and her stories have been published in newspapers and online in the U.S. and Canada. She is a contributor to two books about broadcasting in Eastern Europe since the fall of the Soviet Union. She's been a producer of public affairs, documentary, and science television programs and a professor of broadcasting and multimedia/web design.

Queen of Compassion

Is she the right goddess for you?

"LOVE IS AN *ILLUSION*," MY WISE OLD UNCLE TOLD ME. I SET out to disprove this unpalatable statement. The resulting quest was to take me halfway round the world.

The East! My last Sunday in Singapore. The young man who is my guide speaks to me earnestly. He has only one desire—to take me to a certain temple he knows. He has been saving this visit for the end. I am not enthusiastic and he is not able to make me so.

We leave the hotel and cross the main road; walking is easy and comfortable here. Streets are clean, and the strict laws against pollution have had their effect. A big blue dragon's head towers above a building, but we pass it by.

"The temple is down a back street," he says, "and tourists don't go there."

We go down a narrow road and arrive at a low, plain building. The temple is a bare, rectangular room; the door is half open. Plain wooden benches are stacked in a corner and paint-stained planks lie scattered around. A man is up a ladder; an open pot of paint stands on the floor. The only thing missing is an "out of order" sign.

A smiling woman arrives in a gray robe. There is a hint of gray stubble on the shorn head. She ushers us in.

"You must take your shoes off first," my guide tells me. I don't like having to walk barefoot in this. Soon stuff sticks to the soles of my feet.

"She is a Buddhist nun," he tells me, "and Kuan Yin's voice." (Many of Singapore's temples used to have a resident spiritual medium.)

I do not know who this Kuan Yin is. I cannot even spell the name.

As the temple is being redecorated, the medium cannot work today. My guide informs me that she wears rich robes and full headgear for the formal Sunday service; it is only then that she functions as Kuan Yin's spokesperson and transmits her messages. He did not tell me, then, that he was himself a trance medium in training, and that the goddess had spoken to him.

My guide and the nun speak rapidly together in Chinese. From time to time the young man turns to say something to me in English.

The Buddhist nun goes to the back of the Temple, and returns with sweets and tea.

"She says she does not want you to have come here today for nothing," he says, looking pleased.

The hot tea does me a lot of good and I drink it gratefully, while they talk animatedly in Chinese, with frequent pokes in my direction.

"She says she will pray for you," my interpreter tells me.

The Buddhist nun disappears into the back room, and returns holding an object I cannot identify. The two of them converse in some excitement. No one bothers to translate anything for me. The nun goes to stand behind my chair. Suddenly something hard and wet lands on the back of my neck.

"She has stamped you!" my guide tells me.

Drops begin to trickle down my back. I raise my hand to wipe my neck.

"Don't touch it! You must leave it to dry."

I do not realize that my neck now bears a large round reddish stamp and that I will return to the hotel looking like a prize cheese. Later I discover an article on the web: "Pilgrimage in Contemporary China," wherein Chün Fang Yü relates that "on pilgrimages to sacred sites red seals were stamped on the bags and belts indicating the monasteries the people had visited. When they die, they would be…cremated together with the incense bags and belts. These would serve as 'travel passes,' as one pilgrim put it, and would assure them a safe journey to Paradise."

I see!

The temperature is 30 degrees Centigrade. I feel hot, bothered, and very uncomfortable. There is still stuff sticking to the soles of my feet. The Buddhist nun smiles at me and fetches more tea, thick with sugar. For this I really am grateful. She goes to the back of the temple once more and returns with a gift: it is a small ferryboat.

"It's for the great crossing," my guide tells me.

I don't feel like a crossing—great or small: all I want now is to get back to my hotel.

The Buddhist nun seeks my eyes and smiles at me once more; then she gives me a dark poster with a white deity on it. I roll the poster up and thank the nun. My restlessness increases: I want to leave. But my guide and the nun go on talking—still about me. They are looking very pleased. I can't for the life of me see what there is to be so pleased about.

I get up to go. Just before we leave the nun brings me the gift of a second boat. She smiles at me as she does so. That makes two fragile ferryboats to pack: my safe journey to the farthest shore is now assured.

Time to return to Europe: time to pack. Finally everything fits into my fuchsia traveling bag, except this poster. I look at it again; it's glossy and cheap! Might as well leave it behind; it's only a poster. Or give it to the porter! Perhaps I'll try just one more time: I roll up a towel, roll the poster around that, then roll my skirt around that, and finally squeeze the bundle into my bag.

The poster travels well. By the time I unpack it in Geneva it has been *antiqued*. Lines of fine cracks run across the thick, glossy paper, making it look like parchment. A majestic bejewelled Chinese deity, clad in a flowing white robe, stands barefoot on the back of a long dragon with shiny emerald scales, a belly edged in bronze, and a copper mane. He has ivory antler horns, large onyx eyes, a flaring crimson tongue, sharp white teeth, two long golden whiskers that spread out like feelers from his wide open snout, a wispy green beard, and four ferocious claws. (In China only the emperor was allowed to possess a dragon with *five* claws). Kuan Yin wears a necklace; high above her head her black hair is crested by a tiara and covered by a veil. In her left hand she holds a precious golden vase from which flows some nectar. Her right hand, palm facing outwards, is raised in a sacred gesture (*mudra*).

I frame the poster behind anti-reflection glass, hang it in our living room opposite the front door, and begin to look up at the graceful goddess riding her dragon through the clouds in a blaze of light. From then on the poster presided over our going out and our coming in.

"But who is she?" I had asked my young guide, back there in Singapore, not having caught her name.

"Kuan Yin is a Celestial Bodhisattva whose job it is to help the Buddha. In Sanskrit her name means, 'The One who Hears the Sounds (Cries) of the World and Comes.'"

"But what exactly *is* a bodhisattva?"

"A being who has overcome the world by the practice of strict disciplines (spiritual perfections) and who no longer needs to incarnate. But because of infinite compassion for suffering humanity, a bodhisattva forgoes the bliss of Union with the Divine, and chooses to stay close to the earth, to help all beings unconditionally. In this way Kuan Yin is captain of the *Bark of Salvation* who ferries humans safely across the sea of suffering. She will go to a thousand places, respond to a thousand prayers, alleviate a thousand fears."

"But in Mahayana Buddhism there are two kinds of bodhisattvas: the transcendent, such as Kuan Yin, and the earthly. The second kind is that of the follower who aspires to enlightenment and dedicates him or herself to the service of mankind by endeavoring to be loving and compassionate to all sentient beings alike."

Here it is again—this thing about the bliss of Union with the Divine: I've heard it before!

My life has now claimed five decades. Young loves have come and gone; older love, too. Heart has opened and shut. But I still believe: love cannot be an illusion! I assemble the fragments of memory and experience; suddenly, I'm back at twenty!

"There is an excellent esoteric library in London," my uncle tells me. "As you are looking for Truth, you might find some interesting books there. Go to the Baker Street Underground next to Madame Tussaud's Waxworks, cross the street and walk down Gloucester Road, towards Marble Arch."

In the musty library I borrow an occult novel about the love affair of an immortal. In the hall below some public lectures are about to begin. Next week there's one that's an absolute must. It's on love!

There are ten chairs across, five on each side of the aisle, and eight rows down in the lecture hall. My seat is in the third row on the right, next to a friend—far too near the front.

The speaker, a widow, is around seventy, has white hair down to her shoulders and a powerful build. She has just come back from her second pilgrimage to India where she spent six months with her guru. Her plain black dress is lit by the gaudy brooch that glitters below her neck and captures one's gaze as she begins to speak, till only her voice remains. Vigorously she embarks on the subject of love.

I am still hoping to find someone who will confirm that love is not an illusion; maybe this Russian woman will. I hope she will prove the others wrong.

Love is—she quotes the Scriptures …
Love is—she quotes Eastern texts…

Yes, yes, yes! Go on! Go on!

Love is the most wonderful thing on earth!

I have come to the right place! Her voice warms and begins to glow.

Love is…she continues, and quotes the ultimate heights ever known to humankind.

Great! Great! Great! So, love is *not* an illusion!
I sit back and relax. At last someone has said exactly what I wanted to hear!

Now the speaker is into the heart of her subject. Her body sways with the surge of it. She has experienced the love she describes, and it surges forth for all to see!

"And then, after all the most wondrous experiences, love takes one further, beyond anything ever imagined. And you fly high in the sky—wizz Love!"

I can just see it: Up and Away!

Now a wave surges through *my* body, rises to a crest; spray glistens in the sun. My ribs begin to ache. I dare not look at my friend; we can hardly hold our stifled laughter.

The lecture continues in crescendo. The silver hair is drawn back severely, and the cheap brooch glitters at her neck.

"And I tell you, my friends, LOVE IS ALL."

Here we are, at last! Love is *not* an illusion after all.

Suddenly there is a lull. The speaker's gaze sweeps across the audience, and scrutinizes each of us in turn. There is a long, deep silence.

"But," the passionate voice now flames forth, "there is no such thing as love!"

She begins to speak about her experience in India, at the feet of her guru. "There is no greater love than the union of the soul with the Beloved."

Can't one even find love without having to go through all that with a guru?

"The greatest love affair on earth," she concludes, "is the love of the soul for the Divine."

I emerge from my reverie.

Kuan Yin still rides the dragon with the shiny emerald scales (said to be 117 in number; 36 yin and 81 yang!), and I've grown accustomed to the poster on the wall. It is the first thing I see when I walk through the front door and I've learned to live with her. But everything has changed; now she seems breathtakingly beautiful.

One particularly hard day I wonder: Can it be true, as John Bloefeld suggests in *Bodhisattva of Compassion*, that all one needs to do is to call out Kuan Yin's name, and she'll be here? Is it true that "Rocks, willows, lotus pools, or running water are often indications of her presence. In the chime of bronze or jade, the sigh of wind in the pines, the prattle and tinkle of streams, her voice is heard?"

"Kuan Yin," I call out, "Kuan Yin."

Is she real? Or is she myth? Can an archetypal symbol be taken from one culture and transposed to another?

"Kuan Yin, can you hear me?"

She does not move; she does not speak. But I begin to feel dreamy, happy, consoled. A fragrant mist wafts in. The floor carpets itself in white; the delicate fragrance of gardenia fills the room. I fill with pleasure; welcome its caress. I look around; but I am alone. No one else is home. I look up at Kuan Yin, and my heart beats one with her.

Forgotten words, once whispered to me, now slip back into my mind. *Compassion is the elder sister of love.*

A year later I find myself in Boston for two weeks. I'm walking along the street, with nothing particular in mind. My eye catches the figurine of a white Madonna in the window of a small art and curio shop. I go in to inquire.

"Oh, that's Kuan Yin. We have a book about her. Would you like to browse through it?"

An Oriental gentleman leads me to a table and armchair behind a curtain at the back of the shop, hands me a book, and leaves me to read. A little later he comes back with a cup of green tea. I thank him.

This is fascinating! There is even such a thing as a Kuan Yin initiation into cosmic sound. I order the book and leave.

Spring is in my step. So, Kuan Yin is in Boston, too! I get the feel of a little shrine, somewhere, not far from here. I walk down unfamiliar streets, following the inner trail. After a while I see an orange-robed monk disappearing around the corner. The next day I return to the same area, and walk around. Presently two orange-robed monks appear, but they, too, seem to vanish. I go to the area supermarket and ask the tall security guard.

"Oh yes, I've seen them, too," he says. "The monks seem to be coming from somewhere behind there," he says pointing in the direction of a large block of flats, and I make my way towards them. I recall the fragrance of gardenias. I want to find the Buddhist Madonna; I want to find her here! I loiter around, wondering what to do next. Then I see an old man, and ask him if he knows of a Kuan Yin temple.

"In that building there," he says, indicating a door a few paces away.

I find it on the third floor. A well-rounded monk with a kind face and a day's stubble of gray hair opens the door.

"Kuan Yin?"

His eyes nearly pop out of his head.

"Quan Âm."

"Me, meditation," I say, bowing and joining my hands in greeting.

The Venerable ushers me in.

"Japanese?"

"Vietnam."

The front room serves as temple and meditation room. A tall, white statue of Kuan Yin stands on a cloth-covered table. A trickle of incense rises and wafts through the room.

"Hello," I say to her. "So it's you!"

The Buddhist Master discreetly leaves the room.

I sit down on the floor in front of Kuan Yin and wait. I make no promises; do not bargain. Yet before I call I am answered.

A stack of little cards lies beside the incense. Each is a miniature replica of the poster given to me in the small Kuan Yin Temple in Singapore. When I'm ready to leave, the Venerable gives me one of the little cards and says, "You come tomorrow afternoon, five o'clock. Speak English. Good!"

The following day there were seven pairs of Buddhist sandals by the door. The gray-robed lay members had just completed the closing ritual of a strenuous retreat, and were in the kitchen taking light refreshments, which they immediately offered to share with me. One of the women could speak English and was asked to translate.

We all sat down on the floor.

Then the Venerable's deep, guttural voice burst out: "How did you find us? We haven't been here long; we only moved a few months ago. No European has ever set foot in here before!"

I told the story at great length. How I had seen a statue of Kuan Yin in the art and curio shop, just up the road; how I had followed the trail. How, just one year before that, my guide had taken me to her temple in Singapore; how my neck had been stamped; how I brought the poster to Geneva. And how, a year later, Kuan Yin's fragrance had filled my home.

From time to time the Venerable interjected comments of his own. These were not translated for me, but made everyone smile: at each other—and at me.

It had gotten late: people were tired after the strenuous disciplines of the last days, and needed to get home. As I ended my story the Venerable held me in his forceful gaze, then addressed me thus:

"All this can only mean one thing: you, too, must become a bodhisattva."

He must have meant the second kind, but *still*: thirty-seven practices and five merits!

One by one the members of the group left. I thanked the Venerable and slipped out.

It was to take me years more to *get it*!

The Heart of the Universe answers the call: nothing is demanded; nothing imposed; no bargaining required. Eternal Compassion pulsates—underneath, above and beside—in symbols both of East and West.

Rozalia-Maria Tellenbach is a freelance writer and a member of the Geneva Writers Group. She loves to go to the heart of the matter.

✳

Love Potion No. 9

The ingredients are different in Malaysia.

I AM NOT EXACTLY SURE HOW RIPPING THREE EYELASHES OUT of my head is going to make my husband passionate, but at this point, there doesn't seem to be any turning back. After all, I have just let a fully head-scarved Moslem woman rub ruby oil into my breasts. It's a little late to get tentative.

To be fair, I thought I had merely signed up for a cheap one-hour massage. It's not like I had an option of going to the bar. I am in the state of Terengganu on Malaysia's east coast. Known as the fundamentalist state within the Islamic nation, they take the idea of abstaining to serious levels. Coke is about as good as it gets. Besides, sixty Malaysian ringitts amounts to just over thirty bucks Canadian. It seems like a pretty decent alternative to margaritas. Actually, it's the only option.

The fact that Sari Ra Wati doesn't speak any English, has me lying on the once-pink hotel carpet covered only in a soon-to-be-removed sarong, and is digging into my ovaries through my belly wall is rapidly making up for the savings. When she gets to my legs, I swear she is pushing aside my muscles and bruising the tibias and fibulas directly. So, when she stops long enough to say, "Solly, Auntie," and begins kneading my breasts, I am merely grateful for an end to the pain.

Kneeling behind my head, she pushes me into an upright position. Her thumbs push through my scalp, bracketing her mouth that is waterfalling a rush of Malay syllables into my head. She breathes and blows into my brain. I feel blessed and weak. The words stop.

"Finish." Sari Ra Wati leans back on her heels. "Finish, Auntie."

But really, it's only begun.

Dressed now, I nod and smile and wonder why she's not leaving. I read the red oily bottle, Minyak Panas—a combination of citronella, nutmeg, eucalyptus, *eugenia aromatica*, and paraffin oil. I can only hope no one lights a match.

There is a muffled knock. My translator, Sandra Ngoh-Fonseka has arrived just in time. Ngoh-Fonseka begins, "You mentioned that you would be interested in the spiritual world of Malaysia. This woman has a gift that is passed from mother to daughter. She offers it to you."

Instructions are simple. Go to the lobby and buy a small bottle of water. Pour some in a cup. Scrape left thumbnail and toenail into the water. Pluck three eyelashes and add them to the mix. Right. I opt for scissors, hoping that self-inflicted pain is not required for this particular enchantment.

She takes the cup, sets it on the generic coffee table cum altar, faces east and begins her prayers. Incantations start slow, the la-la, sh-sh sounds of the language soft and melodious, only sounding clunky when she inserts my mispronounced name. The prayers change to pleadings, her body rocking and begging on my behalf. The muezzin's plaintive call to prayer rises to our tenth floor balcony on the hot equatorial air. I am transfixed. I believe.

Many minutes pass. The elixir is poured into an empty bottle. Ngoh-Fonseka translates, "Make your husband's coffee using this water. He will have eyes only for you. And now she will bless the rest of the water for a potion to splash on your face. You must do it every day. When either potion depletes, you can top it up with normal water. It will not lose its potency."

Ngoh-Fonseka smiles. "She wants to know if you want to know a persuasive potion you can make at home?"

In a culture where it is still permissible for a man to have four wives and where women's rights aren't exactly at the forefront of political discussion, it is perfectly logical that such secrets and potions exist. This kind of covert knowledge gives a woman power in her situation, not unlike our North American equivalent of wearing Victoria's Secret red-hot lingerie under our beige clothes.

"Bring it on." I say.

There is a rapid Malaysian discussion. There are smiles and gestures. Finally, I can't stand it any longer. "What? What do I do at home?" Ngoh-Fonseka brings her hand to her mouth, smiling, "Boil your panties and use the water to make your husband a hot drink."

She's ready to tell me more. I can't imagine how I could possibly need any more help after this but Sandra is continuing to translate, "This is something that will *strengthen* your husband." At the word, strengthen, Sandra makes a sudden fist as she stiffens her arm from the elbow.

I am to grate a turnip, pour off the water that separates from it. Pound the sediment with flour and a little water. Drink it down. "When your husband sleeps with you, he will be so satisfied." She smiles and repeats, "...so satisfied."

I stroll down to the lobby. I am feeling pretty fine. Three hours have passed since Sari Ra Wati first appeared at my door.

"Wow. You're glowing. You look like you've had a night of great sex." My traveling companion is right.

I look and feel pretty warm and shiny. Mind you it's 39 degrees Centigrade in the shade, the humidity is about 1,000 percent, and I'm slippery with red-colored paraffin oil, but I think it's more than that. I am powerful in my possession of the potions splashed on my face and stored for future use in my purse.

Look out.

Colleen Friesen is embarking on a second life as a travel writer using her formerly stagnating right brain. She lives in a crooked little house on the seaside in Sechelt, British Columbia with her math-minded left-brained husband, her hyperactive twelve-year-old nephew, and a continuously shedding and sometimes incontinent Dalmatian. Her work has appeared most recently in The Georgia Straight, Vancouver Sun, *and* Coast Reporter *newspapers,* Shared Vision *and* Balanced Life *magazines, and* Whose Panties Are These? More Misadventures from Funny Women on the Road.

IRENE-MARIE SPENCER

✦ ✦ ✦

A Wedding in Ekinlik

This small island town marches to a slow and sedate rhythm.

I AM SITTING IN THE CAFÉ NEAR THE FISHING BOATS, LISTENING to the fishermen with their raspy voices, to the chanting of prayers, to the wooden carts against the earth, to the high-pitched whining of the ship's engine and the churning water. I feel dizzy and radiant at the same time. I gather up my sacks of vegetables, cheese, yogurt, and supplies from the market to go find Ombashi's fishing boat for the twenty-minute crossing to the tiny island of Ekinlik. The crowd from the big ship from Istanbul, which comes every afternoon at two, has finally cleared out, the machine gun guards are now gone, the Turkish street music gone, now only the lapping sea and the dark-skinned boys diving for pennies off the pier.

It is easy to spot the fishermen with their self-assured expressions and weathered faces, standing protectively near their boats on the wooden dock. Ombashi is expecting me. His bright fishing boat is painted turquoise, yellow, and red. His face betrays no emotion of any kind; but I know there is a half-smile there, camouflaged by his prominent features. Ombashi has the face of an eagle. Straddling the boat and the quay, he holds out his hand to me, taking my bag. His every movement has a purpose. I find a spot on the small bow deck. I circle it, like a cat, then sit, gathering up my arms and legs. It is warm out, a day that glistens. I feel drops of sweat in my armpits, dripping down the insides of my blouse. I stretch my legs out and arrange my faded skirt around them, then rub my feet together. The aromas around me make my head spin: the freshness of the sea air laced with wafts of heavy Turkish tobacco, grilled corn, rotting fish, the powerful body odor of these working men, and salt, the salt in the air and the skin. Blinding spots of light reflecting from the swaying dance of clear aquamarine water make me squint.

Ombashi loads on several other people, villagers returning to Ekinlik with their bags of fresh fruit and vegetables, blue propane gas tanks, and plastic water jugs. A villager unties the rope from the dock, and pushes off with one leg. We motor slowly around the huge cement pier, where the ferry from Istanbul still looms above us, casting a behemoth shadow across the water, and then head straight out for the small island about a mile across the water. Ombashi sits perched at the stern, a large angular seabird, motionless except for his arm slightly moving to steer. His sharp blue eyes dart almost imperceptibly over every roll and pitch of the Marmara Sea. I look at him and smile. He doesn't acknowledge me openly, even though I know he sees me. He looks straight ahead, to Ekinlik, but he seems to smile through the straight, immobile line of his lips. He is one who doesn't say much. But what he does say seems to matter. People listen, perking up when he speaks.

The vibration from the boat's motor enters through my heels, buzzes through my body, and reaches full pitch somewhere in the canals of my inner ears. Looking down at the churning water which turns black as we pass under the shadow of a cloud, I see exploding fireworks in the points of light shooting out from the boat's prow. I feel myself shrink, dwarfed by the vibration of the motor and the chant of the cutting water. I am feeling jubilant, and plunge my legs into the glowing Marmara Sea. The sun is warm on my arms, and I breathe in deeply. I feel myself fade away, and I melt into a place that is much, much larger than just me. This is a place full of spells and magic. I've seen blue charm beads everywhere, little beads that look like glass eyes. They ward off the evil eye. I wear them as earrings. You can buy them for pennies in the marketplace, and you see them around the necks of women, on the key chains of the men, hanging from the rearview mirrors of buses, boats, and cars. I think of the Blue Mosque, a giant blue charm, as blue as this sea.

Ombashi lands the boat at the village quay. Landing at the village is like stepping into a fairy tale, with its whitewashed, eighteenth-century stone houses, its single café with red and blue painted tables and chairs, and its small mosque with a pointed minaret off to one side. This island is from another century. As we land, there are a couple of fishermen sitting in the café. They sit and make nets, and the women sit on the porch, their faces solemn yet blissful. I can't remember any of their names, but they all remember mine. They have names which are more like descriptions: *Black Leg, Old Sailor, White One, Moonlight.* I feel embarrassed, shaking hands and embracing these warm and smiling people who call me by name. *Irena*, they call me.

The houses of the village are stone or whitewashed cement, with paisley or faded lavender curtains hanging across the doorways. The wooden beams framing the village houses are severely weather-beaten, full of gouges and splinters, and they keep their windows open, with little pots of globe oregano sitting on the sills or the front step. The women clean the thresholds to their homes daily, sweeping and scrubbing on hands and knees with soap and water, their hair tied back in scarves, and faded print shirt sleeves rolled up to the elbows. The women smile and wave as I pass. I begin to lose any desire to ever leave this island. With no cars, there is no smog, no revving engines, no car alarms going off in the middle of the night.

On Ekinlik, sounds take on a piercing and sharp quality. I can hear better, or maybe it's that I can hear at all for the first time in my life. The sounds of the insects buzzing and chirping, crickets and cicadas, even the flies that land on my arms as I walk from the village to Gülbin's house, seem enormously loud in my ears. The wind, as it heaves and pelts dust against her stone house; the black cow and its calf mooing; the chickens all around the village; the distant motoring of a fishing boat... these are the sounds of this life. Every afternoon there is a tremendous blast from the steamship docking at Avsa. And then the sound of water, all around, a light lapping of flat waves against small beaches, always in the background. It is the prayer, the *ezan*, being sung from the single minaret of the small mosque of Ekinlik, though, which pulls me inside of this place. This is a sound which makes goose bumps rise along the back of my neck, which sends a flood of warmth washing over me, inside and out.

Gülbin is waiting for me to arrive from Avsa with the groceries. She is in the process of tying a bright scarf around her jet-black jaw-length hair as I enter the house. The glass doors which span the entire length of the front room are pushed all the way open to let in the breeze and a view of the sea, which is just down at the foot of the stone stairs. She tells me excitedly as soon as I walk in that there will be a wedding in the village tomorrow, and tonight will be the bride's special ceremony. She says it is something that cannot be missed.

We take a long time getting dressed for this special occasion, yet I have no idea what it will be like. Finally we are ready to walk to the village, at twilight. As the sun disappears behind us, to the other side of the island, we walk in the violet stillness to the beat of the evening crickets, and notice the first stars pricking through the arching cloudless sphere above us. The west wind gusts and fusses with its small hands, caresses my bare calves, and bends the enormous brim of Gülbin's hat into a near perfect ellipse.

All of the women and girls of the village are gathered in the café on the quay, in the darkness. A kind of feminine hush and smallness precedes the ancient ritual. The women gather together and begin to sing a haunting and wistful chorus. I cannot understand the words, but the meanings scrape at my bones, piercing my heart with sharp little pins. Gülbin motions to me to merge in with the women, to take part in the ceremony. We all stand touching, connected, weaving into one tapestry the voices of many unique and strangely beautiful women. They light candles, and together, the women move as a unit, an airy, wispy, floating cloud of tender hearts and open hands, we move, gliding, towards the street of the village, towards the house of the bride.

A young girl, no more than eighteen, emerges from the stone house. She is dressed in white gauze from head to toe, and a long veil is draped over her face and head like the shroud of a corpse. The women circle around her, touching and holding her, their voices melding, drawing her on diaphanous threads toward the open sky. They lead her to the café and begin to chant and dance in circles, their song rising in pitch, their hands opening and closing like emergent, wet butterflies. The women take out pots of henna and paint brushes, and paint round red circles on their palms. Everyone is painted, myself as well. We all surround the bride, painting her palms and the soles of her feet with henna, dancing, singing, and swaying. Then we lift her up above us, in one white flowing fountain, our movements becoming liquid, the voices separating into questions and replies. Gülbin, the village women, and I carry the young, painted bride back to her home, softly lifting her back through the door into the arms of her weeping mother. All of the women then begin to sway and sing, the tears gently making rivulets down their full, transparent cheeks. The door closes, the women stand outside in the dark, some with candles, and sing softly until the moment of separation makes itself felt in unison, wedges softly in our hearts beneath the veils.

When the women reach the dark café near the sea again, they embrace each other, quietly, sadly. Gülbin and I, united by the strong emotion and magic of the ancient ceremony, embrace the village women, and embrace each other. No words seem appropriate. Together, we walk in silence down the dark path, illuminated only by the full, effervescent moon. Together, closing our palms around the red, pulsating circles, we hear the crickets. We reach the house, still wordless, kiss, and go into our separate beds, ready to drift on the memory of the songs, to enter the magic of the red circles, in spiritual preparation for the wedding the following day.

Nothing, not even the mysteries of last night, has prepared me for the wedding day. It is a day that billows with light, a faded white day background against which the intensities of color are blinding. It is early afternoon, and all of the people of the village are gathered near the waterfront. Two of the double-decked fishing boats are decorated with tree branches and giant red bows, to transport the entire population of Ekinlik over to Avsa for the feast and celebration. The music has already started up, the musicians show gold teeth in their broad smiles. The plucked strings of the *saz* vibrate wildly, with a frenzy that jars my thoughts. The village women, dressed in their best flowered skirts and scarves, nod and flow together with a secret knowing. I open my palm. The red circle of henna is still there. It pulses with the promise of eternity in a primitive way. The circle is bloodlike and has something to do with consummation. Gülbin told me that the reason for the painted circles has to do with dreaming, or good luck, but I cannot really pinpoint it. I understand, not needing an explanation.

The men are already dancing. They dance with each other, with a foreboding abandon. The dancing men, the knowing women, move as a large family towards the pier. The boats are ready. The villagers crowd onto them, spilling out over the rails. The weight of all of us rocks the boats violently, and I am terrified that we will capsize. I imagine the entire village swimming and drowning in the sea, a mile from the shore. But the musicians, continuing to play, wedge themselves into the heaving crowd, somehow masking the effect. Gülbin and I squeeze ourselves between the circle of women, and I feel the cool, moist pressure of enormous breasts and ample bodies completely surrounding us. The women shift their bodies as a unit, moving to the music and the careening dance of the boat in the swells. I look up at the sky. It is a vibrant blue, cloudless.

The wedding is to take place in an enclosed waterfront café covered by a huge tent. A few mangy cats prowl around the edges of the outer tables. The light inside is a gaudy, fluorescent green, casting an unearthly, morbid glow on the faces of the wedding guests. Pink and blue crepe paper streamers sag from the corners of the tent, held together in the center above a huge rotating mirrored ball. Specks of light dart and swirl, and make a crazy, streaking grid on the greenish-cast canvas walls of the wedding pavilion. The street musicians are gone.

Now, in the tent, there is a professional band with an electric piano, electrified instruments, and an echo chamber which gives the sequined vocalist a carnivalesque, spooky sound. A shriveled, starving dog has sneaked into the tent, and I turn just in time to see one of the village men send the bony animal flying back outside with a powerful kick.

Gülbin and I order beers. There are small bowls of sunflower seeds and peanuts on the tables. I search the expanse of people and tables with my eyes, until I locate Hakki, a very attractive young man from the village who has been visiting us at Gülbin's house. He sits at a table with some other villagers, drinking a beer and looking directly at me. Embarrassed, I turn away.

The wedding could be taking place in Las Vegas. The ceremony is very short and mundane. The bride has a tawdry look, a village girl wearing too much makeup. The bride and groom stand before a long folding table, and exchange gold rings. Nothing seems very exotic about this Turkish wedding. The greenish atmosphere gives the whole thing a garish, cheapened unreality. The highlight of the wedding is the money dance. The whirling, laughing couple seems to come alive, both of them pinned from head to toe with multicolored bills of Turkish lira. There is a traditional white wedding cake, a champagne toast, rice. This couple had apparently decided on a Western, American-style wedding, something they had admired while watching the much-anticipated, weekly broadcast of American sitcoms on the TV perched above the village café. After dancing to the hollow-sounding wedding music for what seems like hours, they pack the boats and head back across the water to Ekinlik.

I am relieved to get back. The sacredness I had experienced the night before has been lost on Avsa, in the vulgarity of the greenish tent wedding. But back on Ekinlik, the village musicians begin to play. The café, open and full of air and light, woos me back into the mood. And Hakki is there, watching me at a much closer distance. The men dance together, with a visceral, sexual intensity. I wait to see Hakki dance. When he finally does, I feel my stomach knotting and my head lightening as I watch him move, his arms tightly outstretched with fingers snapping, his hips undulating. I feel small points of sweat appear in half-moons under my eyes. Then the women dance, and I dance for Hakki. I dance, feeling the physical force of eyes following my every swerve. I move my hips in a circle, snaking my arms in the Turkish style. I dance with Gülbin, and with other girls of the village. The long afternoon light deepens, golden, reflecting gilt edges around the wooden tables and chairs pushed to the sides of the café. Slowly, even the gold fades into the shadows between the swells on the darkening sea. When I stop dancing, I retreat to the edge of the quay to breathe in the warm, black air.

When the village stops dancing, they divide down the middle, the young men facing the young women. They start to sing a sad and haunting ballad, the girls asking unknown questions with the lightness of their voices, the men responding with their gentle answers. I am transfixed by the profound silence surrounding the song; the voices seem to emerge from a hidden dimension. One young girl's voice seems to take on a physical form as it hangs suspended in the chasm between the village men and women; its beauty is something I can feel with the palms of my outstretched hands.

To the beat of a single drum, the group moves together to the groom's house, where the couple will spend their wedding night. The wedding couple, delivered to their bed with the song of the village, enter the stone house. To the closed wooden door and the candle in the window, the village sings outside the house. To the young bride and the honorable groom, the village sings of the heart. As the wings of the angel fold, the dark hovering form begins to move towards the sea. We walk, me with my arms outstretched linking shoulders with village girls, as we sing, still softly. When we reach the sea, we continue to sing for a long time.

Irene-Marie Spencer writes, paints, and climbs volcanoes in her spare time. The rest of her time is taken up with her four spirited daughters, a husband, two dogs, a cat, five rabbits, two guinea pigs, and two budgies. She hails from Wisconsin, but now lives with her family in New Zealand. This story is an excerpt from a longer body of work entitled Tales of the Moon and Water, *an account of her experiences living in a fishing village on the island of Ekinlik in the Marmara Sea.*

JENNIFER BARCLAY

✶

The Path to Buddha

*The author finds unexpected hospitality in
a traditional Korean monastery.*

I WAS STANDING AT A BUS SHELTER IN THE TOWN OF TOKSAN IN
the pouring rain, trying to figure out where to spend the night,
a campsite or a motel, and how to avoid being drenched to
the skin. It was late June, and rainy season had started. A car
window rolled down and a fine-featured man with a smooth
head and soft gray monk's robes asked "*Odi-gan?*" I was going
to the Buddhist monastery, Sudoksa, I said, though actually I'd
planned to spend the night here and take a bus the next day.
He offered me a ride. As we made our way slowly through
sheets of rain in the air-conditioned car, he put the earpiece of
his cell phone in, and found some classical music on the digital
dial. I tried to cover my bare legs with my backpack.

We passed through a gate, and halfway up a forested mountain arrived under darkening skies. Imposing buildings rose up
from the hillside in the traditional Korean style: long, black-
tiled roofs, and eaves painted in delicate pinks and greens, decorated with flower and animal carvings; sturdy red wooden
pillars, delicate trellised doors with paper windows. Tradition

has it that there's been a temple here on Toksung mountain since 599. We stopped and the monk disappeared into one of the halls, asking me to wait.

Sitting in the car and watching the mist rise from the trees, I couldn't help thinking he was going to emerge embarrassed, having discovered I had no invitation, no right to be here. Instead, he invited me in to eat. When I said I wasn't hungry, a boy of about twelve gave me an umbrella and another monk led me across the sandy courtyard, skirting puddles, past a stone pagoda and toward the Hall of the White Lotus, a residence for monks. Instead of passing by, we walked up some steps to a raised walkway kept dry under the eaves, and doors were drawn open on a bright, bare room. I left my shoes outside as is customary and from behind sliding doors they brought out cushioned quilts and a pink, seed-filled pillow. I was left alone with a bow and a smile.

Incredulous, I spent the night in that perfect simple space, listening to the ceaseless rain and thunder in the hills. Outside my wood-and-paper shutters, which were held back by carved wooden turtles, I saw tall gnarled trees and a giant iron bell silhouetted by lightning. The monks returned a couple of times, once to give me a candle when the storm was bad, and again to check that I was comfortable. "Breakfast is at eight." They conferred. "No, sorry, six." Smiles, bows.

Thanks to my alarm clock, I made it blearily to breakfast in the canteen, having splashed myself with cold water. A monk in brown robes mutely helped me to fill my steel tray with rice, boiled greens, fresh bean sprouts, tofu and mushroom soup, roasted potatoes, and kimchi, all of which were delicious. Breakfast was quiet. Six tiny boys with cropped hair, in t-shirts and shorts, sleepy-eyed but with different expressions like six of the seven dwarfs, were guided to sit near me at the long table. They were "child monks," aged four and five, and had been training here for several months. One looked especially tired and grumpy, and a middle-aged lady gave them thousand-won notes (worth about a dollar) to cheer them up.

The morning was peaceful after the storm, and fog hung close to the hillside. A monk swept a courtyard, but everyone else had disappeared, so I explored. The main temple was a simple wood structure, with a tall ceiling and wooden floor. Five golden statues faced benignly through the open front wall out across the valley, three of them representing the past, present, and future Buddha. Hanging paintings lined the walls, lively scenes of gods and kings. On the roof beams were faint, centuries-old dragon paintings. An inscription said the temple was completed in 1308, the thirty-fourth year of King Ch'ungnyol, during the Koryo Dynasty. Few wooden temples have survived that long in Korea, thanks to repeated Japanese invasions, and then of course the war.

Finding it was still only 7 A.M., I took a path up the moist hillside, vaguely following the tocking of a wooden instrument. Steps led into forest, beside a stream cascading over boulders. Several groups of monks passed me on their way down, smiled happily and wished me a good day. One asked cheerily "Where are you going?" I grinned and shrugged, "Up the mountain!" He laughed, pointed up the steps: "Only two minutes! See you again!" I continued, and fifteen thigh-tightening minutes later realized the monk had a wicked sense of humor.

I thought I'd reached the end of the path when I found a tiny thatched house; an inscription on the rock said it was the hermitage of Man-gong, a Son (Zen) master who lived here in the early twentieth century and helped revive the Buddhist tradition in Korea. Buddhism, introduced from China 1,600 years ago, had a profound impact on Korean thought and culture, though Confucianism, Christianity, and Shamanism are all significant here.

The path continued straight up; although it was tough in the burgeoning heat and humidity, and views down the valley were obscured by clouds, the forest was peaceful. Then suddenly, the path turned, revealing a clearing and the most beautiful statue I had ever seen, standing in the mist against a cliff of pink rock that was covered with moss and ivy. The Buddha stood the height of two men, holding a vial, with an expression of absolute serenity. The trees around held still the moist air. A spring gurgled beside tall bamboo across the clearing. The only sounds were of birds and water.

Later that morning, Kim Moon-Sim, a cheerful woman with short black hair and gold-rimmed glasses, became my guide. She came from Seoul to curate the museum created here in 1999 to promote an understanding of Buddhism and protect the treasures. She spoke English with me, since I spoke barely ten words of Korean. Happily there were some English signs, too; I was one of the museum's first English-speaking visitors. I asked the meaning of something in one of the books on display. Her brow momentarily furrowed, she flipped through a dictionary, then consulted Chung-am, a monk with cropped black hair, in loose gray robes and slippers. He spoke to her in Korean for what seemed a long time. Then he threw up his hands with a laugh, eyes sparkling, and went to play on the multimedia screen: it was too difficult to explain.

Most people who came here were Korean or Japanese or Chinese Buddhists; Sudoksa has produced important Son masters and Dharma teachers. A non-Buddhist Western woman arriving alone, wearing shorts, and carrying a backpack was an oddity, yet I'd met with nothing but uncommon, smiling kindness. Over lunch in the canteen, a soft-spoken man in secular clothes who had invited me to sign the museum's guest book asked if there were many Buddhist temples in Canada. I said I didn't think so.

Kim Moon-Sim told me the 1,080 steps I had taken that morning related to the path to enlightenment. She showed me what to do when I entered a temple, and how to show respect to the monks by putting my hands together and bowing. I was introduced to the lady in the wide-brimmed straw hat who let visitors buy prayer tiles, and the one who looked after the temple, and gifts were pressed on me by Chung-am and Kim Moon-Sim. I tried to buy some keepsakes from the shop to show my gratitude, but they wouldn't let me pay, and apparently I couldn't pay for my room and board, either. These funny, charming, calm people were so generous.

When I was leaving, Chung-am insisted on driving me to town in one of the monks' communal cars. Bright green rice fields descended in tiers from hillsides he told me were named after phoenix and dragons. In Hongsong, he bought me a bus ticket and said goodbye. When he was gone, I walked in a daze for an hour before I could get on a bus.

Jennifer Barclay has published stories on travel and books in The Globe and Mail, The Toronto Star, *and* The Korea Herald, *and is coeditor with Amy Logan of* AWOL: Tales for Travel-Inspired Minds. *She has traveled in twenty countries and currently lives in England.*

ALISON WRIGHT

The Face of Disaster

*A celebrated photojournalist couldn't
tolerate watching the devastation on TV, so
she went to Sri Lanka to bear witness.*

WHEN I ARRIVED IN SRI LANKA, TWO WEEKS HAD PASSED SINCE the tsunami had hit. I found a car and driver named George who, I believe, thought we would be taking a leisurely tour of the tea fields. After a week of my encouraging him to continue for more than 1,600 miles on the worst possible potholed roads, dodging wild elephants, Tamil Tiger insurgents, and a continuous array of soldiers brandishing AK-47s, he calmly inquired, "Madame, should I be buying clothes?"

The devastation rocked us both. The shock seemed to be wearing off for people and the enormity of what had happened to their homes, their lives, their loved ones seemed to be sinking in. Relief was rolling in from all over the world, yet in many places the aid was still unorganized and unavailable. Although millions of dollars had been donated, what these people needed most immediately were just a few rupees to help them get by. I took to folding small amounts of money into squares and discreetly passing them on with the shake of a hand as we parted ways. Very rarely was I ever asked for it. In fact, quite the opposite.

I stopped to photograph one lone man sitting in a chair amidst a pile of rubble. Instantly he called out, "Have seat!" Here he was offering me the one thing left standing in his home. As if that wasn't enough, he shimmied up a tree to get me a coconut and there we stood, on a slab of concrete, drinking coconut milk in what was once his kitchen. Another man bought me tea. A woman gave me shells, the only possessions the ocean had left in her home since sucking away everything else she owned.

I accompanied a young woman who was revisiting the remains of her house for the first time. It was where her two-year-old daughter was ripped from her arms. The mother's face lit up with the memory as she picked up a teddy bear, a child's dress, a baby bottle, before dissolving into tears. Next door a man was chinking through the debris with a small knife looking for any remnants of his life, an identity card, a bank book, a rupee note. Not only did these people have nothing, they were not even sure who they were any more.

Of the 8,000 residents of Batticaloa, 5,000 died. That's 60 percent of its population. The once-thriving beach-front village was surrounded by a lagoon so there was nowhere to run when the giant wave hit, just into more water. Saris and clothing were left embedded in the barbed wire set up to protect against wild animals, where many of the bodies were trapped in its grip. A few remnants were scattered: cooking pots, photographs with cracked glass, clocks stopped when the wave hit at 9:22, Buddhist statues which mysteriously remained standing. But mostly there was just rubble. Everywhere had its own ghosts.

I viewed the beach, cluttered with personal effects. Human bones had started to wash up. A woman walked alongside me who appeared to be in shock. As I turned to ask if she was all right she began madly gesticulating toward the sea, indicating that it had taken her two children. Beside herself with anguish she attempted to throw herself into the ocean. I pulled her back and held her as she wept. Inconsolable, she buried her face in the sand.

Death is certainly more integrated with life in this part of the world, but there was no quantifying the universality of a mother's pain. Many felt the profound guilt of being unable to hold onto their children. Men who managed to grab on to palm trees live with the image of seeing their families swept away before them.

It was the end of the day, a milky dusk. I stopped to photograph an elderly Muslim man, his arms lifted to the heavens while clutching a small prayer book. He chanted prayers over the five freshly dug sand mounds before him, the graves adorned with small white flags flapping in the salty wind. Tears openly flow down his cheeks as he raised his face to confront the sea which had killed his family. Our eyes met and his were so overwhelmed by grief that I was compelled to take his hand. The pain became a shared, palpable connection as he told me this was his wife and four other family members he was burying, their bodies only just found after two weeks. We stood like that for some time, the unlikeliest of people, bound by the rawest of human emotion. There was nothing that I could say. As I eventually turned away I heard his soft voice call out just above a whisper, "Please," he implored, "don't forget about us."

Alison Wright is the photographer and author of Faces of Hope, Children of a Changing World, The Spirit of Tibet: Portrait of a Culture in Exile, *and* A Simple Monk: Writings on the Dalai Lama. *View her work at www.AlisonWright.com.*

Filipina

Can you take the islands out of the girl?

ONE MARCH DAY A FEW YEARS AGO, A FRIEND AND I, AFTER finishing a hike on Japan's Mt. Hiei, waited at a bus stop in the rain. Just as our makeshift newspaper shelters had disintegrated, a crowded bus came ambling toward us on our right; its seats and aisle curiously occupied with Filipina nannies balancing Japanese babies on their tilted hips, or cradling them in their brown-skinned arms—a tell-tale sign of the lower-class in Japan.

The women grew still as we tried to maneuver to the back of the bus without bumping any of the babies with our backpacks or bulky rain jackets, jarring them from the warm solace they found in the brown arms, the comfortable smell of frying oil and cocoa butter and Chanel No. 5 wafting into their noses. The women's eyes settled on my face for a brief second until they realized that I was, in fact, also a Filipina, and at that point their gazes veered elsewhere—to their babies' faces or to the roof of the bus, or to the dripping gold on their wrists. *In blood only*, they could immediately infer from my yellow North Face jacket or my green Salomon hiking boots.

Native Filipinas, or at least the majority who grew up poor in the cities, the ones whose homes were devoid of running water, air conditioning, and flushing toilets, the ones who squatted on their haunches to wash their shapeless housedresses and babies' diaper cloths in a plastic tub filled with murky water, the ones who wheezed at night because their lungs were trying to clear the smog sooting up their little air sacs, usually vowed to live more glamorously if ever they managed to flee the ghetto. I noticed from my several stopovers in Manila on my way to other Asian destinations, that the departing gates at Ninoy Aquino International Airport teemed with smartly-dressed *balikbayan* (Filipinas working abroad) surrounded by boxes distended with *hopia* cakes and *ube* jam, and *turrones de casoy,* edible comforts readily unavailable in their foreign homes. "Glamorous" meant toting around ridiculously expensive Louis Vuitton handbags, and wearing large Chanel sunglasses with the trademark interlocking CC conspicuously in view of anyone who doubted that this girl from the ghetto could have such symbols of stature draped about her body.

These women overlooked me, perhaps because cargo pants and hiking boots did not fit their idea of style, perhaps because they were too busy patting two-shades-too-light pressed powder onto their faces from their Dior compacts, but more than likely because they knew that I was not one of them, could sense it on levels beyond the most obvious: that my gypsy lifestyle required Eddie Bauer over Louis Vuitton; that in fact my raggy traveling clothes, stained with red dirt and tattered at the edges, signified wealth and freedom beyond their grasps; that my own outbound ticket to Hong Kong was for the exploration of back-alley Chinese eateries in Wanchai and the various bird and flower markets on Kowloon—*not* for cleaning toilets and chasing after the insolent children of wealthy Hong Kong residents.

Sometimes blood is just as thin as water.

The wide crevasse between my identity as an American and my Filipino ethnicity began when my father, fresh off a tour of duty for the U.S. Army in Vietnam and sufficiently infused with an intoxicating American Imperialism, made the decision that his children would not be raised to speak Tagalog—thereby driving a wedge into the porous bedrock of young minds, stopping bilingualism and multi-ethnic identity from taking root. ("They are American, they will speak English only.") Though my parents spoke Tagalog to one another, allowing me to absorb it indirectly, they never spoke it to me; so that today, while my comprehension is ample, even reaching levels of humor and irony, my speaking ability is sadly scarce. I am unable to conjure up *hello, goodbye, please,* or *thank you* on my own, but can understand complicated conversations Tagalog-speaking mothers are having with one another about such things as the impudence of their first-generation Filipino-American children. Their audacious sense of entitlement. Their insistence on owning a Sony Play Station, a pair of GUESS? jeans, and a white Jeep Cherokee in which to do their gallivanting.

"I'd like to see Leilani survive one day in Manila. What would she do without a hot shower? Or refrigeration? Does she think that the milk stays cold because she's an American?" my mother grumbled to her sister after one of my particularly greedy episodes: I'd added Coca-Cola to her grocery list, and when she returned with some generic store brand, I was livid—slammed the refrigerator door several times, pouted in front of the T.V. for hours, simply refused to drink any fluids whatsoever for half a day in protest. And yes, I did think that the milk stayed cold because I was an American; it is an advanced Western country after all, and refrigeration is part of the basic package. Along with telephone service, TV reception, electricity, and *real* Coca-Cola.

"I never want her to struggle like we did," she clarified, still in Tagalog, her head turning in my direction. I stared blankly into my book and turned a page, pretending I didn't comprehend what she was saying, or that I even cared. The benefit of not being able to speak your parents' native language is that they can't *make* you understand. Isn't it their fault that you can't?

Seven years after I eavesdropped on that conversation, I was a twenty-two-year-old teaching English in Japan, speaking conversational Japanese, meaning that I was able to summon up *hello, good-bye, please, and thank you* with no problem, unlike Tagalog. I had already ridden the bus crowded with Filipina nannies cradling Japanese babies; heard their whispers in Tagalog, "She is Filipina? She doesn't act Filipina." And had answered them in my head, in the crispest American accent I could muster, "Does acting Filipina mean that I should be acting like a maid?"

Had I actually voiced the insult, its maliciousness would have triggered the women to recoil into the shell of their shame, which they tried to camouflage with haute couture, but the fair babies in their brown arms betrayed them. I would have caused them to backtrack the steps forward they had already taken through the mazes of their inferiority complexes. They would have needed a few moments, or even a lifetime, to find their way around those dark corners again; and I, as a punishment, would be banished to the start of my own maze, despite my flailing protest.

My mother's words flashed upon me violently, like a crack of white-hot lightning: *I never want her to struggle like we did.* Guilt engulfed me as I pictured my mother as a teenager, working two part-time jobs as a secretary, and then dragging her heels to night school before returning home at 11 P.M. Often she found her own mother asleep, her head dangling from her neck, sitting next to a plate of soggy fried *tilapia* and a scoop of rice. "I was waiting for you," my grandmother would say through a fog of exhaustion. "Sit down. Eat your fish." The rest of the house was still. As the girl pinched rice between her fingers, she could see through the screen door that her mother had done four hours' worth of laundry that day, because the ghostly bluish moonlight reflected on the white t-shirts and underwear hanging on the line out back, and because her mother's hands were coated with a thick layer of cocoa butter to help repair the damage from scrubbing out grass and sweat stains barehandedly.

"You didn't use the money I left on the table for the market this morning," my grandmother would inquire, a little groggy.

"No, I didn't. I had some extra from my paycheck. It's O.K., Nai. Use it to buy a *Reader's Digest*." My mother would wake up at 4:30 A.M. so she could go to the market for the day's sustenance—*pan de sal*, *queso*, and *balut* (hard-boiled duck eggs)—and still have enough time to bring in the laundry, finish the last of her English homework (between Shakespeare and grammar, she much preferred to toil through the Bard's *thee*s, *thou*s, and *dost*s), and coax her brothers and sisters from their slumber. When they heard the floor creak from her tiptoeing around the room, putting away their laundry, the young ones started their first whimpers and stirrings to begin the day.

"Carmen, Cristina, get up. Nai has already boiled water for your baths." 6:30 A.M. My mother wouldn't have time to take her own bath. It took two hours to commute from Balut to her job in Makati, through Manila's twisted mass of congested roadways, which surged and coughed huge mushroom clouds of exhaust, as though they suffered from end-stage emphysema. She bounced violently in the back of a crowded jeepney, which stopped every fifty meters to load and unload passengers. She would be late for work again, despite the prayers she made to the Virgin Mary statue roped to the jeepney's grill. She had four hours of sleep.

I never want her to struggle like we did.

But in her endeavor to make sure that I didn't have to toil through the destitution that she suffered; that I didn't have to sleep on straw mats with five other people in a room swathed in mosquito netting; that I didn't have to boil water for a hot bath or work two jobs to support the household, I sprouted a cruel arrogance. In the folds of her promise to ensure that I would never want for anything, in the grooves carved into the keys of my new Jeep Cherokee, in the creases of my antique linen duvet hovering cloud-like over my brass bed, I became lost, disconnected from basic compassion.

So it's my fault.

No, mother, it's mine.

Riding on the bus that rainy day with women who looked like me—who had the same broad nose and thick lips and cocoa skin—who were so far removed from my own reality, was uncomfortable to begin with; but when I allowed my condescension to manifest itself in a comment so despicable that I had reduced myself to the lowest class just by thinking it, the situation became downright painful.

"I'm going to the Philippines," I whispered to my companion, wiping away a stream of rain that had unraveled from my forehead and into my eye.

"Why?"

"I need to get over myself."

A telephone trilling for attention in the middle of the night is never a good thing. "*Moshi moshi?*" I croaked into the receiver as my eyes searched the darkness for the luminous green numbers on the clock: 3:07 A.M.

"They stick up Americans!" It was my mother, in a fit of odd English.

"Ma, please. It's three o'clock in the morning. I have an early flight."

"And by the way. Your grandmother lives in the poorest ghetto in Manila. It's very dirty."

"Ma, I'm going. Goodnight."

"I'm faxing over these travel advisories I pulled off the web. Just…"

"Goodnight, Ma."

They stick up Americans? Did she mean *her* countrymen? My mother's disdainful tone astonished me; the obvious distinction she made between her and *them*, as if she were the Filipina Marie Antoinette standing on her balcony looking down upon the masses of poor people and saying, "Let them eat cake."

Did *they* include the people I observed, my mouth gaping in disbelief from behind the windows of my taxi, bathing *fully dressed* along Jose Rizal Boulevard in Manila, snaking a wet towel through the openings in their clothes, a garden hose draped over their shoulders like a feather boa? Or the children whose filthy bare feet skipped over the railroad ties to pick up daffodils and trash? Or the thousands of beggars whose arms rippled toward me like a diseased hydra, reaching for my hands, trying to grab at my sympathy?

What about that poor young girl I remember from my side trip south of Manila to Cebu; a girl who perched on the edge of the plastic lounge that her older German lover was suntanning upon, twirling his chest hair around her finger, trying to dam her tears while she tuned out his sing-song "I like you, but I'm leaving tomorrow. (And you're not coming with me.)"?

Growing up in American suburbia does not adequately prepare you for witnessing such acts of hopelessness. As I walked by, my toes gripping the warmed sand, I watched the young girl's faith dissolve into fine granules all around her—the fur coats she envisioned keeping her warm against a Munich winter (he told her of the huge snow drifts which piled around his "castle"), along with the Berliner pastries she would have tucked into her tote bag for her children's afternoon snack, being careful not to flatten them with her thick European fashion magazines or else she'd have strawberry jelly everywhere! (She giggled at the thought of this.) I saw the fantasy fall away with each word of his practiced refrain, and still the most sympathy I could muster was to feel embarrassed for her stupidity. Her dreams sieved through my toes now.

I'm sorry that you were such an idiot, my eyes flashed at her, *I'm sorry that the twenty pounds of gold chains slung around the neck of an obese man in a Speedo didn't tip you off.*

"Lani!" my grandmother scolds through the prickly telephone connection after I'd confessed my latest bout of condescension. "Those girl doesn't have your thinking. Those girl are poor."

"Still, Gram. The man was a whale. I can't believe she'd be attracted to him." I am arguing fruitlessly. The careless tumble of my reasoning amounts to little more than wasted dribble, rather than a gracefully pointed argument. I had called to tell her that I would be flying back to Manila the next day, but the way the conversation was progressing, I didn't feel a warm welcome would await me.

"They don't see if man is handsome or not. They see opportunity. You don't know because your parents give you opportunity already." It's true. In comparison, my plate was always piled high with an ever-replenishing, incredibly decadent dessert. So enticing that often, I didn't even bother to use a fork. I shoveled with my hands instead.

My mother and I took the Biblical adage, *Ask and you shall receive,* to towering new heights with layer upon layer of indulgence. When I was younger, I said, "Mama, I need a new doll, purse, glittery nail polish, et cetera. Pretty please?" She replied, "Yes baby. We'll look for something this weekend." And so my toy chest overflowed. When I got older, I said, "Ma, I need a new car, tuition money, a trip to Europe, et cetera. Please." She answered, "That's fine, baby. Start checking on prices." And so my horizons broadened. When I moved out of the house, I said, "Ma, I need money for rent, groceries, et cetera. *Every month*." And she responded, "O.K., baby. I'll write you a check every first and fifteenth." To this day, she still does.

The phone hisses and pops in my ear. I sigh, sensing the futility of this rapidly-declining argument. I'd never be able to justify my reaction toward the deflated young girl without sounding like a snooty American princess, and my grandmother would never be able to understand how such strong antipathy could arise from someone with suffering in her blood, passed down from her parents. In a moment of dead air, my mind sweeps the immediate future for any bit of merciful traction that could possibly redeem me—a flicker of remorse for my comments, perhaps—but instead I see myself flying back to Manila from Cebu with nothing more than a deep tan and a belly full of *buko* pie to gauge the value of my time on the beaches, and a new string bikini, wooden salad bowls, and beaded hair clips implying my preference to view poverty from my imperial perch comfortably padded with American dollars. As long as *my* life brimmed with choices; as long as *I* didn't hope to marry a man who used me to satisfy his yearly quotient of sex; as long as my mother and father were also drunk off privilege—my mother making a clear distinction between her and *them,* my father refusing to speak Tagalog to his children—I could justify my attitude by using my own family as a model for decorum.

Halfway through the dead air, I contemplate my life twenty hours from now: back in Manila, hailing a taxi on Jose Rizal, protected from the beggars by glass windows, unable to transpose my life with theirs because the air conditioning in the cab is running on high and in the streets *they* are dragging in 90-degree heat and 100 percent humidity. It's too big of a leap to make.

Maybe if I slept first.

Maybe if I could pull myself from this odd divergence of Filipino realities I inhabit, if only for an hour, I might recharge enough to take on the daunting task of trading fates. I might be able to surrender my lingerie bag and the automated delicates cycle to imagine living with hands chafed and raw from years of hand-washing clothes. Because then I'd know toiling. I'd know what it feels like to live with a dull ache in my shoulders and in my knees from hunching over a plastic basin for hours on end every day, while my daughter and granddaughter in America merely add soap to a machine and forty-five minutes later they've got clean laundry and soft hands and I'm not even a quarter of the way through my pile and already my fingers will not release from their clenched arrangement without pain.

I might be able to swap my decadent dessert for a simple *pan de sal,* which must be tied to the roof-rafters at night so the mice can't find it. Because then I'd know scarcity. I'd know a dinner table unadorned with variety, and taste buds desensitized in order to allow the imagination to infuse different flavors into the same old thing, or to allow the unappetizing to pass into the throat, because that's all there is to eat, some five-year-old cans of Vienna Sausages the American soldiers brought around at Christmastime.

I might be able to relinquish my backpack for a Louis Vuitton tote, which holds disposable diapers and zwieback

biscuits for those teething babies in my care. Because then I'd
know sacrifice. I'd know that I wiped baby bottoms in Hong
Kong for a living to make enough money to support my
family, so that the five-year-old cans of Vienna Sausages don't
have to be opened for dinner, so that the laundry can be
washed in a machine, so that I could reward myself with a
fashionable handbag because I need something, too.

I might be that girl, the one whose dreams of eating jelly-
filled pastries in Munich have now been taken out to sea by
the surf. Because then I'd know desperation. I'd know that my
exodus from this country takes precedence over something as
vital as basic human respect, or even personal dignity. I'd wish
I could be as small as a grain of sand and stow away to
Germany between the fat man's toes, because if someone ever
said to me, "I like you, but I'm leaving tomorrow (and you're
not coming with me)," I'd feel that small anyway.

Tomorrow I will direct the taxi driver toward my grandmother's squatter-style bungalow, which is more charming
than decrepit with a fuchsia bougainvillea cascading down
from a window box. But my mother would not have this
memory because she fled thirty years ago and hasn't been back
since. Her memories are of glassless window frames and a leaky
roof which would be covered over with a thick plastic sheet
and secured down with cinder blocks during the monsoons.
Her memories are of coming home to a cold fried fish dinner
and fighting her brothers and sisters for a narrow column of
sleeping space on the straw mats. Her memories are of hardship. The only proofs to mark the passage of time here are the
deepening furrows on Gram's skin, and the bougainvillea.

Gram is standing behind the curtain of blooms now, wondering if she'd actually said something to render me speechless,
or if the line has just gone dead. "Lani? You are there? What is
happen?" she demands, and then taps the receiver against the

door frame, in case the void of conversation was actually a malfunction of her telephone.

The droplets of salty guilt forming on my upper lip highly recommend a change in subject, so I say, "You know, Gram, you can speak to me in Tagalog, if it is easier. I will understand you."

"But you cannot return Tagalog. So you are useless," she replies as a sudden breeze sways a line of laundry tinted in the ghostly bluish moonlight.

After returning to America after a four-year stint in Asia, Leilani Marie Labong promptly forgot her backpacking survival skills and slipped back into her habits of royalty. She currently resides in San Francisco, where she avoids public restrooms at all costs, insists on drinking Pellegrino daily, and works as the research editor at the San Francisco lifestyle magazine, 7x7, and national design magazine, California Home of Design.

✦ ✦ ✦

Thin Places

Virginia Woolf wrote in The Waves,
"There are moments when the walls of my
mind grow thin; when nothing is unabsorbed."

MY SKIN WAS LIKE WET TISSUE PAPER. IT PEELED OFF WITH MY socks, pulled off under the damp bandage. It came off between my toes, from the soles of my feet and the edges of my heels. The exposed new skin was raw and tender. There was too much of it to cover and nothing solid or dry to hold down a new bandage. I had never seen anything like it and had no idea what to do. I glanced up with despair and saw the women already lifting their bamboo baskets and filing barefoot into the early morning mist. Pain was preferable to abandonment. Wincing, I pulled on my last dry pair of socks and laced up my soggy boots. I stuffed my jacket into the top of my pack and followed in the direction of the women—day number two on our pilgrimage to Khembalung.

At night in their dreams, shamans and priests from Hedangna, a village in the upper Arun Valley of northeastern Nepal, are said to travel to a cold clear lake on the right shoulder of Khembalung. Witches travel to the ridge as well, but they bathe instead in a lake of blood. When they are done washing, the shamans, witches, and priests stretch out on the rocks, drying themselves in the moonlight and arguing over which of them is the most powerful. Khembalung refers to several places. It is Makalu, the fifth highest mountain in the world and the home, so the villagers in Hedangna say, of Lord Shiva. Khembalung is also a *bhayul*, or hidden valley of Tibetan cosmology, a pure enchanted land set outside the destruction and corruption of time. Here, so the legends say, one will find refuge from the enemies of religion and will attain eternal youth, beauty, strength, and fertility.

These *bhayuls* are physical places hidden deep in the Himalayas and rendered inaccessible by the magic of the Tibetan *yogin* Padmasambhava. Years ago, so the story goes, in the paradisal kingdom of Galdan, Arya Avalokitesvara made a prophecy:

> *Emaho!* In the future, during the epoch of conflict and disputes the land of snows, where live those who follow the way of the great compassion, will be conquered by the demons of ignorance. At that time all the followers of the Arya, to flee from the demons will take refuge in this place which has sprung up from the flowers offered by the most powerful of the gods...It is the castle of the divinities, is the place of the purest prayers, is the natural site of the Vajra. It is surrounded by rocks and snowy mountains, and is known as *mKhanpa lung*, the valley of Artemisia. Everyone who arrives there will go to the paradise of Akanisthah.

At the time when all temples are destroyed, Giacomella Orofino describes, when servants become masters, when "people sacrifice their own animals, drink blood and eat flesh of their own fathers," those disciples of Padmasambhava who "display greatness of heart" will take out the guidebooks hidden thousands of years before and set out to "open" these hidden lands.

The journey to Khembalung crosses the physical landscape, passing by a lake, so the guidebook says, that "by day is like boiling blood and by night like burning fire," through a valley like "the outer curtain of a door," and beneath "a mountain of black slate like untied hair." But what the pilgrims see along the way depends on what they are capable of seeing. Some travelers encounter rocks and trees, snow and empty forest. Others travel over the same terrain and see mysterious landscapes shimmering with jewels, spacious deserts beneath strange skies, and towering mountains floating above clouds of light. The hidden valley itself bestows a spiritual blessing on all who arrive there. How the pilgrims experience that blessing again depends on what they are ready to experience. Most who enter the hidden lands of Khembalung will have a vision of a peaceful and fertile valley with room for a settlement of five hundred people. These pilgrims will receive health and long life, fertility and strength, and all of their desires will be fulfilled.

Though yogis trek beneath the same mountains and enter the same lush, green valley, they also undergo a spiritual transformation on their journey to Khembalung, a death and rebirth that allows them to transcend their usual state of consciousness and awaken to deeper levels of the mind. These pilgrims experience a flash of insight into the nature of reality, a vision that is fleeting, but one that strengthens and deepens their own spiritual journey. The secret journey to Khembalung is reserved only for those who have reached the highest level of spiritual fulfillment. Here, at its most profound level, the hidden valley corresponds to the body and mind of the pilgrim, to the realm where no distinctions are made between oneself and the outside world. Upon entering this innermost realm of the kingdom of Khembalung, the pilgrim acquires clarity of mind and openness of heart, the two qualities needed to attain the ultimate goal of enlightenment.

Few attempt to undertake this journey to the hidden lands. It is too dangerous, and they fear they will never return. But many make pilgrimages to the edges of these valleys, to the "gateways" (Tibetan *gnas sgo*) mentioned in the guidebooks and said to have been hidden by Padmasambhava. Two caves carved out of a granite cliff one thousand feet above the high-altitude summer pastures of Yangle Meadow, a day's walk south of the base of Makalu, are said to be one of the gateways into the hidden valley of Khembalung. Whether they are or not, these caves are believed to be places where gods have been; they are sacred places and are one of the most important pilgrimage sites for Hindus and Buddhists throughout the upper Arun Valley.

Priests and shamans, lamas and yogis may be able to make the journey to Khembalung in their dreams or through intense spiritual practice. Everyone else must get there on foot. And so, at the height of the monsoon, I set out at dawn with twenty-five villagers from Hedangna on a pilgrimage made annually to the Khembalung caves during the August full moon. Most in our group were Yamphu Rai, the original inhabitants of Hedangna, strong wiry people who have spent their lives as subsistence farmers in this remote subtropical Himalayan village.

Yamphu rituals and spiritual beliefs are based on oral texts passed down from the ancestors through the priests and shamans who learn these traditions in their dreams. Although they know that the caves are connected to the hidden valleys of Tibetan cosmology, they consider themselves to be Hindu and refer to the site as Shiva's cave. Two Brahmans from a less remote village to the south also joined us. These men were tall and thin and not at all suited to the long, hard days of walking. One of them complained incessantly, saying the trail was too hard, the trip too difficult. Each time the Brahman complained, Jadu Prasad, one of the oldest Yamphu men in the group who was on his sixth pilgrimage to Khembalung, would reply, "It wouldn't be a pilgrimage if it wasn't difficult." By the end of the trip we were all repeating, again and again, "It wouldn't be a pilgrimage if it wasn't difficult."

Yogis and lamas travel to hidden valleys in search of enlightenment; they hope to escape *samsara* and attain eternal bliss. The Yamphu were going to Khembalung to ask for a son, a daughter, a job, a good harvest. As an anthropologist living in their community, I hoped to learn more about their pilgrimages, about what they did, and found myself mumbling repetitive chants, over and over, to keep myself moving across the rocky terrain.

I carried a down sleeping bag, a Thermarest, a toothbrush, a pack cover, a flashlight, a notebook, iodine, four pairs of socks, long underwear, a synchilla jacket, a camera, rice, and the boots on my feet. Everytime I unpacked and repacked, the women gathered around to comment on each item I had brought. They carried a handwoven woolen blanket, bamboo mat to keep out the rain, rice, some spices, and a pot. They were barefoot. They had small bundles of string and bits of cloth, a shawl, their finest clothing to wear on the day we climbed to the caves, and *raksi,* a type of wine made from millet. That was all.

Each morning we awoke in the dark. We walked all day along steep narrow trails, fording icy streams overflowing from the monsoon rains, and climbing from 5,000 feet in Hedangna over two 16,000-foot passes and up the Barun Valley. In five days, we covered the same distance I had covered in two weeks the previous spring while trekking with family. The villagers would stop only at dusk, when we had reached a cave large enough to hold all twenty-five of us. We ate one meal of rice a day, mixed with wild plants gathered along the trail. While hiking we snacked on roasted corn flour. Occasionally, we drank black tea.

By the third afternoon, we arrived at Yangle Meadow, the grazing lands at 13,000 feet below the Khembalung caves. We sat on the grassy floor of the narrow valley, flanked on either side by towering granite cliffs. Our words were swallowed by the roar of the Barun River, which carved its way through the center of the valley. Jadu Prasad pointed out some invisible trail going straight up the vertical rock face: the path to the caves. I sat silently. A chill that had been with me the entire trip slowly crept up from my stomach. The two oldest women in the group, both in their seventies, looked at the cliff and then looked at me. "Don't go," they said. "Don't do it. The trail is too hard. Stay below and wait."

I know how to rock climb, I know what to be afraid of, and I shared their concern. "If these grandmothers can do it, of course you can," Jadu Prasad said. Having spent much of the past year trying to keep up with these same grandmothers while collecting firewood and stinging nettle in the jungles around Hedangna, I wasn't so sure. But the men promised we would all go together the next morning and they would look out for me. If I could go with them, I agreed, I would give it a try. We lifted our loads and went in search of a dry cave for the night.

The next morning we again awoke in the dark. It was drizzling. It had rained all night, and I had slept fitfully, dreaming of slippery mud and slippery rocks. I again asked Jadu Prasad if he thought I could make it and he again reassured me, so I went with the women to bathe. The women were used to doing things on their own; they were strong, and they assumed

I was equally strong. I couldn't count on them for help on the trail. After a perfunctory bath in the icy water, I returned to an empty cave. I waited, thinking the men must have gone to bathe as well.

Finally, one man returned. He was surprised to see me, said the men had already left, and that he had just come back to get something he had forgotten. I grabbed my bag and scrambled after him. We walked silently and rapidly through the drizzle, turning off the main trail onto a narrow overgrown path that climbed toward the cliff. We caught up with Jadu Prasad and the two Brahmans. They greeted us as we approached and told me that the trail was too slippery for my boots, that I should go barefoot; they then returned to their discussion of whether the two menstruating women should climb to the sacred caves. I was curious to hear what they had to say, but was distracted by the trail and, now, by my bare feet. Until now I had never thought of the cold. The soles of my feet were numb, so numb I didn't notice the stones underneath.

Soon the trail disappeared into the base of the rock. Those ahead had been slowed by the climb, and the women coming from behind caught up with us. Hands gripping the rock, we slowly followed the others up the cliff. Along with our group of twenty-five from Hedangna, there were Bhotes (Tibetans) from the northern Arun Valley and Chetris (Hindus) from the south. Together, sixty or more people were making their way up the rockface.

In the West, we climb rocks with rope and protection. We wear soft rubber under our feet. We are on the rock, yet not on the rock. With these pilgrims I climbed to the Khembalung caves barefoot, with no rope. Perched on a tiny ledge, Jadu Prasad reached down to pull me over a difficult section. I clutched his hand as he hauled me up the cliff, not letting myself think about what he in turn was holding on to. At a particularly difficult part, one of the grandmothers looked at me with concern and suggested I go down. But then a man appeared with a twelve-foot piece of rope. He knelt above the difficult section and held the rope as I used it to climb up the crack.

Once, at a Quaker wedding I attended, the father of the groom talked about thin places, about places where one's nerve endings are bare. We take pilgrimages to thin places, to places where gods have made their mark on the land. As the legends of the hidden valleys make clear, these journeys are internal as much as they are external. How thin the place seems to us depends on who we are and where we come from; most important, it depends on what we bring and what we can relinquish in order to make our journey.

I often joined the women in the fields in Hedangna, helping with digging and planting and cutting and carrying, doing whatever I could to create something in common for us to share. Though I was slower and clumsier, they welcomed the free labor and perhaps the novelty of having me around. During breaks in the work, when we were gathered on a rock or under a tree, the women, old and young, would reach for my hands and rub their fingers slowly across my skin. They would turn over my hand and feel the palm, pulling the fingers up close to their eyes, and they would comment to each other on how smooth and white it was. Then they would hold up their own hands and feet, which were tough and dark, next to mine and shake their heads. They lived by their hands, they would say, and I lived by my head.

The women in Hedangna want skin like mine. They want some padding in their lives, want to be able to stay inside for a while and let their bodies become smooth and white and soft. I went to Hedangna because I wanted skin like theirs. I wanted its thickness and its toughness, a toughness that seemed to be a sign of an internal strength, a thickening from the inside that allowed them to get by without a lot of external support. Their dark, callused skin enabled them to walk through their lives barefoot, enduring, not avoiding, the sharpness and the pain encountered along the way.

I was raised in a world where the answer to a problem or the solution to pain was always out there, around the next corner, in the next place or next job or next year. I was educated away from my home, taught to believe there was more to be gained by moving forward than by staying put. I came to Hedangna, a community where people still farm the land their ancestors cleared eleven generations ago, because I wanted to learn what it took to stay at home. I wondered what life was like without the leather and the plastic. I came to Hedangna because I wanted to relearn what it meant to live from the inside, with my hands and my feet and my heart—because I wanted to remember what their ways of living have never let them forget. And as I climbed the rock face to the Khembalung caves, I found myself entering one of the thinnest places I had ever been.

Two hours after leaving the valley floor, the trail leveled, and we began to climb the final section through thick clumps of juniper. Spiky roots and sharp stones under the juniper bushes made me aware of my bare feet, by now used to the cold. While climbing, we had only been able to see the rock immediately ahead and the valley dropping out below. As we came over the last incline, the most sacred site in the upper Arun Valley—the Khembalung caves—suddenly loomed before us: an immense amphitheater carved out of the cliff with a torrent of water pouring from an opening at the top of the cave. Buddhists say Padmasambhava meditated here on his way to Tibet. Hindus say Shiva bathed here on the evening before his wedding to Parvati. Now, snatches from the high-pitched chants of the Chetri pilgrims drifted down from the base of the amphitheater.

We approached the cave from below, first stopping at a smaller stone cairn to hang offerings of narrow thin bits of colored cotton cloth. Then, in single file, we walked through the waterfall. Those before me stood directly under the torrent and drenched themselves in the freezing water. It was still drizzling, and cold. Already chilled, I skirted the edges, hoping no one would notice, and followed the others up the last rocky stretch and into the cave.

The air inside was cold and dry and laced with the sweet smell of burning juniper. Red and green, blue and yellow prayer flags brought by the Bhotes and attached to long sticks rose out of a pile of stones in the center of the cave. Smaller bits of cloth were attached to sticks or rocks. String candles, clumps of wildflowers, red *tika* powder, coins, even a watch were placed haphazardly on the pile of stones beneath the prayer flags.

Until now, people had been quiet, focused on the trail and the destination. Once in the amphitheater, the atmosphere changed. There was work to be done, and everyone set out busily to do it. Two women pulled out clumps of string that they coiled into bundles, dipped in *ghee*, and lit as candles. One couple carefully placed a small tin trident below the prayer flags. A young man who had come on the pilgrimage to assist his mother sat off to the side, staring at the opening in the top of the cave through which the water flowed. There was no way people could have made this hole or the waterfall, he told me. It could only have been made by a god. That is why we had to give offerings. A middle-aged man who had moved to Hedangna from southern Nepal paused in his preparations to scan over the amphitheater. He had heard about this place for a long time, he told me, since he was young. "Now that we are

finally here," he said, "we have to take our time and make sure
we do things right."

The time spent in the cave was not what I think of as
spiritual. There were too many people, too much commotion,
too much concern about this piece of string, that piece of
cloth. I was too preoccupied with how we were going to get
back down the cliff. But the cave was awesome. Now the
voices and din echoed off its high ceiling, but I imagined what
it would be like to be there alone, with only the sound of the
wind and the torrent of water spraying against the rock.
Outside, the ground dropped out abruptly and steeply, and all
I could see was the Barun River, silver and silent, winding its
way through the distant and green meadows far below.

We finished at Shiva's cave, walked down a narrow path
through the juniper, around the ridge to a smaller cave set in
the rockface. For Hindus, this is the cave where she is said to
have bathed. For Buddhists, this cave is where Padmasambhava
and his consort, Yeshe Tsogyel, are said to have stayed on their
way from India to Tibet. We took turns crawling into a space
that would hold only three or four at a time. The air was
pungent from the burning butter. Light from string butter
candles set on the floor illuminated exposed chunks of quartz
crystals along the inside of the cave. The rest of the cave was in
shadows. Several red plastic bangles and a white cotton shirt
sewn by a tailor in Hedangna had been placed amidst the usual
bits of cloth and coins: offerings brought by a couple seeking
a child.

Outside, more juniper was burned. One of the Brahmans
chanted prayers for the well-being of our group; we tossed bits
of uncooked rice into the juniper smoke, and the Brahman
wiped the ashes on our foreheads as a blessing, a *tika*. We then
began the descent. Not until we reached the dirt trail coming
up from the valley floor, two hours later, did I begin to relax.

I paused to pull my boots back on and followed the others back to the cave where we had spent the previous night. The women who had been unable to go to the sacred caves because they were menstruating sat by a smoldering, smoky fire. They added some wood to the coals to heat water for tea, and we snacked on roasted corn flour mixed with sugar. The two oldest women said they were too tired to continue north up the valley and that they would wait for us there. We packed our loads and set out once again.

The valley floor was brilliant green from the summer rains, and there was finally a bit of blue sky. The air on my bare feet that morning had dried the skin, and the raw parts felt less painful. With the climb to the caves over, I felt carefree for the first time in days. As we walked up the valley, one man speculated that the weather had turned because of the particularly strong *dharma* (spiritual practice) of someone in our group. The idea that sun and rain responded to our thoughts and actions reassured me somehow and made me feel less exposed in this vast landscape. We walked until early evening and spent that night in a huge open cave at 15,000 feet. The next morning we climbed the remaining few hours so that we could bathe in the headwaters of the Barun on the morning of the full moon.

The next evening, another cave, another long day walking in more misty rain. There had been confusion over a bag I had left behind with the grandmothers, who we discovered had decided to head home before us. One of the women reprimanded me for not taking responsibility for my own things. A man who had told me the previous day to leave the extra weight behind looked at me with disdain and said that he had told me he would carry the bag. I turned and walked off to the river's edge to fill my water bottle. It was dusk, and the sky was still overcast. I stood on the banks of the Barun River, alone. I thought about how hard I was trying—trying to walk fast

enough, to say the right thing, to understand the right way—
trying to get it right. In Hedangna, I had novels to read and a
tiny room with a door I could shut, a door that, oddly enough,
was what protected me from this stark realization of my solitude.

For the past five days, these barriers had been stripped away,
and this sudden and complete exposure made me acutely
aware of the gap between my world and the world of my companions. I stared at the cold gray rapids thundering through the
cold gray fog. Why was I here, alone, in the middle of
nowhere? Why did I keep going out on my own into the wind
and the rain and the wet?

I inhaled the cold, moist air and searched the shadows
beneath the Khembalung caves, searched the thick fir trees
clinging to the edges of the valley floor. The mist moved swift-
ly and silently along the banks of the Barun. The silty river
roared. Then the clouds suddenly opened and a shaft of light
broke through the fog, turning the gray water silver, the black
fir a deep green. An angular cliff appeared out of the clouds
high overhead. The red-gray granite, softened by the yellow
evening light, was framed by the heavy dark clouds. And then,
just as suddenly, the fog closed in again, and night fell.

I took a deep breath and turned to walk back to the cave to
help prepare dinner. In the cave, a younger woman came over
to tell me that they were all with their families and neighbors,
that for them it was as if they had never left home. She said that
they had forgotten that it was different for me, that sometimes,
she thought, I must feel lonely or homesick, and that she
hoped I was O.K.

During the whole trip, I felt an ache in my chest, a longing
that would not go away. I thought there must be a place, somewhere, where I could be held, here, no *here*, on the inside. If
only I could get to that place, I was sure, the yearning would
disappear. Now I realize that this feeling of aloneness is not

something that ever goes away. It is always there, underneath the words spoken, inside my boots. It's what comes up in thin places. It's what you feel when the skin peels off your feet.

Three months earlier at a cremation in Hedangna, as we watched the burned body float down the Arun River, the mother of the dead man held up her hand in front of me. It was cracked and dark. "We all feel love," she told me. "We all feel pain. We all bleed when we are cut. It is only the *mindhum* (oral tradition) that is different." The skin contains the blood, preventing it from spilling over; it creates the distinctions that enable us to live. But the skin can become too thick. It can keep us from seeing blood underneath, from sensing what Roberto Calasso calls the "connection of everything with everything, which alone gives meaning to life." It can keep us from experiencing the sacred.

We make pilgrimages to sacred places, but the places themselves are not inherently sacred. We enter the sacred when we let go of the fear of being exposed: only when I gave up trying to hide what was inside did the boundaries between us begin to dissolve. And in the moment I felt most alone, I realized I was never alone. The sacred, as Calasso writes, is always there "waiting to wake us and be seen by us, like a tree waiting to greet our newly opened eyes." It is simply up to us to let ourselves see.

Having reached our destination, everyone was suddenly in a hurry to begin the trip home. Rice fields needed to be weeded, millet planted, houses looked after. We left early the following morning and walked twelve hours, over a 15,000-foot scree pass, and then descended steeply past grazing yaks and shepherds' huts. We walked on after dark for an hour, searching for a place to spend the night. Finally, ten of us crowded into a small empty bamboo hut. I had a mat, so I kicked away the cow and goat dung, spread it out on the dank floor of the attached livestock shelter, and tried to sleep. We again woke before dawn and started walking hard and fast until we reached another shepherd's hut where we stopped to drink sour buttermilk. Since climbing to the caves, I had given up bandaging or even looking at my feet, but by this time, I was no longer the only one limping. The women leaned heavily on walking sticks and groaned with each step. We joked and laughed to keep our minds off the pain.

The trail continued to descend steeply. Yaks gave way to water buffalo and cows, and we began to meet shepherds from Hedangna. Finally, we could see the village, far down the ridge. We had been rushing, and now the women wanted to linger, to hold on to the remaining bits of time that were outside regular, routine time. We paused on top of the ridge to eat the last of our corn flour. One woman sighed and said she was so happy up here, in the meadows and the mountains, that she didn't want to go home. Two women separated the tiny wildflowers they had collected from the fields beyond Yangle Meadow to bring as gifts for friends who had had to stay home. Two others divided a bottle of water, taken from the headwaters of the Barun. The sun was beginning to set.

We began the last stretch, down and down. We came across leeches for the first time but were too tired to pull them off. An hour later we entered the edges of the village, in the dark. I was the only one with a torch and my batteries were weak, so our pace slowed to a crawl. The trail wound beneath thick clumps of bamboo towering over the stone and mud houses. People broke off from the group as we passed the narrow paths to their homes. Eventually, it was only the two oldest women and myself, walking down to the houses at the bottom of the village. We finally arrived, I dropped my pack and leaned it against the stone wall. Someone went inside to cook rice. The children gathered around, and I sat on the mud porch to unlace my boots. My socks were wet with blood. I carefully peeled them off so the air could begin the slow process of healing—and thickening—the exposed raw skin.

Ann Armbrecht Forbes teaches in the Environmental Studies Department at Dartmouth College and is the author of Settlements of Hope. *This essay is part of a book she is currently writing about her work in northeastern Nepal.*

JANNA L. GRABER

✦ ✦ ✦

Thailand's Lost Children

They help her find herself.

IT'S ALMOST NINE P.M. AND CHIANG RAI'S NIGHT BAZAAR IS still swarming with people. A group of young girls performs a traditional Thai dance in the market square, their lithe arms swirling in graceful chorus. Most locals don't bother to watch, too busy with friends and catching up on the weekly gossip.

Dozens of vendors line the walkways, hawking everything from iron cookware to traditional Thai clothing. They raise hopeful eyes to my daughter, Kirstin, and me, as we worm our way through the market's narrow aisles. The melodic tones of the Thai language are an unintelligible, yet soothing buzz in my ears, and for a moment, the English thoughts running through my head seem foreign.

Ten-year-old Kirstin doesn't seem to notice the newness, the strangeness of it all. She giggles with excitement, holding tight to my hand while she marches ahead, as if in search of some great treasure.

Here in this tiny square of Northern Thailand, our lives in Colorado seem distant, opaque. In the warm night air, I sense something I can't quite identify. A slower pace of life, perhaps? A feeling of safety? Whatever it is, I am starting to relax, intrigued with the world around me.

I can nearly forget that this is not just a simple vacation; ignore the fact that I have come here to write about the sex trade.

"Come on!" Kirstin says, pulling me toward the rich smell of spicy food. The colorful dishes, neatly displayed, all look so appetizing, except for the plates of grilled crickets, beetles, and grasshoppers.

"Wanna try some, mom?" my oldest daughter asks, a mischievous tone in her voice.

"Maybe later," I say. "Right now, I can't stand the thought of eating bug legs."

There are limits, after all, to one's adventurous spirit.

Kirstin and I are obviously outsiders, the only blonds in the market. But the Thai are kind and welcoming, and Kirstin mirrors their pleasant grins. We stop at a jewelry stand where I look over several gold necklaces.

"It's so cheap," Kirstin exclaims, after asking the prices.

The American dollar is strong here, making our purchases quite affordable. And while all economic strata are found here in Thailand, the majority of people live comfortable, simple lives.

While I pore over the necklaces, the middle-aged sales-woman smiles and admires Kirstin's golden locks. We don't understand her words, but the stroking of the hair and friendly pat on the head is universal. A complimentary child's bracelet is tossed in on top of our purchase. Kirstin hugs it to her body as we walk away.

"The Thai seem to like children," I remark to my friend, Nancy, who joins us later at the market.

"Of course," she replies. "The Thai love their children and

the children of others as well; kids are something to be treasured here."

I nod my head, deferring to Nancy's wisdom. She has, after all, lived in Thailand for several years, raising two sons with her husband. Still, I am confused. Her take on Thailand's purported adoration of children seems at odds with its thriving child prostitution. I open my mouth to ask about this paradox, but Nancy turns down another aisle.

When I reach her, she is speaking with four young women resting on a blanket, their handcrafts in neat rows in front of them. They are wearing dresses covered in intricate beadwork, and vibrant headdresses adorned with coins and beads sit atop their heads. Shy smiles reveal red gums and teeth from chewing betel nut leaves, a popular habit.

The women speak to each other and Nancy in clipped sounds foreign to my ears, quite different from the Thai language.

"They are Akha," Nancy says.

Instantly, I'm intrigued.

The Akha are one of six distinct hill tribes living in the nearby hills of Northern Thailand. Each of the tribes has its own language and culture. Considered outsiders in their own country, the tribes lead remote, primitive lives. Village homes are often made of bamboo and thatched roofs, most without electricity or running water.

Rejected by the Thai, many of the 540,000 tribal people do not possess Thai citizenship, as documenting births in grass huts, far from modern hospitals is difficult. Lack of official status denies the villages fundamental rights, like education, voting, and land ownership.

As an agrarian society, the inability to own land is problematic for the hill tribes. As soil is depleted, tribes migrate between the steep hills of Thailand and neighboring countries. Recent government mandates force those who stay in Thailand to cultivate the same plot of land over and over, a distinct change from former ways.

The pressures of modernization have intensified hardships for the Akha, the level of poverty making the villagers more susceptible to the social ills of civilized cultures. The least educated and poorest of the hill tribes, the Akha maintain the highest rate of drug addiction and infant mortality in Thailand. Opium addiction, and, sadly, child prostitution are huge issues for the hill tribe.

I'm here to write an article for a Chicago paper on child prostitution. It's a problem that has plagued many nations, but in Thailand, it has reached endemic proportions.

"Why would you want to write about *that*?" a friend back home had asked before I left.

My reasoning is not exactly logical. I'm hoping that more media exposure about the consequences of prostitution will shrink the allure of this social blight. Personally, I'm searching for a glimmer of hope, a fine shimmer of light that illuminates the goodness of humanity.

But that won't be easy to find. Young children are prized commodities in the sex tourism trade in Thailand. Despite the government's efforts—they've spent millions of dollars on programs and law enforcement—relief agencies estimate that there are over 2 million prostitutes in Thailand, 800,000 of them under the age of sixteen. New laws allow for foreigners who use prostitutes to be punished in their home countries, but few of the thousands of sex tourists who come here each year worry about such possible consequences.

Glancing at my daughter, her fresh face shining with innocence, I am sickened. What kind of person willingly takes that away from a child?

Across the border in Burma, a mere half-hour drive from Chiang Rai, the situation is even more complex for the hill tribes. A coup d'état in the 1960s obliterated Burma's once prosperous society. Taking the name "Myanmar," the military shut down universities and plunged the country into poverty and civil unrest. Now, refugees from Burma stream across the Thai border.

Another country known for poverty and conflict, Laos is another half-hour drive to the north. The three countries meet in a fertile area called the Golden Triangle; it was once the opium-producing capital of the world. Many of the children in the sex trade come from Laos or Burma, Nancy had told me earlier. Living in severe poverty, they cross the border believing they will find jobs as waitresses or dishwashers. Instead, they are forced into a despicable profession, deceived by malicious, greedy adults.

"Can I buy this, mom?" Kirstin asks, holding up a doll clothed in the same Akha dress of the women merchants.

The porcelain doll feels cool to my touch.

"You'll have to be careful with it," I say. "It's very fragile."

The word resonates in my mind. Each child comes into the world a delicate flower, unsullied and buoyant with dreams so easily crushed, lost to unchecked compulsions and incomprehensible cruelty. I look at Kirstin, hoping she will never encounter the violence and hardship so many children here have. An intense feeling of protectiveness overwhelms me; I want to keep all of the evils of the world from my child. So once again, I question.

Was I wise to bring Kirstin along on this trip? Child prostitution is a challenging subject for an adult, and even more so for a ten-year-old girl. Though I knew the trip would be challenging, I selfishly wanted Kirstin with me as our busy lives—school, sports, church—leave little opportunity for one-on-one time with my kids. I wanted to spend time with Kirstin away from her siblings, the normal distractions of life, and beyond the normal "mommy" role. And I was tired of traveling alone in search of stories. Thailand, I had been told, was a safe and wonderful place.

"Why not bring the family along?" Nancy had suggested. While there weren't funds for five airplane tickets, there was enough for one more.

Although Kirstin won't be privy to the interviews, she knows the topic I'm here to research, and about some of the girls that we may meet. We've had simple conversations, at her age level, about what we might see, but Kirstin is still struggling to understand.

"How can they stand to do that, mom?" she asks when I try to explain the sex trade.

I have no answer.

I have the same questions myself.

How do I explain that there are parents or aunties and uncles who willingly sell their children into sex slavery? That other children, with no parents or means of support, take to the streets to fill their empty stomachs? That others prostitute themselves for drug money or to fuel a lavish lifestyle?

Rooted in poverty and primal human behavior, child prostitution seems an insurmountable problem. How can it be addressed?

I pose this question to Nancy, who thinks a moment before answering.

"By helping one life at a time," she says.

Nancy has spent the last ten years doing just that. Originally an interpreter for the deaf, she spent several years working on Christian social welfare projects before moving to Thailand.

"When I first saw Bangkok, I thought, 'I can't love this dirty city,'" says Nancy. "You would see the sidewalk moving and realize it was cockroaches. It was awful."

But then Nancy was sent to the picturesque hill country of

Northern Thailand, where she spent several months working at a new girls' home.

"The first time I read the reports on child prostitution, I went to bed and wept for an hour," Nancy says. "It just broke my heart. I had never felt a burden like that before. But I couldn't figure out what I could do about it, because the whole subject scared me. I had always been a good girl, and never got in trouble or been around it. Still, I liked the idea of some kind of preventive approach."

That's why, when Nancy was asked to return as the home's "house mother," she gladly agreed.

"I had always been a born mother," she says, laughing. "As a child, I was the one reminding other kids to zip their coats and keep their hats on. My mother used to say to me, 'Nancy, they already have mothers at home.'"

It wasn't easy.

"I didn't speak the language, and at times I wondered what I was doing here," Nancy says. "Because of my hearing loss, the doctor doubted I could ever learn a tonal language. But I kept trying. The girls would have an argument and I would use a dictionary and pictures just to figure out what they were fighting about. In the end, we'd all end up laughing anyway."

"Within a year," Nancy continues, "I could hold my own in Thai. I spent time comforting girls, making sure they did their homework and meeting their needs. The main thing is that the girls knew that someone truly cared for them. For many of them, that was a new experience."

Nancy was working on a village project when she met a handsome young Akha man named A-Je, the man who later would become her husband.

"When I saw A-Je with his people, I was so impressed," she says, a smile inching from her lips. "I turned to a friend and remarked that if he were a Westerner I would marry him in a minute. I just never imagined I would marry a man from the hill tribes."

But the two worked together on several social projects, eventually falling in love.

"One day, A-Je went down this list with me," Nancy says. "He said he came from the lowest tribe, and that he owned nothing but a bike, a degree, and a heart to serve God. Though he wanted to study in America, he felt called to help his people here. That meant if I married him, I would have to give up my country and my ways."

I consider the difficulty of that decision—one that Nancy easily made.

"Since A-Je's father was the tribal chief of a large village, over one thousand people came to our two-day wedding," Nancy says. "I had to prove myself as a wife, cutting down a tree and feeding chickens during the event."

I can hardly picture that one.

"The American ceremony in Colorado was just as hard on A-Je," Nancy says. "We had to kiss in front of the whole congregation, and he about passed out."

As the first Akha ever to graduate from university, A-Je, a Christian minister, works full time for his people. He and Nancy run a children's home for tribal children rescued from the sex trade or are at risk of being lost to it. I can understand why he is compelled to help. But I'm curious to see how A-Je, with his jeans, sunglasses, and fine education, blends with the tribal villagers.

Finished with our purchases, Nancy directs Kirstin and me down a side street. It is dark and shadowy. Such places in the States are not always safe, so my senses are heightened to danger.

"Is this O.K.?" I ask, referring to the dark alleys and the red lights of the go-go bars up ahead.

Three young men walk in the shadows behind us. I can't help but wonder if they plan to do us harm. I pull Kirstin close. But this is Northern Thailand, and Nancy assures me that we are safe. She stops in front of a bar, and I turn to see what she sees.

Young girls, some in their early teens, others approaching twenty, congregate outside the bars. Dressed in jeans and t-shirts, a few wearing short skirts, they look like average teenagers.

"They're prostitutes," Nancy says, a sad note in her voice.

The announcement shocks me. The girls don't look anything like the prostitutes I've seen in American movies.

But the girls are rooted to their spots in front of the bars, a dead giveaway, Nancy says. We walk down further, passing dozens of young girls—and boys—who make this their profession.

As we walk past one bar, the girls out front notice Nancy's Akha bag with its recognizable stitching. It's a slow night, so they call out "hello" in Akha. They are shocked when Nancy responds in their native tongue, since very few people can speak the Akha language.

There are three young prostitutes, the youngest possibly thirteen; the oldest about nineteen. They admire Nancy's bag, and then turn their attention to Kirstin.

One strokes Kirstin's locks, the other drapes an arm around her and looks into her large blue eyes. Kirstin can't understand their words, and at first, she pulls away from them in fright. But Nancy shows no fear or disgust, only kindness and compassion. She continues to exchange pleasantries with the teens. My daughter picks up on Nancy's calm manner and grins shyly back at the girls.

"She looks like a little doll!" the oldest one exclaims.

Nancy tells them that we are visiting from America. They

smile. Why are we here? Do we like it? Does Kirstin like her straight blond hair?

We end up taking pictures of the girls with Kirstin, posed and smiling in the middle. The girls smile, too, perhaps sadly, and I wonder if they sense our meeting has made my heart heavy. I wonder about the dreams each of them has given up.

Eventually, it's time to move on. We wave goodbye and continue on down the sidewalk. Here and there on the streets, I notice foreign men who seem to have local "girlfriends." These men buy their "girlfriends" clothing, Nancy tells me, and shower them with gifts. Still, it is a business arrangement— a girlfriend for the week. As I pass one such girl, who has an Australian's arm draped possessively around her, I look into her face. She is trying to look happy, but the sadness fills her eyes. I can't help the matronly feeling of protectiveness that wells up inside me. I want to run back to the Australian and yell and scream and kick. "Why are you doing this?" I want to cry. "Can't you see you're hurting her?"

But I push the anger down and move my eyes away and back over to Kirstin, who is clinging to my hand in silence. There is a somber look in her eyes. She seems to have sensed the gravity of what we're seeing; still, I don't think she truly grasps all that has transpired here tonight.

"Why don't they just go home?" she asks of the girls we spoke to. "Why don't they stop it, if they don't like it?"

I try to explain that some may not have good homes to go home to; that maybe this is the only way they think they can earn a living.

A look of shocked realization crosses Kirstin's face. It is, perhaps, the first time she has considered what she has—a family, a home, and parents who support her.

I'm struck by the strange dichotomy of Thailand: in a country where child prostitution is a huge problem, those children born into stable homes are loved and well provided for. It's obvious from looking around at families on the streets and out shopping, that children play a vital role in Thai society. Their innocent manners seem to delight those around them.

But those who are born into poverty or to drug-addicted parents face a different fate. The lure of wealth from prostitution is strong, even if it is a child who is forced to be the bread earner.

When we return to our hotel room an hour later, Kirstin and I call home. She speaks with her dad, regaling all of our adventures so far. The sadness that had covered her face has disappeared and now she is her usual, happy self.

"Should I tell him about talking with the prostitutes," she whispers to me, holding her hand over the phone mouthpiece.

"Let's wait till later," I reply, not wanting to shock her father.

That night, I dream of the girls with sad faces.

The next morning dawns bright, a perfect day for heading upriver to the Karen tribal village of Ruammit. We plan to explore the village and pursue one of Kirstin's dreams—riding an elephant. A-Je is busy at the children's home, so Nancy is our guide for the day. We hire a boat and driver in Ban Thatorn. Nancy's boys, seven-year-old Zion and four-year-old Silas, come along.

The long, slim craft doesn't look very steady, but we're soon skimming up the Mae Kok. Within minutes, the city is behind us. Tall mountains covered with green trees and thick grasses rise from the riverbanks, no people or animals in sight, except for one lone hawk circling overhead. Our driver keeps his eyes straight ahead. We come upon several men in their underwear fishing rocks from the river to sell later in the city. They ignore us completely.

The hum of the motor is soothing, like a lullaby, and Kirstin puts her head on my shoulder. Nancy's boys do the same with her. We are a contented lot, pleased to be together, the lush river banks passing by.

Eventually, the hills grow larger and I see my first tribal village high up on the mountainside. The huts, most of them on bamboo stilts, look like little wooden dots in the emerald-forested land.

A few minutes later, Kirstin sits up and points with excitement.

"Mom!" she exclaims. "Look!"

Following her finger, I see several elephants in the river, playing in the water. At least ten of them huddle together near the bank, paying no mind to us.

Scrambling ashore, we're immediately greeted by two men struggling to hold onto a fifteen-foot boa constrictor. Smiling, they ask if I'd like to have my picture taken with the snake draped around me. I glance at the massive creature writhing about on their shoulders, and shake my head no. Kirstin walks far around the big snake.

Behind the men, several elephants are walking around freely. It's unnerving when they reach out their massive trunks, looking for a handout. One animal reaches its trunk to Kirstin, who shrieks and grabs my hand.

Nancy, who has clearly been here dozens of times, pushes the elephants' trunks away and makes her way past. Kirstin clings to my hand as we follow cautiously behind, while Zion rushes to buy a bunch of bananas to feed the beasts. This is a treat for the boys, who are happy and at ease here.

Nancy speaks to the Karen villagers in Thai, who also speak this as their second language. "It's 150 baht for an elephant ride," she says. "Give it a try!"

Kirstin takes a determined breath, and walks over to the elephants. We purchase a ride from the villagers, and then mount rickety stairs to a high wooden platform. Gingerly, we crawl onto a rough chair that has been tied to the elephant's back. The handler hops on the creature's head, and we're off.

Not prepared for the creature's jilted footsteps, I support myself with both arms to keep from being thrown into Kirstin. She giggles.

"This is hard, mom!" she exclaims. "It's kind of bouncy!"

As we make our way down the narrow lanes of the Karen village, chickens dart in front of us, and dogs run about. Occasionally, the elephant handler stops to talk with an acquaintance; at other times the elephant halts to pull at a grassy snack. Nothing hurries here.

I can see into several of the stilted huts, where women are cooking or stitching. Kirstin looks as well. Does she notice there are no lights or toilets? How different this must seem from our home in Colorado. Do the straw walls and dirt floors shock her? My daughter says nothing, but I can see she is deep in thought.

Settled in the foothills, the Karen tribes depend on farming and hunting for game. The women dress in colorful blouse-sarong combinations, their long hair often pulled back in buns or covered with white scarves.

My body is stiff after the elephant ride, but the soreness is forgotten when we stop at a local village store-restaurant. Aside from the rice, I have never seen most of the food we are served. A tad spicy and quite delicious, at two dollars a plate, it's a bargain. Kirstin and I smile at each other over our plates of food.

"Wasn't that cool?" she asks, still thinking about the elephant ride.

Perhaps this will be one of those memories that will linger in the back of her mind, resurfacing years later when she has children of her own. I'm grateful to be a part of that memory; to have this precious time with my oldest daughter.

We walk around the dirt roads, looking at shops and talking

with villagers. I watch one young woman set out chilies in the sun to dry, while her son plays in the dirt beside her. A contented look consumes her face as she cares for the little one. Further down the lane, we pass men standing outside of their homes, looks of boredom on their faces. Pieces of unmatched clothing are hung on bamboo lines behind them.

Many of the homes seem empty; others have a chair here, a table there. Kirstin's eyes are wide as she soaks the scenes in. This is her first glance at the unrelenting grip of poverty. She is quiet as we head back to the riverbank, where our driver is waiting.

The ride back to town is chilly, and I'm glad I have a jacket. Kirstin snuggles close for warmth, and within minutes, is sound asleep. Zion and Silas are fast asleep, too. Smiling at each other, Nancy and I pull our children close. My mind plays back the scene in the village. I wonder what it is like to raise children there.

Is it harder to raise children when you don't have all the comforts that materialistic goods can offer? Or it is simpler without the distractions of having to provide stylish clothing, constant entertainment, and a lovely home? A child's happiness does not come from things bought with cash, but from the love and support of a caring family. Perhaps, like mothers everywhere, Akha women simply try to make the best possible life for their children; meeting their basic needs, protecting them from harm, and loving them as only parents can. Aren't these common bonds of motherhood, whether lived out in a stately mansion or a simple hut, universal?

A few days later, Nancy, Kirstin and I make our way to the Thai city of Tachilek, just across from the border in Burma. Dozens of vendors line the streets, offering tea and clothing at rock-bottom prices. There is plenty to buy, but we are here to visit the Akha in Burma.

"Sometimes, it's not safe to cross," Nancy says. "There is often shooting and fighting between the Karen and the Burmese military. Sometimes, whole villages are wiped out."

Today is a good day, however. In a border procedure I don't understand, we leave our passports with the Thai, and carry copies over to the Burmese. We pay US$5 each to cross, and we must be back to Thailand by 6 P.M.

"Keep your eyes straight ahead, don't talk to anyone, and just look like you know where you're going," Nancy says as we cross the bridge joining the two countries.

But it's hard to keep our eyes straight. There are dozens of children, tiny bodies thin and dirty, begging on the bridge.

"We'll give them money when we cross back," Nancy says. "Don't do it now or they will keep following us."

A child of about six follows us anyway. A young baby, barely old enough to hold its head up, is tied to his back. My heart can't stand the sight, and Kirstin, who is holding my hand fiercely, has a shocked look on her face. Her grip on my hand is so tight that it hurts. I glance at Nancy, who looks like she wants to weep.

"There are just more children than we can help," she says, as if trying to explain.

Burma seems like it is from another long-past era. Donkey-pulled carts piled high with hay amble up the road. A few old cars are parked on the streets, but there is little traffic. An ox-drawn cart moves slowly past us. Villagers in sarongs and large straw hats pass us. I look for stores and signs of commerce, but only see one such place, about the size of a 7-11 store. There is little to buy in the window.

It is dangerous for the Akha here to meet with us, but Nancy's friends, a family of four, welcome us with open arms. Several young Akha friends, dressed in sarongs, have joined them.

Inside a plain two-story house, home to over twenty people, we are spirited to a long table piled with tasty food gathered from meager rations. There is little else in the room. Yet everyone smiles and laughs. We can't understand the Akha chatter around us, but Kirstin and I feel welcomed.

"Eat more!" one of the older mothers motions to Kirstin, then piles more rice on her plate. Throughout the day, this same mother looks out for Kirstin's every need, even cracking a pile of sunflowers for my daughter when she can't do it herself. Touched by her thoughtfulness, I try in stumbling Akha to thank this kind woman.

After lunch, the young people move the chairs and gather in two lines. Nancy translates for us as they sing and dance Akha songs of their Christian faith. Obvious joy covers their faces. Kirstin and I are silent, for the experience is overwhelming.

"Mom, they had absolutely nothing!" Kirstin later says as we cross back into Thailand. "But they still seemed so happy."

So happy. With nothing but each other, a roof over their heads, and a few meager belongings.

My daughter has learned an important life lesson. For that matter, so have I.

Later that week, Nancy drives me to meet with Kusumal Rachawong, a Thai woman who is the local director for End Child Prostitution in Asian Tourism (ECPAT). I like Kusumal, who is in her mid-30s and passionate about her work, immediately. She offers me tea and we sit down to talk.

Kirstin has come along, but Kusumal reads the look on my face. I don't want my daughter to hear more than she has to.

"Kirstin, why don't you come over here and have a look at these books," Kusumal offers.

While Kirstin reads, Kusumal reports the facts.

"Formal reports claim that prostitution numbers have gone

down in Thailand, but that's not true," she says. "Brothels have been shut down, so prostitution has gone underground. You can find young girls and boys at karaoke and go-go bars, massage parlors, and hotels," she says.

AIDS is a constant threat, she says. There are 14,000 children under age fifteen living with HIV/AIDS in Thailand. "But many child sex workers are not tested for AIDS," Kusumal adds with a note of gloom. "This generation is in denial. I fear they will die young."

ECPAT has also found formal links with the tourism trade. "The pimp will bring a photo album of girls to hotels for the customer to choose," Kusumal says. "Then, the girl goes to the customer." Thailand's sex trade reputation has become so well known that men (and sometimes women) from America, Australia, Great Britain, Asia, and other developed countries come to Thailand specifically for sex tourism. That creates even more demand for the sex trade. It is a vicious cycle that many feel helpless to break.

"It's difficult to do prevention if we don't know where the children are," Kusumal adds. "They are easily hidden at go-go bars, massage parlors, and behind photo albums."

I look over at Kirstin. She is looking at the book, but I know that she is straining to hear our words. A lump forms in my throat as she turns the pages. Is it just me? Or does she seem to have matured during this trip? Recently, I have begun to see glimpses of the young woman she will become; the words and comments that seem to come from a girl much older than she is; the times when she jumps up in exuberance, only to pull back in sophisticated restraint. Kirstin seems to be changing, turning away from the child toward the young woman inside her, hovering uncertain somewhere between.

Kusumal's voice grows weary as our conversation continues. She talks of children who have been rescued from prostitution who require great amounts of therapy, long after the last trick. The sex trade leaves deep scars on the innocent lives it taints.

"The real truth is that we have no alternative to offer them," Kusumal adds. "Many are so desperately poor. Prostitution offers good money."

As Nancy and I slide into the front seat of her truck later, she mentions Kusumal's comment.

"How sad," she says. "When there is nothing better to offer."

"But you wait," Nancy continues. "When you meet the girls at our home you will see that they have something much, much better now."

Kirstin perks up at the mention of the children's home.

"Finally," she says, "I can meet someone my age!"

When we pull into the children's home later that week, we see dozens of the residents outside playing basketball. Nearly eighty tribal girls live at the home, ranging from age seven to twenty three. All of them attend Thai school, and take courses in English and their native Akha. They are dressed in worn, but neat clothing. I can hear laughter and quick chatter.

"They built that court themselves," Nancy says, pointing out the large, slightly uneven concrete court. "We told them we could only pay for the materials, so they put in the concrete themselves."

A group of girls comes to greet Nancy, their faces beaming. They hug her when she gets out of the car. Kirstin looks at the girls through the car window. The girls stare back.

The children have come here under varying circumstances. Some were rescued, like the eight-year-old whose father tried to sell her into prostitution to support his opium addiction; others have lost both parents to AIDS and were at risk of being sold to the sex trade by relatives.

"And that girl," Nancy says, pointing to a twelve-year-old, "came to us when the house was full. Her uncle brought her in because her parents had died of AIDS, and said he didn't want the girl. She was hiding behind him, crying. I just melted and I took her anyway."

Nancy turns her attention to the group of girls, speaking in words I can't understand.

"These are our girls," she says, with obvious affection and pride.

"Nice to meet you," one ten-year-old says meekly, holding out her hand to me. A few others come toward me, grinning. One little girl with short black hair and mischievous eyes slips her arms around my waist.

"Hello!" she says brightly.

The girls immediately surround Kirstin, giggling and covering their mouths with their hands.

Kirstin tosses me a questioning look.

"They like your hair," Nancy says.

One of the girls bravely reaches out her hand to stroke Kirstin's hair and soon there are more tiny brown arms stroking her head. I search for concern on my daughter's face, but she senses the girls' kindness, and laughs.

Another girl motions for Kirstin to come play basketball with them. "Can I go with them, mom?" she asks.

"Of course," I say, shooing her off to play.

Nancy and I walk into one of the simple eating rooms of the house. There are no screens on the wide open windows, and the chilly night air wafts in. The home has no heat or hot water, so I keep my coat on like everyone else in the room.

From my perch near the window, I can see Kirstin and the girls at play.

There are happy shouts, and playful teases coming from the court. A peaceful feeling permeates this home, a contrast from the streets.

I look over at Nancy, who is holding one of the little ones

on her lap. A-Je and Nancy are surrogate parents to over eighty girls, living out their Christian faith by pouring their love—and lives—into these young women. This is not a "typical" family, but it is indeed a family. There is an inner strength instilled in those who come from a loving family, no matter what its composition.

A lovely young woman comes into the room, two small girls holding her hands. "This is A-Gaw," Nancy says, as the young woman smiles back. "She is one of the reasons we do what we do."

A-Gaw offers me some warm tea, which I gladly accept, and sits down across the table. In a quiet voice, with Nancy translating, she begins to tell her story.

"When I was fourteen, I came home to find my sixteen-year-old sister, Mukda, gone," she says. "No one would tell me where she went. But I saw from the sad helpless look on my mother's face that something terrible had happened."

A-Gaw pauses, as if the story cuts too deeply. "Later, I found out that my father, who is an opium addict, had sold her into prostitution. She died of AIDS five years later."

Nancy reaches over and puts her hand on A-Gaw's.

Trying to help her daughter the only way she knew how, A-Gaw's mother brought the fourteen-year-old to the girls' home. "My mother was happy that I would have an education," says A-Gaw. "My father did not even notice I had left."

Now twenty-five and a college graduate, A-Gaw has decided to give back what she has been given and has become an assistant house mother.

"I have been there," she says. "I know what it's like not to have anyone care about your needs. Here the girls find that care. Akha people live in such hopelessness. You constantly hear of disasters—this one into prostitution, that one died of AIDS. When they come here, the girls get some of their childhood back and they have hope that maybe they never had before."

Hope, faith, and a sense of family, ingredients that have helped hundreds of lives, including this once-wounded young teen, who now bestows love on other girls in the same situation.

Nancy gives me a knowing look. She sees that I finally understand.

The door opens abruptly and several younger girls spill into the room. Kirstin is in the center, hair now in two neat braids.

"Molleigh did my hair for me," she says, nodding to the girl beside her.

"And look what Molleigh made me," she adds, holding up some beautiful needlework.

"Can we come back here tomorrow?" my daughter asks.

I nod, and she heads back outside with the girls.

Through the window, my eyes follow these girls who will soon become women, hopeful futures spreading out before them. Kirstin's arm is linked in Molleigh's. Several other girls skip alongside them. Language barriers, economic and cultural differences don't seem to matter; tonight Kirstin has found a kindred spirit.

A sense of gratitude washes over me, and I'm grateful that I've brought my daughter to Thailand. For it is here that she has began to grasp truths that some take a lifetime to learn.

Further out into the night, I know there are other girls, girls who weep in pain and disgust or whose hardened eyes no longer cry from the brutality of their world. I think of the girls at the go-go bar. Do they ever dream of different lives?

I look back at A-Gaw, whose laughter betrays a genuine happiness, a sense of purpose from giving, and I know there is hope.

Tomorrow there will be more girls to interview, more heartache to see. But tonight, in a place where money is scarce but love abundant, I have seen the smiles of contented lives.

As the moon rises into the cloudless sky, I hear more giggles. The girls, most with straight shiny black hair and one with locks the color of honey, are playing basketball again. I look at Kirstin, whose petite frame has seemed to grow on this trip, and wonder if she knows how proud of her I am.

A whispering breeze sweeps through the window and into the room. I catch the smell of wildflowers. I stop for a moment and make a mental memory. It is a beautiful night to be in Thailand.

Janna Graber is a freelance journalist and senior editor at Go World Travel Magazine *(www.goworldtravel.com). She has covered news and travel stories in more than twenty-five countries for* Parade, *the* Chicago Tribune, Denver Post, *and* Alaska Airlines Magazine. *Her favorite part of travel is meeting other people.*

PHYLLIS MAZZOCCHI

* * *

The Holy Nectar
of Immortality

*Break your mirrors, leave your attachments
in the dust, and live.*

"BEWARE OF WILD MONKEYS," I WAS WARNED. SOMEHOW, I HAD foolishly relegated those words of advice to a minor side note on the typewritten priority list I prepared for my journey to India. Now that self-admonition reverberates of life and death proportions to me, as I stand frozen in my tracks staring down the colossal monkey about to pounce on me from the roof of my ashram cell.

Shifting his weight from one limb to the next with the edginess of a puma about to stalk its prey, the primate eyes my modest dinner of bread and tea. The expression on his face is a cross between the innocence of a child's playful mischief and the calculation of a killer. His furry gray coat is rounded at the neck with a white collar of soft spiky hairs, and for a moment I consider that he is actually quite beautiful, but I don't have time to think about that now. Two more monkeys join in on the foray; the shrill of their battle cries rousing me from my paralysis. I make a race for the door of my cell and slam it shut. I even block the door with a chair. *Whew!*

I'm here in Rishikesh for the Kumbha Mela. An event that occurs only once every twelve years on the Hindu calendar, the Festival of the Kumbha commemorates the mythological struggle between the gods for the Holy Nectar of Immortality and is marked by the entry of the planet Jupiter into the constellation of Aquarius. Representing the guru or teacher, the cyclical arrival of the planet Jupiter into the Aquarian skies portends a year-long period of enlightenment and good fortune. A letter of introduction from my local yoga center in Los Angeles, along with a prerequisite donation, has earned me the opportunity to be housed in an ashram on the banks of the Ganges. From here, I can easily visit the nearby city of Hardwar. Known as the "City of God" and the "Gateway to the Himalayas," this crowded settlement along a stretch of the River Ganga has been host to the Kumbha Mela for twenty-five centuries. Perhaps I may gain some spiritual revelation here, but so far my experience of India has fallen far short of enlightenment.

Traveling alone through the cities of Bombay, Delhi, Agra, and now Rishikesh, I have been poked, grabbed, followed, and harassed. I have had my stamps stolen at the post office, been cheated at the money exchange, propositioned by total strangers, and abandoned by my driver on a desolate road. The curious tug at my long hair. The enterprising jangle beads in front of my face. The beggars grab at my skirt to kiss my feet. I have been on guard for two weeks now, shielding myself against an onslaught of malefactors; this, in a country known for it's spiritualism throughout the world. I did not expect this. Was I so naïve?

To add to my distress, I have unknowingly arrived during the three high holy days of the festival. Reports say that over 1 million pilgrims have already reached Hardwar. There is a food shortage and no transportation out of the area. I am literally stranded here with wild monkeys on my roof and a tarantula on my wall. A tarantula on my wall??

Yikes! I head for the Deet spray, the only weapon I can fathom in my panicked mind. Gripping the nozzle with a ferocity I never knew was in me, I aim it at the venomous intruder. *"Eeehhhhhh!"* I wail in horror as I spew a nonstop dose just inches away from the spider, whose body mass is as big as a small fist.

"No, no, you must stop! We do not kill God's creatures!" These are the soft-spoken but urgent words that are my introduction to Mataji, the petite bald-headed woman of the cloth, whose cell I will share for the duration of my stay at the ashram.

"But, it's a taran..." I begin to protest, feeling a bit stunned by her entrance and slightly embarrassed to have been caught in the throes of such a heinous mission. I shrink back from the door and release the can to the ground, the tarantula remaining unfazed.

"All living things are God's creatures," she said in an airy whisper, almost as if talking to herself. Then calmly gathering the tails of her orange robes in a makeshift cradle, she fearlessly scoops the spider off the wall in one gentle sweep. With a steadiness of purpose only the confidence of faith could bring, she is out the door to the open courtyard, her bare feet plodding ground still muddy from a morning of rain. I watch as she deliberates her options in the sparse flowerless bush. Pacing from left to right, then left again until all at once she drops the folds of her orange skirt and with mumbled words I cannot decipher, releases the spider to a tangle of leafy vines.

When nightfall arrives in Rishikesh, there really isn't much to do. There is no street activity to speak of, and there are no local cafés to frequent. Up here at the ashram, only the bank of the river is about you, the sight of it now blackened into the moonless sky. In the windowless cell I share with Mataji, an oil lamp provides the only light. The room is truly a monk's chamber, a no-frills, basic shelter for prayer and meditation that is just large enough to hold the two beds that are placed opposite each other on either side of the doorway. Hard beds they are, at that. Constructed from your basic wooden slats, I have only a white sheet to provide what little cushioning I will sleep with tonight.

Mataji sits cross-legged in a lotus pose. Her black horn-rimmed glasses fall down to the middle of her nose, giving her a seriousness of demeanor that belies the childlike features of her pixie face. Born in Sri Lanka, she has been cloistered at the ashram for fifteen years, dedicating her life and will to the call of the religious life in the same way that a nun would enter a convent and commit herself to the church. The name Mataji means *mother* in Hindi and is more of a title than a given name, comparable to *sister* in the Christian order. I'm curious about her age, but don't ask.

"Where is your family? Your husband or your mother?" The tone of her voice expresses what I imagine is her full horror at my being a woman traveling alone. Knowing that the Indian point of view on this is in direct opposition to my American values, I give her the answer that I know she will not be able to accept. "I am not traveling with a husband or a mother. In America, it is common for a woman to travel without her family."

Her words are sparse and voiced with an innocent quality when she responds. "In India, this would not be proper."

No doubt. I have had my share of hassles as a woman traveling solo. Despite following all the rules of dress code and protocol, I'd been dodging the bullet since Day One in India. This is not an easy place for females. I had, in fact, been very distressed at witnessing the treatment of the Hindu women and children themselves. I'd seen the beggar trade made "business" with female children maimed or burned so as to make a more pitiful specimen for tourists; mothers who were virtual outcasts in their family for not giving birth to a boy; and young girls who were only fed after all the males in the family had eaten.

"Why are females treated so poorly in India?" I ask. Mataji's eyes open wide. She seems stunned by my question. It was a very Western question to ask and perhaps impertinent of me, but I had been struggling with such issues since my first day here. Hard as I tried, I could not rationalize the ethics of Hinduism and its theorems of "cause and effect" with the awful realities in practice on the streets.

"I have never seen the things you speak of," Mataji's answers flatly. Is it possible she has been so isolated that she is totally unaware of any corruption outside the ashram walls?

"I assure you that such things are happening every day." I reveal what has been my deep disappointment at my experience in India. "I came to India to study Hinduism, but where is Hinduism if not in the practice of daily living?"

Mataji stares straight down at the floorboard, deep in thought for what seems a minute or more. When she looks up again, she peers straight into my eyes through the glare of her lenses and chooses her words carefully. "The people…these people you speak of have lost their way. They are lost now, but they will return eventually. They will return to Hinduism because this is their roots." Is it blind faith, the purity of an innocent mind, or the clarity of vision? I am not sure.

A lizard plops down from the ceiling and slithers across the floor. Even in the shadows of night I can recognize the antics of this familiar reptile. I learned to appreciate them at my hotel in Delhi when I realized that they ate the insects that crawled about and bit me while I slept. Mataji cups her hands to her forehead in a silent gesture and then turns off the oil lamp. I take it as a signal to stop talking and go to sleep. How different our lives are, I think to myself. The disparity of our ways made transparent for the second time tonight.

The voice is high-pitched and smooth, gently vibrating with delicate emotion. I must be dreaming, I think. It can't be morning yet. I groan and turn over, my back aching from the board of a bed I've slept on. I squint at my wristwatch to see the time. It is 4 A.M. and Mataji is awake and singing to the accompaniment of a small stringed hand organ.

"You have a beautiful voice."

"I don't sing very often. I shouldn't be singing now. It makes me very emotional and I am working for a less emotional plane." Admonishing herself for falling victim to such a temptation of the senses, she ceases her singing and hastily places the hand organ under her bed.

I let out a huge yawn and turn over attempting to go back to sleep, but not a chance! It all falls into place now. The purpose of my roommate assignment becomes evident as Mataji makes it clear that she will be my escort for the duration of my stay at the ashram. There will be no going it alone here. I will be put on a schedule of meditation and study. "Where I go, you will go," she says emphatically.

And so, our day begins at 4 A.M. with a visit to Swami Atananda for a full hour of sitar performance. Bracing myself upright in traditional cross-legged posture, I can feel the cement floor beneath me, still cold in the dark hours of early dawn. The softly strung notes of Swami Atananda's sitar are rapid and furious, escalating from middle to high and back again like a flurry of snowflakes in a windstorm. The rhythmic trail of the music resounds through my body in the most gentle of spells, and I willingly surrender myself to it.

In the Meditation Hall, we are joined by a group of twenty or so devotees for the 5 A.M. hour of contemplation and silence. I can barely stay awake, but I struggle to concentrate on

my breath and clear my mind of invasive thoughts. Fidgeting
and squirming in my knees-bent lotus position, I am hard-
pressed to sit still with all the insect bites I received last night.
I glance over at Mataji to my right, who looks entirely focused
and serene. Then suddenly, I have a revelation. It occurs to me
that everyone's eyes are closed and that no one will notice if
mine are open. I seize the opportunity to reach into my tote bag
and retrieve a palm-size hand mirror to inspect the itchy welt
on the back of my shoulder. One, two, oh dear, there are three
red blotches I can see so far! I raise the mirror for a better view,
and then…comes the eerie sensation of eyes upon me. It is
Mataji, the reproach of her stare having caught me red-hand-
ed and guilty of inattention in the Meditation Hall. Now, she
will think I am not a serious student, I fret. I throw Mataji a
nervous smile that says "sorry" and stash the mirror in my bag.

At the sunrise ceremony in the small garden temple over-
looking the courtyard, the sweet scent of sandalwood incense
cuts the foul of musty air, a repose from the omnipresent odor
of death and decay one learns to live with in India. A clan of
orange-robed swamis, their baritone chants joining together
in a solicitous wail of the mantra, touch their palms to the
ground in a synchronized gesture of humility. I can't understand any of the words that I hear, but somehow I comprehend
their meaning.

When its over, Mataji beckons with a wave of her hand. I
follow her, anticipating my next instruction, but there is a
strange expression on her face that I cannot translate. It is the
look of someone who wants to ask a question. What does it
mean? I trail along at her elbow as she leads me on a short path
at the back of the temple shrine. She stops, then turns to look
behind us; her eyes racing left to right, the sleuthing of her
body language speaking of discomfort. She seems to be searching for a place where no one will find us, a zone of privacy, but

why? What's going on? As I take a seat beside her on a block of broken concrete, I can only wonder what I've done wrong now, when in a hush, her voice implores… "The mirror…"

"The mirror?" I can feel my body flinch backwards in a knee-jerk reaction.

"The mirror," she repeats. "May I see it?"

First the singing and now the mirror! Has my presence somehow stirred the forbidden? I rummage through my tote bag to dig out the small compact-mirror and offer it to her open hand. A souvenir from Paris, its faux porcelain lid sports a little pink Eiffel Tower. How inappropriate it seems at this moment, I think to myself.

"Uhhh!" A huge gasp from Mataji.

I realize that I have handed her the mirror with the magnified side face up. She takes a moment to compose herself and with a hard swallow confesses, "I have not seen my face in fifteen years."

I'm still stunned and I'm sure my mouth is half open. I flip the mirror to the smaller view.

Moving in what seems like slow-motion time, Mataji removes the large horn-rimmed glasses that cover so much of her petite face and proceeded to examine each of her eyes in the mirror, one at a time. I watch in silence as she fingers the surface of her suntanned skin, carefully tracing every crease line of the past fifteen years. Are they wrinkles born of sunwear or of sadness? I don't know.

Mataji heaves a huge sigh. It is the only sound I ever hear her make as she continues her inspection, scrutinizing her mouth, chin, and neck, the tentativeness of her unsteady hands exposing a gentleness tinged with fear. I try to imagine how she must feel, but I have no comparison in my own life. What I do know is that she had exposed a vulnerability to me—and more importantly, has trusted me to hold that vulnerability in confidence and care for it. I feel privileged to do so.

Suddenly, the strike of the temple bell beckons from the hall. Sensing that our stolen time is nearing an end, Mataji performs her final act of inspection at a hurried pace as she bends forward, holds the mirror high above herself and examines her shaven head. Then, finally breaking her gaze from the face she might never have seen again, she nods to me in a gesture that says "thank you" and returns the mirror without a word.

Thousands of years ago, both Gods and Demons worked in tandem, spinning the depths of the Milky Ocean in an effort to find the coveted *amrita,* the holy nectar of immortality. But once the *kumbha* (pot) of holy nectar was finally retrieved, the Gods and Demons turned against each other, waging a fierce battle in the heavens for possession of the sacred ambrosia. For twelve days and twelve nights, the struggle between the primeval forces of good and evil raged, spilling drops of the precious liquid at four different spots in India—one of which was the waters of the ancient city of Hardwar. And so it is, that once every twelve years, in a ritual celebrated since the second century B.C., pilgrims from India and the world converge onto the banks of the Ganges in a *mela* (festival) to celebrate this blessed event.

By the look of it, time has stood still in Hardwar. I could be arriving at the Kumbha Mela a hundred years ago and I'm certain it would have looked exactly the same. Mataji instructs me to stick close at her heel and not get separated. It is the main bathing day of the festival, and the streets are jam-packed with people, all pushing, shoving, and eager to make it to the riverbank. If history stands to repeat itself, millions of the faithful are here today, hoping to bathe themselves in the purifying waters of the Ganges at the same spot where the holy nectar of *amrita* is said to have fallen. Yogis, mystics, musicians, and tourists intermingle with camels, oxcarts, and cows. For many, it is the pilgrimage of a lifetime. To make one's way to this anointed city and to cleanse oneself in its waters is to cleanse one's soul of the past and achieve immortality.

A nude monk with a flowing white beard right down to his toes walks ahead with a somewhat glazed look on his face. Might he be one of the cave sadhus to come out of his hermit existence on this special occasion? Sari-swathed women, their foreheads marked with the red dot of the Third Eye and their hands ornamented with delicate henna designs, dance to the music of the snake charmer's flute. A mob of squealing children surrounds a magician performing magic tricks while a fakir pokes pins through his cheek in a test of endurance. The appearance of an elephant elicits an uproar from the crowd. Its head is decorated with a mask of red and yellow rhinestones and on its back is a makeshift float of sorts made from what appears to be human limbs, six of them in all. I pause to mop my forehead, dripping with perspiration. The heat and dust are almost unbearable. The smell is the smell of India—a combination of death, feces, and filth hanging heavy in the humid air. I feel certain I will never see or experience such sights again.

"The people who have lost their way will return eventually. They will return to Hinduism because this is their roots."

Mataji's words echo through my mind. I think about my time spent in India—the disappointment, the disillusionment, the fall of my expectations. What lesson is there to learn from this experience? I looked to Mataji for answers, but she really had no answers. She saw no conflict and she had no quarrel. Her sights were set on the transcendent, and in the pursuit, her sense of stalwart faith prevailed. There isn't much I understand about Mataji's world. Most of it is a world I cannot tolerate, and yet I feel a common ground with her. We connected in ways that broached our vulnerabilities and tested our courage.

We shared in a search for self-understanding and we shared in the camaraderie of friends. We were worlds apart and yet not wholly unalike, and this outweighed the differences in our lives.

It is time. Mataji marches out and leads me by the arm. I can swear that I recognize the same steadiness of purpose about her that I first saw when she released that migrant spider to the garden. Together we walk down the sandy hillside to the edge of the River Ganga. Nearby, a local barber shaves the heads of worshipers who will offer their hair to the river today. Mataji lifts her orange robe and I my *lungi*. At the ashram, we were fed alongside beggars and lepers, and now we bathe together: poor men, sages, and voyagers alike united in a mass of humankind. Together we step into the same waters where countless ashes of the dead have floated to their rest. Together, we immerse our bodies in the holy nectar of *amrit* as did the same hopeful pilgrims who stood at this spot centuries before us. Here in this moment, we revel. And in this moment, there are no questions, there are no judgements. Perhaps, I have learned something after all.

Phyllis Mazzocchi was born and raised in New York City, but spent half her life working in the entertainment business in Los Angeles. Her writing has appeared in Great Expeditions Magazine, The New York Poetry Foundation *anthology, and* Many Voices, Many Lands. *Her hobbies include music, stone carving, B&W photography, reading, and traveling solo all over the world. She is the winner of the Frankenstein Travel Award for most horrific travel experience.*

JANE MARSHALL

✦ ✦ ✦

Trigger Happy in Cambodia

Let the darkness enrich you.

COILS OF BARBED WIRE UPON CONCRETE WALLS SURROUNDED the compound, though the guards who had once flanked its perimeter were now only ghosts and shadows. The woman who asked me for money in broken English and the pamphlets and books that she sold looked gaudy and out of place, even disrespectful considering their home. I was inside Security-21, a school turned torture chamber, and now a tourist attraction for those with strong stomachs. My eyes fell upon a building and my legs carried me to it. From the outside it was a typical school building, long, two-storied with numerous small rooms, but as I looked inside I saw what no children should see. The rectangular room held nothing but a metal bed frame with unknown devices strewn along its springs, and a photograph strung up on the wall. The picture described what the room no longer could; a man lay on the same bed with shackles on his arms and legs, his fat and muscle eaten by time and grief. His hair was thin and dirty and his eyes…my eyes fell to the floor for reprieve but they were met with decades-old bloodstains and I backed away. This was the interrogation building.

I grew up in Canada in a comfortable home, without threat of war, free from the fear of having my body explode from land-mine contact, and far removed from threats such as the Pol Pot regime, an extreme communist movement that was responsible for some 2 million deaths in less than five years. I did not have to worry about being arrested and executed in a place like S-21. Before entering Cambodia I had spent months sunning myself on Thailand's beaches, thinking of nothing more challenging than accidentally ordering squid rather than chicken for my lunch by the sea. From Thailand, Cambodia sounded intriguing, like tough travel. I knew nothing. My understanding of Cambodia encompassed little more than the vague knowledge of land mines, and that Phnom Penh, the capital city, was fairly dangerous. Who put those nasty land mines in the fields? I could not have told you. And I could not understand why my hands would shake at the end of each day I spent there, as I washed my supper of rice down with Angkor beer, or why I felt dizzy each morning when I opened my eyes and found myself looking through the guesthouse's barred window in downtown Phnom Penh. We knew that place was risky, yet it was so easy to get our visas.

Luckily my feelings of unease did not inhibit me from exploring the city, despite the guesthouse clerk who warned us, "No walk at night. You take cab to restaurant and bar, take cab home. I sleep here, let you in."

And he did. He slept inside the iron bars that held out beggars and other unwanteds on a dirty little couch or the floor with his body curled in a position that made his bony knees flare out and accentuated his joints. We woke him each night to get into the guesthouse and he never seemed to mind. One morning, I convinced my friend Krystyna to explore S-21, or Tuol Sleng, the war museum. How else was I going to learn to feel comfortable, to feel less like an ignorant idiot, blind to why Phnom Penh was so poor and sad? I ached to know why so many beggars were picking through the remains of the market that was set up each night behind our guesthouse, eating rotting litchi and crushed bananas, and why when friends in the street stopped laughing together their eyes would cloud over and their faces would close. So we set off.

Without thinking, I approached another tourist who stood behind me at S-21's interrogation room.

"Are photographs allowed?" I inquired. She looked at me with disgusted, judgmental eyes and answered my question without words. She was crying. Quickly, I left the interrogation wing and moved on to the next building to escape her and the image she held of me: a disrespectful tourist with a fetish for gore. She did not know that I was just stupid.

A feeling of displacement washed over me as I walked to the next building where the long-term prisoners had been held. The day was bright and hot, but the aura was dark. Clouds should have been casting shadows and brimming with drops that needed to spill, but instead the hot Cambodian sun blazed hard on the concrete schoolyard and scorched the shadows that lurked in my imagination. The only reprieve was under the palm fronds that lined the compound, or in the deteriorating buildings.

A sign of scrolling Cambodian script that was translated into English was posted to remind prisoners of the rules:

1. Do not be a fool for you are a chap who dares to thwart the revolution.
2. You must immediately answer my questions without wasting time to reflect.
3. While getting lashes or electrification you must not cry at all.

If you do not follow all of the above rules, you shall get many lashes of electric wire.

This holding section was identical to the interrogation building but was filled with brick cells that measured less than two square meters. People lived here, sometimes for months, with their legs shackled to iron bars as though the tiny cell was not confining enough. They reminded me of kennels, but with the constant recognition of school floor tiles, the ones from the 1940s and 1950s that look like grocery store floors, and I could not forget reality. Humans were held here. The museum's pamphlet explained that iron buckets or empty ammunition containers were placed in each cage for defecation and urination. Imagine feeling the urgency of a certain pressure on the bladder and then being forced to ask permission before relieving it. They could not move their bowels without asking or they would be beaten severely. What would I do if I had no control over my own bodily functions? Would I still feel human?

Krystyna looked dazed and I knew it was not from the heat. "Let's keep moving," she whispered.

In the third building, faces, some almost smiling, others trampled and emaciated, stared at us from the walls. Back in the late 1970s the prison guards had taken pictures of each prisoner at S-21. They took accurate records—photographs, interviews, documents—the process was calculated. I walked in slow circles, drawn sporadically to the hundreds of faces that were beaten and banished from this world, women with shiny brown eyes, children with tousled hair, men lying on the ground half dead, all crystallized in time. We quickly left and their eyes followed.

From the second story I looked through barbed wire into the compound. Though now rusting, it was strung meticulously across the balcony to prevent prisoners from jumping to their deaths. I imagined watching soldiers in the compound and seeing the children who had been trained to torture. Apparently their young age at training allowed them to achieve what was beyond the cruel ability of the adults. Playground equipment was set up in the center and used to hang prisoners upside-down while their faces were forced into containers of excrement. Childhood had a different meaning and I tried to block out mine because it made me feel guilty.

Pol Pot, the general of the communist Khmer Rouge movement that was responsible for approximately 2 million deaths between 1975 and 1979, was a name I had never heard before. Since my return from Cambodia I have learned that his army trained children to torture and murder Cambodians. If they did not follow orders, their short lives would be ended. Over twenty thousand humans were tortured at S-21 in the name of the Khmer Rouge revolution. How does a country move beyond such a past when over two-thirds of its people suffer from post-traumatic stress syndrome? Many of its citizens had to choose plastic arms and legs from storerooms in Thai refugee camps because the Khmer Rouge had hacked theirs off. Looking back I hope I can understand why Cambodia seemed edgy and dark, even on its sunny days, and why there were so many begging on the streets and picking through the trash because of their loss of land, livelihood, and appendages.

The next image to fill my view was a photograph of a woman. She was seated with her back against some kind of machine and its metallic arms reached out to her temples. She had beautiful long black hair, though matted and dirty, but her eyes held nothing in them. The sockets dared not look down, because worse than torture is the torture of loved ones. Her baby rested on her lap. The machine was designed to send powerful electrical impulses through the body, to punish those who would not talk or opposed the Khmer Rouge revolution. This last building was filled with artifacts of torture and paintings that depicted the methods used. I will never forget the last painting I saw before leaving the building, and I understood why my boyfriend Mike had decided not to come to this place.

The painting hung near the exit door and when I saw it I laughed out loud. It felt similar to having the urge to laugh at a funeral, when the mind takes a break from reality and tries to find some reprieve. Through the sun that streaked in the open door I saw soldiers with bayonettes, poised upwards to the sky, ready to take aim at their target. They were in a forest, and women were poised on the verge of…I do not know what. I cannot imagine what they were thinking. Their babies had been ripped from their arms and the soldiers were throwing them high into the air and shooting them. They were shooting babies. How can a mother survive? I guess those ones did not.

Krystyna looked at the painting briefly and we left the compound, hopped on a moped, and watched in awe as images skittered across the available space left in our minds. People sold rice from their stands, drove by in Mercedes, begged with arms or stumps, and tried to sell us pomelos when we reached red lights. They all seemed different to me now.

After a cold shower and some water we went for dinner with Mike and his friend Dan and found a restaurant that was brimming with people, their drunken joyous faces bubbling with laughter and their cheeks plump with rice. The contrast of this exuberant group to my mood was welcome, and we sat at a large plastic table in some bright red chairs and ordered beer. Mike and Dan's experience revealed Cambodia's bizarre transition from past to present. They had found a shooting ground and paid $20 (American currency of course) to fire thirty rounds of ammunition from a machine gun.

Apparently the building was a large brick bunker with a

standard patio door entrance. Sitting on one side of the door was a large pot filled with local flowers, and inside was a large cushion for resting on while releasing bullets.

"The guy held my shoulder from behind, and I unloaded thirty rounds from an AK-47!" Mike exclaimed. "It happens so fast, all of a sudden thirty rounds are gone from the gun. You can shoot that in less than two seconds."

Danny laughed and said, "Yeah, and guess what else you can do there? You can have a live chicken for a target! Not only that, but for $200 they let a cow out into the field and you can blow it up with a rocket launcher."

I was laughing hard by this point. "Who in the hell would want to blow up a cow?" I asked.

"Oh, I think it would be cool," Danny replied. And with that I realized how Cambodia is going to come out of its slump. With its lack of rules and the ability to let imaginative tourists spend hoards of money to try their hands at destruction, Cambodia will make money and begin to rebuild itself. The average yearly income in Cambodia is approximately $230, so to let a "rich" foreigner pay 87 percent of an annual income for kicks seems like a good way to make money. I had to admit, there was a certain appeal to Mike and Dan's story, and I wondered what it would feel like as I spat out the bullets at top speed from a cold, heavy machine. So why not provide tourists with thrills that they cannot find in Canada or America? Who has ever heard of going to a carnival and paying to shoot a live chicken? If you hit it, would you win a stuffed animal?

One morning in Siem Reap, a small town in Cambodia, Krystyna, Mike, and I walked to a local outdoor food stand for breakfast. We ordered the standard breakfast food of fried rice and stared at the river. It sounds lovely, but the river was brimming with bits of colorful refuse. As we ate under the canopy, four boys aged four to eight walked toward us and stopped at the edge of the shade. They were homeless children, covered in dirt, dressed in bright mismatched cotton clothes and holding plastic bags. The store owners did not seem to be upset when the boys held the bags to their mouths and began to sniff the fumes inside. My fork stopped on its way to my mouth and I stared as they got high from the glue. They wanted our attention, and one boy stared at me with his round brown eyes that had now clouded over, the spirit within them on a distant planet where hunger could not affect it. I was disgusted. They stood with their heads falling backwards and their mouths hanging open, so high they could not speak, and in a moment I hated them. I hated that a four-year-old needed to huff glue, and that the restaurant owners did not seem to care. I could not eat. I hated them and loved them at the same time; part of me wanted to hold them and scrub them clean of all the dirtiness that surrounded them, and the other part wanted to yell at them and kick them out of my perception of reality. As we left, they came at us and begged for money, which we did not give them, and then they finished our food, grabbing handfuls of the rice and shoving it into their mouths before the restaurant owners could throw them out. They were starving; I felt empty, too.

Cambodia surprised and frightened me. Before 1975 it was a growing, productive, prosperous country like Canada, but four years of communist terror shook its foundations to the core. Chickens snacked on people's corpses and pregnant women were speared with bayonets, all in the name of a cause. Today, Cambodia's people are still recovering from the horror they witnessed and are picking up their lives. The remnants, the limbless beggars who cannot work, the children sniffing glue, and the rampant rise of prostitution fueled by tourists are offset by the sparks of hope seen in busy restaurants and the vendors working to sell their wares. I saw things I did not know were real in this world, or possible, and I saw how humans cope and move on.

Back home in Canada, I remember how lucky I am to be able to sleep in a bed without the fear of a soldier coming to the door to steal me away, but I also remember that life can so easily change.

Jane Marshall is a graduate of the University of Alberta with a major in English. She lives in Alberta, Canada, with her husband and young son.

MARYBETH BOND

* * *

Returning to Paradise

Life, liberty, and the pursuit of happiness.

THIS WAS ALL MY IDEA. AND THERE WERE MANY MOMENTS before we boarded the twenty-five-hour flight for Bali via Taiwan when I thought I was crazy. Like when our fourteen-year-old daughter, J. C., announced we just *had* to get a hotel with a pool and internet access so she could lounge by day and email her friends by night. Or when eleven-year-old Annalyse whined, "Why can't we just go to Hawaii?"

But I wanted to return to the island paradise I had discovered twenty years before husband and children filled my life. Yes, I had been warned: "When you get a taste of island paradise, enjoy it once, because you can't return. It will never be as good." I knew the risks of returning, yet memories of Bali, seductive as a Siren's call, were luring me back to this gracious isle beyond the South Pacific.

Traveling with backpack and on a student's budget, I visited Bali the first time in the early 1980s. On the crowded, touristy beach in Kuta, I met another woman who was traveling alone. We agreed to flee the commercial coast and whoop it up cruising by motorcycle on the roller coaster of dirt roads along the northern shore and up to the base of the volcanoes. Along the way, we kept a wary eye out for the lethargic cows and dogs reluctant to give up their comfy spots in the middle of the road.

In the hills outside Ubud, we negotiated narrow footpaths amid terraced rice fields to a remote and simple guest home. The elderly owners, Katoot and Naoman, were childless, a great tragedy for a Balinese couple. "God gave us you—our young visitors—instead," they said. "You are our children to watch over and to make happy."

At night the croaking frogs in the irrigation ditches lulled us to sleep. For breakfast, Katoot, our host mother, brought us fresh homemade yogurt with sliced papaya and mango. We spent our days bumping along dirt paths on our motorcycle, visiting local festivals, temples, artists' workshops, and even an elaborate cremation. At night, Katoot gave us long massages while our host father, Naoman, softly played his gamelan for our pleasure. Our guestroom had no running water or shower, so we bathed like the locals, in a steep valley under a waterfall, during the morning "ladies hour."

That was my first trip to Bali, and years later, as a wife, mom, and travel writer who has trekked, climbed, dived, and cycled through seventy countries, it was to Bali that I longed to return. I wanted my family to experience it, too.

Bali has developed significantly over the past two decades. Each year, it draws tourists of all ages and interests. Many visitors return again and again for Bali's beaches, culture, superb resorts, good surfing, cheap shopping, and the intact Balinese culture steeped in traditions of music, dance, and religious ceremonies.

Yet Bali's charm, I knew, lies not in its beaches, towering volcanic mountains, or luscious green terraced rice fields, but in its people. For me, paradise could only be captured a second time if my family and I got to know and were welcomed by the Balinese.

I didn't search for Katoot or Naoman or try to recreate the same experiences. They belong to another trip, another age, a closed photo album in my mind.

This time around we decided to pamper ourselves and the girls and stay in a luxury hotel at Jimbaran Bay, a wonderful relief after the long trans-Pacific flights and layovers. J. C. and Annalyse gave it a "thumbs-up" after they checked out the TV, video collection, free internet access, and ocean view from their own villa. They fought over who would sleep on which Balinese bed (under mosquito nets), they raced each other to jump into the private plunge pool, and denuded the tropical garden of melon-sized, pink hibiscus flowers to wear in their hair. They quickly discovered the main pool with its infinity-edge (water cascaded over a fall to soaking pools and hot and cold whirlpools below). They soaked or swam in each pool before making their way to the beach. We found them lounging by the water's edge and bribed them with mango milk shakes into joining us for a catamaran sail around the bay. Then we switched to boogie boards to surf in the large waves.

A successful family vacation offers something for everyone every day. Dad read four novels in the shade on the beach. Mom took an Asian cuisine cooking class and learned how to cook with lemongrass and Thai basil, and prepare Hot and Sour Prawn Soup, *gyoza*, and *soba* noodles. The teens alternated between watching videos on the TV, bodysurfing, playing in the pools, getting their hair braided in cornrows and painting their nails. One afternoon we hired a driver and car to take us to a crowded, commercial beach so the girls could go parasailing. They loved it, we tolerated it. We bought elaborate, colorful kites in the shape of majestic ships and tried to fly them along the beach.

We were enjoying a different paradise than the budget Bali I had discovered and grown to love two decades before. But then, I am a different person now. As a mother and wife, much of my own pleasure comes from seeing my children and husband happy.

Yet I couldn't help but wonder whether the charming old Bali of decades ago still existed. If so, I knew we had to get away from the deluxe resorts and the beach to find it.

Unlike my first trip to Bali, motorcycle travel today is considered very dangerous for tourists due to the chaotic and dense traffic on the roads. If we wanted to explore the island and stay in more modest and authentically Balinese lodging, we would need a driver. You can hire a driver and car from your hotel, the local tourist office, or simply choose one of the many drivers waiting on the side of the road.

We wanted a driver who spoke good English, so he could show us his Bali and stay with us as we traveled around the island. So on the recommendation of friends, during our pre-trip planning I had emailed a young man who had toured with them for three weeks the year before.

Made (mah-day) met us at our hotel and became a part of our family for the next week. He was personable, kind, and patient; his English was good enough to help us with any situation. We shared dinner, dominoes, jokes, and stories every night. With Made at the wheel of the minivan borrowed from his older brother, we were a multicultural family of spontaneous travelers. It was easy for Made to find a hotel room near ours every night, for which we paid. Together we tromped through markets, visited temples, and ate in local thatch-roofed restaurants where Made knew the owner, the cook, and the waitress. Together we ate leisurely meals in lush gardens filled with carvings and statues of frogs, gods, and goddesses. The girls sipped fresh mango smoothies, munched on *satay*, fried noodles, and pizza, while we feasted on the Indonesian rice table, with duck roasted in banana leaves, prawns, and spicy curries. We ventured out to the north shore to dive and snorkel on the protected coral reefs of the West Bali National Park. Amid a dervish of rainbow-colored fish we glimpsed lionfish and shark.

Best of all, Made liked us and invited us into his life and home. Outside the bustling artists' village of Ubud, he took us to see the "real Bali" that I had so longed to visit again. With Made in the lead, we trekked along steep slopes, through a maze of frog-green rice fields, down to a muddy river where young boys were bathing and women were digging sand from the riverbed to be used in construction; shoveling it into baskets, they carried the sand on their heads up the gorge. When the young boys first saw our teenage girls, they held their hands over their private parts and stared, but after many smiles, waves, and cheers, they returned to their play and ignored our passing on the rope and bamboo suspension bridge above them. J. C. and Annalyse giggled and waved.

We climbed up a steep slope, through banana groves, mango, coffee, and cocoa trees to the village where Made lived, where we were treated as honored guests. His mother wore the traditional long Balinese skirt and her best Maidenform bra. "Why doesn't she wear clothes?" asked our oldest. "She's wearing more than she usually does, just for us," I replied.

Our hostess brought us leaf mats to sit on while we watched Made's barefoot, bare-chested uncle shimmy up a nearby coconut tree with a machete. We watched him grapple with the branches until, half an hour later, he descended with three perfectly ripe coconuts. He lopped off the tops with his machete and offered us a refreshingly cool drink of coconut milk.

Made's aunt quietly came out of the kitchen with three delicate bamboo trays filled with rice, purple bougainvillea, and fragrant frangipani flowers. She gently laid these small offerings at the base of stone statues outside the family temple. Made explained that Balinese women make and give offerings numerous times each day. This offering was made after food was cooked but before the meal was enjoyed.

This simple gesture, I thought, embodies the spirit of Bali that pervades the island. Their culture surrounds you, in the music, dance, and religion. You see it in Balinese faces, you feel it in Balinese dances.

Later in the day we drove to see one of the most important ceremonial events in Balinese culture—the cremation of a body. Regretfully, we missed the ceremony by a day, so Made, terribly upset to see us disappointed and always eager to please, cheerfully offered to take us to the wedding of his close friend. At the Balinese wedding we were seated on chairs like royal guests. Well-dressed women and men insisted we take their seats in the front rows. An elderly woman sitting next to Annalyse smiled, nodded, and took our daughter's hand and gently held it in her lap during the ceremony. After recovering from her initial surprise and discomfort, Annalyse quietly responded with nods and smiles.

We were served snacks, like peanuts and chips and soft drinks. When the religious ceremony was over, the tiny, beautiful bride and her groom came to welcome us and chat.

On the twenty-five-hour journey back to the USA, I thought about our daily lives at home. So dominated by routines, job stresses, and the different demands of each child, we can easily lose perspective on what is most important to us. When traveling, my husband and girls and I converge back into the core of this magical relationship that is family. In Bali we depended on each other for guidance, help, and fun. We got to know each other better, as well as the gracious Balinese people. We found the magical Bali intact, off the beaten path. And when we returned home, all was new and we were closer and more connected.

Now I know paradise can be revisited. I saw it through the eyes of my children. Fourteen-year-old J. C. summed it up when she said, "Everone here takes happy pills. Let's take some home."

I guess we did.

Marybeth Bond is the editor of numerous Travelers' Tales anthologies, including A Woman's World, A Mother's World, *and* A Woman's Europe, *and the author of* Gutsy Women *and* Gutsy Mamas. *She is also the Adventure Editor for* TravelGirl *Magazine. Her work can be viewed at www.gutsytraveler.com.*

A M Y   G R E I M A N N   C A R L S O N

*　*　*

The Moss of Time

A blond barbarian rolls on wondering why not?

I BURY MY HEAD UNDER MY PILLOW. THE BLARING EXERCISE music of the Mitsubishi factory across the street stabs the down feathers as my mind tries to begin the day. It is no use pretending sleep on this early Saturday morning. I roll out of my futon onto the *tatami* floor and lie face down with my nose on the grass mat. I like to wake up this way. I dream of being in an open mountain meadow. The smell embraces me. I feel free, full of space. "*Ichi. Ni. San. Shi. Go…*" blasts me back into the reality of my small apartment, #501, across from the busy Ozone Train Station just over the wall from the Mitsubishi Plant where workers do synchronized jumping jacks in their bright orange jumpsuits. Their colorful gyrations remind me—tonight is *oki gomi*…that's right!

This thought springs me from the sweet smelling mat almost as fast as a rabbit darting from a fox, only I am not being chased, but pulled by this once-a-month event in which foreigners meet to root through a mountain of Japanese trash. I pad into my tiny kitchenette to make myself some tea and put out a fresh *gokiburi hoi hoi*. These cockroach hotels are necessary here in this tightly packed bit of humanity. Small, sweetened cardboard boxes attract flying Japanese cockroaches. They buzz through the air en route to their hotel. But once inside, they can't get out. I sip tea while I construct this death trap and wait for my *ofuro* to heat. I melt into the tub like butter in the warm sun. But, alas, I can't linger for Nashimoto will come at 9:00 to pick me up and bring me to a tea ceremony at a neighborhood shrine.

After a quick breakfast, I sweep up toast crumbs and skip down the four flights of concrete steps to the street. Why four when I live in #501? "Four" in Japanese is the same word for "death"—*shi*—so no #401. I stop short as uniformed kids on bicycles speed by ringing their bells yelling *gaijin*, foreigner. I hate that. Businessmen scurry to catch the 9:00 train that has just pulled into the station. A farmer, pulling a cart filled with daikon radish and other vegetables makes his neighborhood rounds. Mom from the corner "mom-&-pop-have-everything" store sweeps the sidewalk in front. She waves at me, the foreigner. They all know I live upstairs in the Takayama Building, somewhere. I am their exotic, long-nosed, blond female. No way can I blend into the current of black hair rushing by me on the street. I don't even try anymore.

"Amysan," I hear Nashimoto. "Amysan."

"*Ohaio gozaimasu*. Good morning my friend." I reply, giving a slight bow.

"Let us go. We don't want to be late." She hurries me toward the subway entrance. Down, down we go. Silent doors slide open and we enter the train. Sitting, I can actually touch my feet to the floor. Amazing. I am short everywhere but in Japan. We whoosh through the dark tunnel. The train rocks. My eyes close. Feeling a tap, Nashimoto motions me to follow her. We have arrived.

Up into the light, we squint. A short walk through a neighborhood maze of concrete walls, ceramic tile roofs, and futons hanging from open windows finds us at the entrance to a wooden shrine. An ancient *tori* gate greets us, its arch beckoning us to pass beneath it into the stillness within. We step from the current of modern-day frenzy back into the moss of time. A bamboo water pipe fills with water, tips, and lightly taps a rock in a creek running through the garden. Maple trees, small and delicate, drape their leafy fingers over the green moss, immaculately manicured. Every stone placed. Every rock matters. All is right with the world.

We enter a polished wooden *genkan* made with clear pine— no knots. Leaving our shoes in this gleaming foyer, we step up into the sweet smell of fresh *tatami* mat. A delicate butterfly appears from around a corner and lights on a scroll full of waterfalls. A lady, equally as delicate, flits toward us in a kimono patterned in cherry blossoms.

"*Ohaio gozaimasu,*" accompanies a bow, and with the sweep of a billowing sleeve, she ushers us into the inner sanctum where others are gathered in a semi circle sitting on the floor. The ceremony begins. Bow once to your left, once to your right. Whisk the tea with an angled wrist. Tap the bowl three times. Bow. Serve. Turn the bowl three times. Finish the tea in three sips. Bow. Just as I relax into the rhythm, my legs cramp. No blood left in my feet. Despite the mindfulness going on here and the concentration needed to not make a mistake in the formality, my knotted knees remind me of tonight's escapade. Distraction sets in. I need my legs to climb the mountain. The *oki gomi* awaits as my thoughts pull me out of the ceremony and into the evening.

"*Sayonara,*" Nashimotosan, "*Sayonara.*"

By day, *Ochanoyu*, the tea ceremony. By night, the *oki gomi*. The big garbage. Finally it is time. It is dark. I scuttle to the park surrounded by closed paper doors behind concrete walls. A mountain of big tossed "junk" stands waiting for us, the foreign cockroaches. Like bugs in the heat of summer, we come out at night and crawl over the heap of discarded debris, searching for nibbles to take home to our hovels. The dark mound of jagged peaks rises in the night cityscape alive with crawling bodies. Meeting at this monthly mountain of broken washing machines, TV sets, microwaves, bicycles, desks, lamps, and all things big, the foreign community bonds in the street-light while rummaging for treasure among the "used" and the free, toasting our finds with cold Kirin beer.

This night I find what I've been looking for. A canary yellow, fat-tired monstrosity with bent spokes and a tweaked seat. Just for me. I need a bike. Both of mine have been stolen. I dance with glee, dragging my new set of wheels off the pile, ringing the bell on its handlebars with gusto.

"Shhhhhh," my fellow cockroaches warn. No lights come on. Good. The king of the *gomi* offers to fix my find. A bloke from Australia not only makes a business from this pile but also furnishes his apartment with its garbage jewels. Why not? We exchange addresses as I watch him limp my canary away.

The following week he calls, "Come and get it!" I race to his apartment for the unveiling. "Ta da," he exclaims as he yanks the white cloth off his re-creation. I recoil in horror, then fall down laughing. Taking a deep breath, I finally calm long enough to rationalize, "They stare at me, the foreigner; anyway, I might as well give them something to look at." There, rolled out before me, stands an *oki gomi* masterpiece, with bits of garbage protruding from every part of my yellow bike—old tennis balls stuck in the newly straightened spokes, pinwheels attached to the handlebars, a variety of bells for different occasions screwed into the frame, a luggage rack jutting off the rear, reflectors everywhere possible, and a seat with a back. No one was going to steal this bicycle! I thank him profusely for his magic, as I ride proudly out onto the street. The wheels roll effortlessly: the seat is sturdy, and the handlebars straight. All is right with the world. Even with the cockroaches.

Here in a culture synonymous with ancient beauty and purity sits a mountain of the thrown away. Here in a culture that honors tradition, steeped in the tea ceremony and the samurai code, *zazen* and a national anthem that sings of the danger of rolling stones gathering no moss, people throw away the slightly blemished and want everything new. Perhaps the need for perfect trumps the ancient and thrives in the obsession for purity? Build with absolutely knot free wood; fold paper without any extra creases; eat perfect fruit; turn, three times, the tea bowl. Maybe this is why the big garbage pile exists: to maintain perfection. But then what of the venerated old? The time honored? The moss covered stones? How can a society so steeped in antiquity, be so quick to throw away?

I roll proudly home on my decorated wheels, a bike restored to glory. My neighbors snicker. I smile and wave. They wave back. "*Gaijin*," they say shaking their heads as they return to polishing their clear pine *genkan*.

Amy Greimann Carlson, writer, editor, teacher, has spent her life playing with words, kids, and nature. She has coedited A Woman's Path, Travelers' Tales Japan, *and* The Gift of Birds; *written pieces for* Travelers' Tales, Guidepost, *and* Birdcage Press, *a children's educational game publisher; taught seventh grade Language Arts; and now offers Writing: The Spirited Craft workshops in the Pacific Northwest to adults needing to reconnect with their 'kid' liness. She lives on a mountainside in Leavenworth, Washington with her husband and rabbit.*

MONICA CAPPUCCINI

* * *

In Search of the Perfect Yurt

She travels the ancient paths of the Silk Road.

MY FRIEND'S FOUR GERMAN RELATIVES SEEM TO HAVE BEEN born with a gene that sparks a desire to connect with remote cultures. Creature comforts are in no way important. In fact, the more grueling the day, the more inedible the food, the more disgusting the toilets (what toilets?), the dustier, muddier the roads, the more insect-infested the accommodation, well, the happier they are. Twelve-hour days spent hurtling inside a jeep over pothole-ridden roads? Wonderful! No showers or toilets for three days? Fantastic!

I agreed to join my friend on an adventure tour to China's northwest frontier because I'd been there more than twenty years ago, and she needed help running the tour. We were setting out on the fabled Silk Road in Xinjiang Province, wedged in by the "stans" of Central Asia, because we were in search of the perfect yurt: the tent-like dwelling favored by the Mongol and Turkish peoples of Central Asia. This cylindrical structure, made of pliable wooden poles arranged in lattice style, is typically covered with waterproof felt or animal skins and is still the portable summer home of the descendants of Genghis Khan.

Xinjiang is home to many ethnic Muslim tribes, the largest of which, the Uygur, (pronounced Wigger) make up 47 percent of what is called the "minority" population even though the Han Chinese account for only 25 percent of the whole citizenry. The names of many other ethnic groups evoke peoples of hot-blooded heroism and times of tempestuous romance: Kazakh, Mongol, Manchu, Tatar. Legendary figures such as Genghis and Kublai Khan, Tamerlane and Babur savaged their way through this region from the twelfth to the sixteenth centuries, uniting much of Central Asia and bringing Islam to the predominantly pagan population. Their descendents are now mostly sheepherders, who will be found in the high pastures at this time of year and whose hospitality is legendary—for a price, naturally.

And here I am with the four German adventurers. We begin our quest with a flight from Urumqi, the capital, to Altay in the far north of the province. From there we travel by jeep to Birjin and head for Kanas Lake—Kazakh country. The very name is captivating, because Kazakhs are famous for their yurts.

Before setting out we shop for fresh fruits, vegetables, and bread at a local market, which of course entertains the Germans who revel in the process of bargaining for the ideal eggplant. But it is we who are the curiosity, and the vendors delight in the repartee and gentle ribbing they give us at what they feel is an unnatural excitement over the size and color of an ordinary tomato. We stop for a picnic lunch by a stream where a drunken yet endearing Kazakh wants to take all of us women as wives—and, truthfully, he *is* entitled to several. Charming as he is, none of us is tempted. Torrential rain ends his courtship and our picnic, and turns the roads slick with mud. Hadji, our Uygar guide, takes an unmarked road, which leads us to a Kazakh village nestled in lush high pasture. But instead of the traditional felt yurts, these farmers have occupied wooden huts in Mongol style. Well, that's progress for you.

Hadji haggles fiercely with one family over the cost of a night's stay. It is obvious that the asking price is high, but we all know that we are in no position to argue—we are quite literally in the middle of nowhere. These negotiations involve the women rather than the men. They are intimidating, and I suppose that is their right because they seem to do all the work.

Hadji also agrees on a price for the purchase of a sheep, which will be killed and cooked for our dinner. A few of us do not have the stomach to watch the kill, but I observe that nothing is wasted. The male of the family sees to the slaughter, and then the women take over. They laboriously clean out the stomach, colon, and miles of intestine, to be recycled into sausage and other delectables. The fat is much prized and there seems to be a lot of it.

After such a production, one would think that the result would be a delicious, aromatic meal. But there is no imagination in its preparation—the meat is quite simply boiled until chewable, and chew one must, and chew, chew, and chew. There are no accompanying vegetables, no seasonings, no utensils; one simply grabs a bone and gnaws away. The Germans are, of course, in cultural experience heaven.

Our wooden yurt is simple and comprises two rooms. Not exactly what we had expected—iron-frame beds and modern appliances everywhere: TV, microwave oven, rice cooker, boom box, all covered with small tablecloths and no means of using them. Electricity, when there is any, comes from a generator, or more amazingly, from solar panels on the roof which, true to form, leaks. This begins to dampen the spirit of even the indomitable Germans.

That night, the wail of the alarm system on one of the jeeps awakens us several times. Who knows what has triggered this, but we stay stubbornly indoors as we hear people stumbling around outside. Besides, it is very cold and raining heavily. And then the police arrive. A five-star official and two rather stiff-looking soldiers who could be twelve years old. They want to see our passports and keep Hadji for some time. We speculate that someone must have complained about the noise, which is really silly considering that we are miles from anywhere and no one has a phone. We later learn that they are searching for a fugitive who is on the loose and apparently trying to cross the border into Kazakhstan. This brings home to us how sensitive an area this is, so close to many former Soviet states as well as to Pakistan.

The morning brings a cartoon blue sky and a perfect rainbow whose iridescent colors seem to cascade right onto our muddy doorstep. But lest this should in any way lighten our hearts, another drama starts to unfold. Our host and lady of the house is demanding an exorbitant amount of money (around $90) for the use of her chopsticks, pots and pans, and firewood. Here we are, in an unspoiled village, in an as yet undiscovered area, and we are being held hostage for the price of simple necessities.

Hadji is outraged and embarrassed. He takes his responsibility for hospitality very seriously, as most Muslims do. He refuses to pay up, insisting that someone fetch the mayor who is the arbiter of all village disputes. I do not think that it will make any difference. These local people will support each other as they should, and we will have no other choice but to pay.

We wait and wait.

The action unfolds, ebbing and flowing depending on who is shouting at whom. The whole village is now caught up in this drama and it is far more entertaining to sit and watch it being played out than go for a walk around the lake. It is certainly much more culturally illuminating. For a moment I wonder if this "show" has been put on for our benefit.

The compound takes on a festive air as people arrive with their families, decked out in their brightest, most luridly colored outfits as befits any self-respecting Kazakh. Everyone is smiling, all curious about us. There is no animosity and we are having a wonderful time. But the wooden gates to the compound remain shut.

A fierce-looking woman appears, bellowing into a walkie-talkie and we think that she is from the local prefecture, so we try to engage her in the dispute, but she refuses to get involved. Smart woman. She's probably just bellowing at her husband.

And suddenly the mayor arrives, a surprisingly tall, elegant man in a smart gray suit. The consummate politician, within five minutes he has negotiated a reasonable settlement between Hadji and our landlady, shaken everyone's hand, and gently prodded us back into our jeeps; the gate miraculously opens and we are on our way to general applause.

Our first yurt. Is it too early for a beer?

We arrive late at the national park at Lake Kanas. We are not allowed to drive into the park, so must off-load our luggage in pouring rain, take a local bus, off-load our luggage again ten minutes later. A long schlep takes us to what looks like an open-air snack bar but is in fact the reception area; there is more schlepping until we finally collapse on the creaky beds of our very own charming, wooden, unheated mountain chalet. My Germans, God bless them, do not utter the word "yurt." We are quite content with this dry place. I sleep well and snugly with a full body armor of silk underwear, one goose-down comforter, one wool blanket, and a hugely padded Cultural Revolution coat provided for our comfort and walking pleasure.

Our days invariably start with morning constitutionals — the only way to describe how my Germans hail the day. But even their enthusiasm for the great outdoors cannot match that of the hoards of Chinese tourists here, all predisposed to having a good time. Their shameless enjoyment is infectious. They swarm around the lake, skipping behind the tour leaders who carry colored flags and bullhorns.

Things have certainly changed since I was here in 1980. Everyone seems quite prosperous with obvious disposable income. One could almost be anywhere in the world, by any beautiful mountain lake, especially when you look at the young people: jeans, brand-name clothing, digital cameras, cell phones, even sun block. It's good to see, if a little frightening, the speed of development and how quickly the Chinese have become such prodigious consumers.

It seems that the Chinese, flush with the gains of a fast growing economy, are enthusiastically embracing the earthly pleasures of the modern world: fashionable clothes, gadgetry, and vacations. And one can sense their pleasure at the new-found freedom money has given them. But it is not all about self-indulgence. There are encouraging signs of a growing need to protect and beautify their environment. Trees are being planted in the thousands—along highways, along city streets, three deep in some instances, giving even the most sterile, industrial towns a softer, greener, more cared-for feel.

As we race through village after village, chucking up so much dust that one can barely make out the road ahead, flashes of color catch our attention: the red of a geranium struggling in a rusty pot, the vivid yellow of marigolds, deep purple and crimson petunias. And in the larger cities, flowers everywhere, grassy areas for people to enjoy with their families, set aside solely for recreation and the contemplation of nature. A happy change from decades ago. Poorer nations, whose people are struggling to survive, do not think to plant flowers.

We head south to the area around Karamay and Serim

Lake—our last chance to find the perfect yurt because after Karamay we will leave the mountain pastures and head towards the harsher landscapes that border the Taklimakan Desert and the official Silk Road.

Our 260-mile drive takes ten hours but the last half hour makes the long drive worth it as we approach the lake under a threatening sky. The light is heavy and opaque in the gathering storm. Lightning sparks on the horizon and peals of thunder follow. The lake is so calm that it looks like an immense mirage.

We reach the main village and again, to our astonishment, find it teeming with Chinese tourists who, despite the threat of a ferocious thunderstorm, are diligently queuing up for high-speed boat rides on the lake. The local vendors along the shore, however, are packing up and running for cover. We find what one can only describe as a "Yurt Motel": twenty prefabricated and permanent concrete structures covered badly in faded plastic. An adjacent restaurant advertises local fish delicacies and karaoke.

My Germans are dismayed at the thought of spending a night here, and look at these modern accommodations with disdain. I can't say I blame them. We are also dangerously low on beer, so the situation calls for drastic measures. Hadji leads us out of town and into the driving rainstorm, along a dirt road, and we are rewarded by finding a wonderful Kazakh family who agrees to take us in. They graciously show us their "spare" yurt which has until now been inhabited by several family members.

The drab exterior of the yurt belies its inner warmth and coziness. As we step inside, the rain thunders down in full force, and then hail starts, bouncing softly off the felt roof. A stove with an ingenious pipe chimney that snakes its way to a hole in the roof is quickly set up. Coal is used as fuel because wood is scarce. A tin kettle of gigantic proportion is placed on the stove to heat water for tea and it begins to boil in a miraculously short time. We are warm and feel most welcome. Tapestries of felt in lurid reds, purples, and black line the walls, topped by a sequined frieze that catches the light from the single twenty-five-watt bulb that hangs down from the center. Given the weakness of its wattage no one seems worried about electrocution. The cotton mats are soft on our bare feet, and around the bright blue central wooden table are huge duvets, triple folded to provide sofa-like seating and which transform into covers for our sleep. Stuffed with camel hair, they must weigh fifty pounds, but will keep us warm when the fire dies and we become enveloped in the mountain fog that is already stalking us from the lake. I feel as if I have been invited into the most lavish of sultan's palaces.

Our host family cooks our meal in a separate tent, a simple repast of vegetables, which we have brought with us, and a little mutton. The warm beer tastes like the best Margeaux, and the rain sounds like a symphony. We sleep the sleep of milk-fed babes, lulled into dreams by the thunder and rain.

Because of our late arrival and general haste to get inside out of the storm, we had not paid much attention to our location. Our spot could not be more picturesque: the yurt sits on a slight rise from the Serim Lake, facing it fully. Snowcapped mountains soar to our right, and we are nestled in a fir-rimmed valley. The sun is glorious after the rain, but the resulting mud is a real mess—no one escapes a tumble to the great delight of the children. We must really look quite frightful: on the road for two days, no bathrooms, no change of clothes, and now half covered in mud. My Germans are positively beaming, as am I.

After all, we've had the perfect night's sleep in the perfect location in, finally, the perfect yurt.

Born in London, Monica Cappuccini arrived in the U.S. in 1972 and spent the next thirty years traveling in search of the perfect adventure for herself and for clients in her travel industry business. She lives in Palo Alto, California where she continues to promote tribal and ethnic tours.

* * *

Tsunami

A sixteen-year-old from California ponders the
catastrophe that barely missed her family.

A MASS OF MUDDY WATER SWIRLS FEROCIOUSLY AROUND THE pool and moves rapidly towards the building. The voice of the woman filming it whispers, "O.K., boys, this is starting to scare me, let's go…" and the clip goes dead.

We saw this particular shot, perhaps ten times, when the tsunami first hit the shores of southern Thailand. We sat stunned before the television, unable to move. How could something so destructive happen so quickly? How could so many people lose their lives! It seemed almost unreal, especially from our hotel room, 100 miles from Phuket, on the Thai island paradise of Koh Samui.

My family has a knack for choosing unusual vacation destinations. Greece, Luxemburg, and Zanzibar aren't your typical family's idea of a relaxing vacation, yet that is what we do. This year we ventured to the south of Thailand to soak up the sun and paddle about in the warm water. But this fun-in-the-sun vacation took a devastating twist when a thirty-foot-tall tsunami struck.

We were relaxing on the beach on the afternoon of December 26th when a Thai woman rushed up to my mother and implored her, "Sir, sir, we have phone call for you." The call was from Dad in our hotel room. Ten minutes later my usually bouncy mom staggered back and informed my sister and me that a tsunami had hit southern Thailand. A tsunami? That's the kind of thing you learn about in science class. I thought a tsunami was a freak occurrence that only happened when a volcano erupted.

At the moment we did not know it, but our vacation was effectively over. We were scheduled to leave Koh Samui the next day for Krabi to spend a week scuba diving, snorkeling, and sea kayaking on the nearby island of Koh Phi Phi, then travel by car to Kao Lakh for a week on the beach. As we soon learned, the Phuket and Krabi airports were closed; our hotel in Krabi was badly damaged; hundreds had died on Koh Phi Phi; and thousands had died at Kao Lakh. We stayed on Koh Samui.

On first hearing about the it, I didn't realize how big or devasting a tsunami could be, and even wondered if anyone had a chance to surf it. *Johnny Tsunami,* an old Disney channel favorite came to mind. But when we flipped on the TV, horrific images flashed across the screen. To my dismay, hundreds of people sustained far more than twisted ankles and broken arms. People were dying by the thousands. By the next morning, the media reported more than 3,500 dead and 6,000 missing in Thailand alone. Thirty-five hundred dead and 6,000 missing! Those numbers were so big it was almost impossible to imagine. That is every person in my high school, multiplied by six! The news clip of the wave washing over the pool and the woman speaking to her children etched itself into my mind.

A few days passed and tsunami survivors stared trickling into our hotel on Koh Samui. People sat by the pool with bandages and black eyes and cuts on their faces. It was most surreal, knowing that they had narrowly escaped the claws of death, and now they sat; glassy-eyed, stunned, and tanning by a pool. Everyone was in a somber mood. On New Year's Eve, Malaysia issued a national decree asking people to forgo celebrations in a display of solidarity with the victims of the tsunami. At our New Year's dinner, the announcer began with a moment of silence to commemorate the lost ones.

This somber mood affected every aspect of our vacation. Despite the safe location of our little island, no one really felt like paddling about in the ocean. I imagined it would be similar to when I swam off the Normandy beaches several years ago—acceptable, but uncomfortable. For days we heard story after story of narrow escapes and heroic rescues, but the most upsetting accounts were those of the missing people. When we were finally able to leave Koh Samui, five days after the tsunami, we had to fly to the Phuket airport for an eight-hour layover, before flying on to Kuala Lumpur. The Phuket airport was transformed into what I understand St. Paul's Chapel in New York became after 9/11—"information central" for those trying to find loved ones. There were missing-person signs, posters, pictures, and pleadings covering every wall and bulletin board of the terminal. My mother likened it to a war zone. Dozens of foreign embassies hastily set up emergency facilities in the airport; Swiss, Korean, Japanese, German, and U.K. relief helpers with their search-and-rescue dogs swarmed the airport; helicopters flew back and forth day and night. We spoke to a British mother and her ten-year-old daughter who had been on a Phuket beach when the tsunami hit. The daughter was so traumatized that she could do no more than stare at us with her thumb in her mouth, trembling. Small Scandinavian children peered out from the missing person posters. Sadly, it was clear at that point (five days after the tsunami) that most of these persons would never return. The experience was extremely disturbing.

Now I am back in my cozy room in Marin County, California; it all seems so far away. But when I turn on the television and those same troubling images keep popping up, I am returned to Phuket, to that sense of terror, of desperation, that I felt. Out there, in Asia, the terror remains a reality: people are still desperately seeking food, water, and shelter. And here I sit.

I am stunned at the effect seemingly insignificant decisions had in saving our lives. We considered staying in Phuket through Christmas, but decided instead to spend one night in Phuket, then fly the next day to Koh Samui to decompress. As we later learned, the hotel we stayed at in Phuket was destroyed by the tsunami. Before we left Marin, we tried to get reservations in Krabi and Koh Phi Phi for December 24−27, but the resorts were full so we decided to stay on Koh Samui through December 27, then fly to Krabi and Koh Phi Phi when more rooms were available, then drive north to Kao Lakh. Hundreds died at Koh Phi Phi. The resort where we had reservations to stay in Kao Lakh was destroyed and thousands died. Had any of those plans been altered by a single day, I might not be here to tell this story.

By sheer luck, my family remained out of danger. Others were not so lucky, and I grieve for them. I just know that I am grateful for my good fortune.

Julieclaire Sheppard is a junior at St. Ignatius High School in San Francisco. She was traveling with her family when the tsunami struck.

DIANA DIVECHA

$\star$ $\star$ $\star$

Homemaking

The hearth is where you place your feet,
your attention, and love.

KEMP'S CORNER IS A SPRAWLING AND CACOPHONOUS INTER-section in Bombay where five roads meet and two more arch overhead. Every child that has grown up on Cumballa Hill, including my husband, knows Kemp's Corner for Modern Warehouse, India Cane House, and Kemp's Pharmacy. Thrumming at the edge of a posh residential neighborhood of embassies, upscale apartment buildings, and romantic but decrepit Victorian mansions, the intersection is a main through-way down into the commercial districts of the city. From my mother-in-law's flat nearby, my family and I travel through Kemp's Corner several times on errands before I realize that among the thousands of moving throngs, a young woman and three babies make their home in the middle of the intersection. An island of stillness in the middle of the traffic merry-go-round, this little matriarchal family lives in the shade of the flyover at the foot of one of the immense pillars that support the road structure soaring overhead. The pillar rests on a six-inch-high concrete block about five feet by seven feet, so that on any side of the pillar, the family has about one to three feet in which to maneuver. Her only possessions are a few cooking vessels, some clothing, and three small, faded, and threadbare hammocks which hang on the metal grate wrapping the concrete pillar. Blocking out an obvious lack of privacy, she performs her domestic chores behind an invisible wall erected by will and necessity, yet transparent to passersby. Surrounded by honking cars, exhaust fumes, and dirt, she folds fabric, grinds spices, and empties a bag of belongings, tasks I might do inside my own home. I am transfixed by this woman and the blasé horror of her situation, and I begin to watch for her from my air-conditioned car as we drive a hand's length from her babies.

I've come to Bombay countless times in the last twenty-two years. I am married to a man from India, and every alternate year we travel here from Berkeley with our two growing daughters to visit our extended family. Touring the massive Gateway to India, the colonial Victoria Terminus Station, and the stately Taj Mahal Hotel once is enough for me, but I am endlessly drawn to the patterns of domestic life I see in Bombay. A "homely" person or "householder," as Indians would say, I am fascinated by how people organize family life. I am compelled by essential questions of homemaking: how to live in balance, how to maximize resources, what to prioritize, how to organize materials and time, how to define roles, how to live well with others. Frequent travels to India offer rich opportunities to refract my American domestic experience through the stories and experiences of my Indian friends and family, examining commonalities and differences, always with an eye for fine-tuning my own skills.

My widowed mother-in-law, Malu, lives in a modest ninth-floor flat with her sister and two aging servants. Her home is organized around entertaining, with a gracious living room, small dining area, and terrace where guests are warmly ushered when they arrive. Couches, chairs, and cushions are always neat and waiting for use; snacks and drinks are readily available. Malu's home is decorated simply with her own pottery, photos of her grandchildren, artwork of friends, and traditional Indian folk art. From Malu and her friends, I have learned the art of easy and warm hospitality and have come to appreciate traditional Indian decorative arts. Bombay is known for its glamour and high society, and I have seen extravagant homes filled with antique carved wooden furniture, hand-tied carpets, silver boxes, and paintings with real gold, staffed with armies of servants lucky enough to have found work in this city. But the beautiful magazine homes with their teen hangouts, home offices, and exercise rooms do not draw my interest as much as the homemaking at the other end of the spectrum.

In this city of 17 million people on an island the size of the San Francisco peninsula, one-third live in slums or on the street. Scene after scene of streetside domestic life threads through this cosmopolitan city of Bollywood glamour, high society, and the thriving Indian stock exchange. In the suburbs, tiny hovels made of concrete, corrugated metal, or cardboard line the streets for miles, cheek by jowl, butted up against taller commercial buildings. Some are open to the street; some have tiny doorways hung with faded cloth; all are three feet from the speeding, spewing trucks and cars that rush down the busy roads. The suburbs give way to the slums, where on a previous trip we visited a young girl and her family that we sponsored, hoping to make a dent in India's poverty by providing electricity, water, health care, and education to one family. After we witnessed their vibrancy in a hovel the size of our bathroom with fewer belongings than we had in our carry-on bags, our lesson became one of simplifying our lives. The U.N. estimates that a family in an "underdeveloped" country such as India leaves a footprint of impact on the Earth equivalent to a size seven, while a family in an industrialized Western country trods the Earth with a size forty-two. Afterward, we vowed to reduce our shoe size, and at home our ten-year-old initiated a strict recycling program as we began downsizing in a variety of ways.

On a trip back through Kemp's Corner, I look closely at the young mother tending a fire, stirring a pot, and keeping an eye on the little ones who toddle about bare-bottomed precariously near the edge of traffic. She is not more than seventeen, and her hair, unlike the shimmery black hair of wealthy women, is brown, tufted, matted, and caked with dust. Still, it is long and tied back, a bow to conventional grooming. She has attractive features, with smooth dark-wheatish skin, straight teeth, and a slim figure wrapped in her sari. The ubiquitous silver bangles, which all women, no matter how poor, seem to have, glint on both wrists. I wonder what she thinks about, how she feels, whether she is angry or complacent, simple or verbal. I wonder how she coaxes the children to sleep in those hammocks, if she sings to them or just places them there. I wonder if she lies down on the concrete underneath the hammocks. I wonder where she gets more food and whether the traffic cop hassles her and threatens to send the children to orphanages. I wonder what the children do when boredom strikes. I wonder how several lives can be conducted in such a small space surrounded by moving cars. The stone on my chest threatens to crush my heart.

From childhood, I turned anything I could into a home, even an abandoned mail truck my father scavenged and parked in the back yard. It was my private play home to which I invited friends. Later followed a long string of dormitory rooms and apartments. In graduate school I made a home for a month out of a seedy motel room—setting up my sewing machine and ironing board, hot plate and dishes, with my

pepper spray ready at hand. Now, having established a traditional family home, I turn trips into domestic scenes, never
traveling without my hot pot, tea, and laundry detergent,
urging the children to take turns making a meal in a hot pot
and stomping the laundry in the hotel bathtub. But in the last
few years my homemaking has run into conflict. After giving
up a successful professional career in academia to raise my
family, I repeatedly run into the demeaning messages of a
society at odds with family life. Though generally steady, I
wobble some days as a fellow academic assumes, incorrectly,
that I must have left after failing to get tenure, as if being at
home is a choice only failed professional women would make.
Or a family member wonders aloud when I'll decide what to
do with my life as if caring for a family is not something.
Between fending off the oppression aimed at women and trying
to constructively channel my intense ambition, I sometimes
fear I will still sink despite all my material advantages.

One late afternoon, the woman under the flyover makes
tea in a tiny pot over a tiny fire on the concrete, a composed,
genteel act standing in harsh contrast to the traffic chaos that
surrounds her. My gaze lingers on her graceful hands, and I
imagine the taste of her *chai* tea made from the dregs of tea
leaves, heavily spiced, milky and sweet. A handful of bare-
bottomed little ones toddle about on the confined concrete
base: One baby teeters at the edge and pees over into the road
while I sit at the stoplight. Other babies play, rubbing their
hands in the dust. Cars, trucks, human pull-carts, and pedestrians rush around all sides of this home on the median strip,
like a river roaring around a boulder in midstream. I hold my
breath, ready to jump out of the car if the peeing little one
falls into the traffic—surely he'd be crushed. There is no man
in sight except the pot-bellied, khaki-uniformed police officer directing traffic twenty feet away, in the middle of the

intersecting roads. Bombay is the fifth most populous city in
the world, and people flock from the villages to this city of
dreams in hope of work. Instead they find themselves struggling "to stay ahead of squalor" as Rohinton Mistry says in *A
Fine Balance*, his devastating novel about poverty in Bombay.
Like a game of musical chairs gone bad, some are left without
a place to land but a median strip in the middle of a busy
intersection.

When I see impoverished Indian women work in their
small metal hovels or out on the sidewalk, I wonder if I would
be able to make a home and care for a family on a patch of
pavement…sort of like wondering what it would be like to
jump off a high cliff onto a rocky shore below. The logistics
alone would be daunting: The urban poor face more challenges than even the rural poor, who can at least grow food.
Life on the street is a cash economy, and street dwellers often
pay more for water than the wealthy, who have it piped into
their homes. With far more people per square inch in the
cities, diseases are more virulent, there are fewer places for
human waste, and bugs carrying malaria have shorter distances
to travel to find a human host. "Bugs and shit," economists say,
are the worst threats to the urban poor in developing countries. And women on the streets incur extra risks, constantly
vulnerable to attacks and threats by corrupt and violent men.
But it is the will to go on day after grinding day that would
surely elude me, and I think utter defeat would quickly over-
take my stamina. Through what points do these streetside
homemakers thread their dignity, hope, and sense of purpose?
What psychic muscle do they use to find the will to sweep
their sidewalk floors amid 17 million people, day after day?

With 5 million people living in slums or out on the streets,
the social service needs in Bombay are overwhelming. Every
adult woman I know volunteers somewhere, teaching at

orphanages, donating medical care in slums, bringing attention to the plight of prostitutes by writing about them, or selling artwork to raise money, all desperately trying to knit together any kind of safety net for families in need. Yet these efforts are ephemeral filaments, and in a country that worships goddesses right alongside their gods, millions of women and children are left to survive by their wits. There is little hope of a social service rescue, a handout, or a government entitlement.

For our brief ten days in Bombay, my children and I keep an eye on the family under the flyover. Sometimes they eat, sometimes they sit, once they are absent, but their hammocks and belongings remain; we worry about them until we see them again. I wonder how it is that the effort mustered by this young woman to hold together a group of children on the base of a pillar, feeding them and preventing them from running into cars, is not more honored, respected, and revered. Or even noticed. In the West, a home is a shelter that can offer entertainment, serve as an extension of the self, or provide an occupation. But under the flyover, homemaking is expressed in its rawest, perhaps its most transcendent form. Devoid of material trappings, it is only an invisible force field that says, "I am here for you. Together we will occupy this physical space, and I will see to your needs as well as I can." Along with prayers for their safety, I bless this family for showing me the divinity and sheer essence of this everyday job, done by millions of women, that is made invisible by the world around them. The travel writer Pico Iyer says that the great thing about travel is that it takes you to places in yourself where you've never been. And indeed, the woman struggling to keep a home together under the flyover takes my hand every time I pass by, reminding me that the inner will to organize food and sleep and shelter, even under the flyover, is fierce and majestic. Every day she makes a home out of nothing, really nothing except her very own life force, just her physical presence, holding together her little corner of the fabric of this society.

Diana Divecha lives in Berkeley, California with her Indian-born husband and two teenage daughters. She is a developmental psychologist who left a university position in order to deeply experience raising her bicultural family. She writes on family and culture, and is currently working on a book about child development.

LINDA LEAMING

Carried Away in Bhutan

She experienced not just the wheel of karma, but the wheels.

I CAME TO BHUTAN TEN YEARS AGO TO PUNCTUATE A TWO-month trip I was taking through India. "A nice diversion," is how the travel agent had pitched it. It was. And it still is.

Like many who come to this tiny Himalayan country, I was instantly attracted to the Bhutanese people, their remarkable physical beauty, easy charm and propensity to laugh. I traveled in Bhutan for two weeks, all the way to the country's far east and back to Paro in the west. On my way east, I stopped in Punakha for two-and-a-half days of sightseeing. Punakha valley was warm and unusually sunny, that is to say not rainy, as it was August and the Monsoons were supposed to be in full force. I stayed at a hotel on the top of a mountain at the southern end of the valley. It was low season for tourists and I was the only customer at the hotel. It was amusing to have the entire staff at the hotel, which numbered about twenty, focused entirely on me. So much so that I merely had to look in the direction of an empty glass at dinner and four waiters would rush toward the table armed with pitchers of water.

My first day there, I was ready to shake off India and have an excursion on my own. I decided to walk down the hotel road to where it intersected with the main road that ran through the valley. I took the valley road past the imposing Punakha Dzong at the confluence of the Mo Chuu and Po Chuu—the mother and father rivers—and through to the other side of the valley. When I set off I had no idea how long it would take, but Bhutan is a place where I always feel like walking. It is suited to travel at the most leisurely of paces. And unlike India, where I had been traveling for about a month, I could let my guard down. There were no beggars. The Bhutanese were polite and smiling. They seemed delighted to see me, but mostly they left me alone.

A rudimentary motor road meandered through the heart-stoppingly beautiful Himalayan valley of Punakha, and paralleled the wide Mo Chuu, or "mother river," which began to flow as glacial run-off above Gasa to the north, then into Punakha and inevitably, I imagine, to India. The long valley curled around lush mountains terraced with bright green rice paddies. It had been raining all summer, so all of the vegetation looked ready to explode with emerald ripeness. There were leafy, geometrical orange groves, which made nice counterpoint to unruly, red poinsettia trees. Farmhouses and the occasional palace belonging to this or that member of the Bhutanese Royal Family, painted with the distinctive Bhutanese Buddhist iconography, dotted the fields. Gold-roofed Buddhist temples appeared here and there, usually high up in the mountains above the farmland. The air was delicious, clean, and sweet-smelling. I remember feeling it was a day where anything could happen and I felt light-headed and giddy. It might have been the altitude, but it didn't really matter: Bhutan made me happier than any place I had ever been.

✳

It was so easy to be happy. Children stopped their play to watch and wave to me shyly, but with obvious delight, as I passed by the occasional house at the side of the road. One boy, the bravest of the children, stood as if at attention as I walked by his house saying formally but improbably, "Hello Englishman!" I smiled, said hello, and threw in a wave. He smiled and waved back, rewarded for his effort. I was clearly the most interesting thing to have come down the road in a while. They were so hopelessly charming, and I felt drunk with good will, the cerulean blue sky, the mountain air, and the sparkling sun that was so intense it made confetti everywhere.

As if on cue, a herd of cows meandered past. I imagined being a cowherd in Bhutan. Or a cow. How would it be to walk this charming road every day? I have to say it didn't sound bad. I am a hopeless daydreamer, and this seemed an excellent qualification for life, any life, in Bhutan.

Before I knew it I was almost two hours into my walk and the valley walls on either side of the road had become steeper, the mountains more imposing. I couldn't remember how long it had been since I had seen any people—or cows. Although the scenery was still breathtaking, it was clear that I should turn around and head back to the hotel and the lunch that would surely be waiting for me. The combination of high altitude and exercise had made me very hungry. But before I turned back I thought it would be a good idea to go down to the river's edge—about fifty feet to the right of the narrow road. There the Mo Chuu was wide but shallow, with clear water flowing over smooth brown stones. I had heard its rushing like an endless loop of white noise all the while I was walking. It had been calling me. Before I knew it, I was beside the river with my shoes and socks off and my pants rolled to my knees. This must have been what I'd had in mind all along. Who could pass up dipping one's feet in the icy cold water during a longish walk through a beautiful valley in Bhutan? I inched my toes and then my feet into the startling wet, and I was just thinking how slippery the stones were and how I should be careful and try not to fall when—boom, I fell.

Laughing, I pulled myself up out of the water and as I put my weight on my left foot, a sharp pain went up my leg from the ankle. I quit laughing. It felt twisted. Not badly twisted, but the thought of walking all the way back to the hotel, including the last twenty minutes up a mountain road made me wince with pain. Now my wonderful walk had taken a turn. I sat on the riverbank and examined my ankle and foot. The ankle was already starting to swell and I cupped it in my hands and felt heat.

As I struggled to put my socks and shoes back on, I tried to keep calm and upbeat by thinking of worse predicaments I'd gotten myself into. But I couldn't think of any. Getting hurt or sick is what every woman traveling alone dreads—not being able to go on. I got my boots on and the support of my boot on the twisted ankle made it feel a little better. This is not so bad, I thought. But it was, and it hurt like hell and I couldn't stop limping.

I made it back to the road. There were no cars around, or trucks or people, or even dogs. There were always dogs around in Bhutan. Where was everybody? I limped along the road for a few minutes, telling myself that it was okay, but I felt silly, walking a little like The Mummy in those old movies. Even hurt, I still felt safe in Bhutan. I wasn't lost. Eventually the people at the hotel would come looking for me. I was all they had. But if I could just walk, get back to the hotel on my own somehow. If I could get down the road just a little bit then maybe I could find a car, a truck, a tractor, something mobile to give me a lift. The thing that upset me most was thinking of hobbling by the children who were playing in front of their houses. I didn't want to limp past them, wounded, and spoil the picture. I tried to cheer myself up imagining walking past on my hands like a circus act. Or maybe I would meet up with the cows again and could ride one. They seemed docile enough.

The ankle and ensuing pain became a focal point, and I could hardly enjoy the scenery. Now fully miserable, I had to stop and rest, get off the ankle and so I sat on a rock at the side of the road, near a small temple that was partially obscured by an enormous, room-sized boulder in front of it.

I sat there for I don't know how long, and it was clear that no one was coming, and I was hungry and hurting. With great effort, I made myself get up and start walking again. Almost at once, I heard the sound of a motor—it was a motorcycle, behind me. I stopped and put my arm out and waved the air like I'd seen hitchhikers do in Bhutan. A man wearing a black helmet with visor and a gho, the handsome national dress of Bhutanese men, passed me slowly. He didn't even look at me.

Then the oddest thing: he went down the road a few feet and he swung the motorcycle around and came back to where I was standing. "Where going?" he said.

I hobbled toward him. "You want me to get on?" I asked. "Can I get on? You're giving me a lift?" I paused. He said nothing. I had asked too many questions. "Oh, please let me get on," I said as I positioned my good leg to take my full weight and I swung my bad leg over the back of the bike. I was afraid he would get away.

Now only inches away at the front of the bike, he turned his head sideways and said again, "Where going?"

"The hotel on the mountain," I said and pointed up. "Zangtopelri."

He let out a big laugh.

As I learned later, Zangtopelri, besides being the name of the hotel on the mountain in Punakha, is the heavenly abode of Guru Rinpoche, the patron saint of Bhutan.

It felt like I was going to heaven on the back of the bike. I was thrilled to be mobile, off my ankle and riding in the open air. It was my lucky day. This kind man, this wonderful man, was giving me a lift. He drove deliberately and expertly, avoiding potholes and bumps, and he even seemed to slow down as we passed a house with the children playing outside. They were busy pushing a small boy in a cardboard box around the yard. They looked up, and, seeing me again, this time on the back of a motorcycle, they shrieked with delight.

One little girl called out "Hello my darling!" as she waved furiously. They all giggled and waved and smiled these amazing, delighted, whole-face smiles. Me too, as I waved wildly with one hand and grabbed the fabric of the man's gho with the other. All of us, the children and me, waved and smiled because we were old friends. My heart melted.

We got to the hotel and I hobbled off the bike and began another assault of questions. "Was this out of your way? How can I thank you? Will you come in and have tea? What can I do? Can I give you lunch?"

"*Me jhu. Me jhu,*" he said. No thank you.

I remember feeling like I didn't want him to leave. I didn't want this dramatic rescue to end. I dug in my pant's pocket and pulled out a wadded 500 *ngultrem* note—not an insubstantial sum in Bhutan. I tried to give it to this man with the motorcycle. He was still astride his bike, wearing his helmet with the black visor and so I couldn't see his face very well, but I did see him purse his mouth below the visor and turn his head slightly, as if he was offended by my offer of filthy lucre. He wouldn't take the money.

I couldn't think of anything else. "Thank you," I said.

"Welcome," he said, smiled, and drove away.

A couple of days reading in the lobby of Guru Rinpoche's heavenly abode with my foot elevated, the staff swarming around me like bees, and my ankle was fine. After Bhutan, I went back to India and traveled in the south for a month or so. Then I met friends in Italy. I remember sitting at a café at the Piazza Duomo in Florence, talking to them about Bhutan. I'd even gotten my film from Bhutan developed in Italy and I made them look at the pictures.

"Don't start with the Bhutan stuff," they teased. "What about India? Weren't you in India for two months? Look around you. You're in Italy now."

"I'm going back," I said.

Great, they said and offered to stuff me in a cannon and shoot me back to Bhutan. But I couldn't help myself. I was already carried away.

The next few years I came back to Bhutan several more times on holiday, and the next year, I got a job teaching English at a traditional art school just outside of Thimphu. Teaching at that school made me radiant with happiness. At thirty-nine, firmly ensconced in middle age, I felt I had found the center of the universe. The other teachers were all Bhutanese tangkha artists, woodcarvers slate carvers, weavers and embroiderers, all making this highly refined but obscure and wonderful Buddhist art. The students, charming, studious and intensely focused, worked all day drawing, painting and praying, and they spent about an hour and a half a day with me learning English.

The second year I taught at the school, I married one of my coworkers, a *tangkha lopen* or teacher, a painter of Buddhist iconographic images. He was talented, shy and enormously kind. It was the first marriage for both of us.

My husband's name is Namgay and he is uncomplicated,

but surprising.

As he is Buddhist, he believes our karma brought us together as it has before in other *samsaras* and it will countless times again as we are born and reborn. Maybe in the next life I'll be his mother; after that, he'll be my dog. It doesn't matter to him. What matters is we'll be together. This he doesn't doubt. His conviction is convincing and now I'm inclined to agree.

I hesitate to tell the rest of the story, because it is enough just to say I have found a home and a voice and a wonderful, albeit quiet life among the people and mountains of Bhutan. Living here has taught me to slow down and pay attention to the signs of life and life force that are so abundant. But sometimes I still have to be hit over the head.

One day, about two years after we married, Namgay said something that stunned me. I can't recall what we were talking about, but he asked me if I remembered the day he gave me a lift?

"What do you mean?" I asked. "What lift?"

"On my motorcycle."

"You don't have a motorcycle."

"Before. That day you hurt your ankle."

"What? That was years ago. In Punakha. How did you know I sprained my ankle?"

"Because," he said sweetly and completely matter-of-factly, "I gave you a lift."

"No! That was you," I cried. "*That* was you? On the motor-cycle?" After so many years, the picture of him riding up on the bike was still vivid, that day when he rescued me on the road. The helmet shade obscured his features, except the lips. But I have certainly seen those lips since. Of course it was he.

And now I understand that life is full of these moments, these life altering, happy coincidences. They probably happen much more than we think or are aware of, especially when we are traveling, loosed from our moorings, if you will. And I know that if a day comes and you're in a place that seems absolutely magical, when you feel like anything can happen, you just have to go with it: go ahead and let yourself get carried away.

Linda Leaming lives beside a river outside of Thimphu, Bhutan.
Her writing has appeared in numerous magazines and newspapers,
including The Guardian Weekly, Cimarron Review, Greensboro
Review *and* Tashi Delek. *Currently, she writes and edits for the*
Centre for Bhutan Studies and is completing a book about Bhutan
from which this story is excerpted. In 100 years she hopes to be a
redheaded ghost in some valley in Bhutan.

Acknowledgments

Many people have influenced me and my work on this book—courageous friends, singular strangers, and most importantly my mother, who always believed in me and thus taught me to believe in myself. Thanks to Dad, as well as Mom, for taking us on long car trips across the USA, giving us roots and wings, and exposing us to the world beyond Ohio.

I have been inspired, advised, encouraged, and soothed by my patient, supportive husband, Gary Sheppard. I have been tolerated and forgiven my absences in mind and body by my heart's great joy, my daughters Julieclaire and Annalyse. Simply, sincerely, thank you.

Some time ago, on a journey over the Himalayas from Tibet to Nepal, I developed a friendship with two wonderfully crazy, entrepreneurial writers, James O'Reilly and Larry Habegger, the editors of the Travelers' Tales series. Under a tropical moon on the shores of the Pacific in Mexico six years later, we began and ended the evening, as we had so often before, sharing travelers' stories. During our chats we decided to work together on an anthology about contemporary women travelers. Heartfelt thanks to James and Larry, friends as well as the series editors. A special thanks to their loved ones Wenda O'Reilly and Paula McCabe for bearing with us and giving their invaluable feminine points of view. My gratitude to Susan Brady who kept us all organized andon time during production.

Finally, my deepest appreciation to all the women who are included in this book, for giving us new stories to live by and strengthening our resolve and courage to step out the door.

—Marybeth Bond

"Waltz at the End of Earth" by Paula McDonald published with permission from the author. Copyright © 1995 by Paula McDonald.

About the Editor

Marybeth Bond has not always been a Gutsy Woman. During summer camp, at the age of ten, she was nicknamed "Misty" because she had a bad case of homesickness. Not one of her counselors would have predicted the bright travel career that lay ahead.

Now a nationally recognized travel expert, speaker, and media personality known as the "Gutsy Traveler," she is the award winning author/editor of seven women's travel books including the national bestseller, *A Woman's World*, winner of the prestigious Lowell Thomas Gold Medal for Best Travel Book from the Society of American Travel Writers Foundation.

Marybeth has walked, hiked, climbed, cycled, and kayaked her way through six continents and more than seventy countries. Her travels have taken her from the depths of the Flores Sea to the summit of Mt. Kilimanjaro, across the Himalayas *and* the Sahara Desert. She made her first gutsy decision when she left a successful corporate career, put her worldly possessions in storage, and bought a one-way ticket to Bangkok. While some thought (and told her) she was nuts, she traveled "single and solo" for two years around the world. It was during her travels that she discovered the "gutsy woman" within herself and had the time of her life.

Marybeth continues to criss-cross the globe educating, enlightening, and empowering others to explore it through travel. Whether your idea of a "gutsy traveler" is taking your first plane ride across the Atlantic, navigating the promenades of Paris, or rafting in the Rockies, Marybeth's travel tips, know-how, and practical advice will guide you along the way.

A highly sought after speaker, Marybeth has addressed numerous consumer groups, corporations, and industry insiders about the amazing benefits of travel. She's also appeared on more than 250 network and cable media outlets including CBS, ABC, FOX, NBC, CNN, NPR to name a few. She was a featured guest on *The Oprah Winfrey Show*, where she discussed with Oprah how it is through travel that women can refresh, renew, and recharge themselves and be ready to take on the world.

Currently Marybeth is Adventure Editor for *TravelGirl Magazine* and a travel correspondent for iVillage.com and USAToday.com. Her articles have been published in magazines and newspapers around the country.

Marybeth is a member of National Association of Journalists and Authors and the Society of American Travel Writers and was an advisor for Northwestern University's Medill School of Journalism.

She now lives in Northern California with her husband (whom she met while trekking in Nepal!), two daughters and the family dog. Please visit her web site at www.gutsy-traveler.com for more news, updates, and travel advice from Marybeth.

TRAVELERS' TALES

THE POWER OF A GOOD STORY

New Releases

THE BEST TRAVEL WRITING 2005 $16.95
True Stories from Around the World
Edited by James O'Reilly, Larry Habegger & Sean O'Reilly
The second in a new annual series presenting fresh, lively storytelling
and compelling narrative to make the reader laugh, weep, and buy a
plane ticket.

IT'S A DOG'S WORLD $14.95
True Stories of Travel with Man's Best Friend
Edited by Christine Hunsicker
Introduction by Maria Goodavage
Hilarious and heart warming stories of traveling with canine companions.

A SENSE OF PLACE $18.95
**Great Travel Writers Talk About Their Craft, Lives,
and Inspiration**
By Michael Shapiro
A stunning collection of interviews with the world's leading travel writers,
including: Isabel Allende, Bill Bryson, Tim Cahill, Arthur Frommer, Pico Iyer,
Peter Matthiessen, Frances Mayes, Jan Morris, Redmond O'Hanlon, Jonathan
Raban, Paul Theroux, Simon Winchester, and many more.

WHOSE PANTIES ARE THESE? $14.95
More Misadventures from Funny Women on the Road
Edited by Jennifer L. Leo
Following on the high heels of the award-winning bestseller *Sand in My
Bra and other Misadventures* comes another collection of hilarious travel
stories by women.

SAFETY AND SECURITY FOR WOMEN $14.95
WHO TRAVEL
(SECOND EDITION)
By Sheila Swan & Peter Laufer
"A cache of valuable advice."   —*The Christian Science Monitor*

A WOMAN'S PASSION FOR TRAVEL $17.95
True Stories of World Wanderlust
Edited by Marybeth Bond & Pamela Michael
"A diverse and gripping series of stories!"   —Arlene Blum, author of
Annapurna: A Woman's Place

THE GIFT OF TRAVEL $14.95
Inspiring Stories from Around the World
Edited by Larry Habegger, James O'Reilly & Sean O'Reilly
"Like gourmet chefs in a French market, the editors of Travelers' Tales pick, sift,
and prod their way through the weighty shelves of contemporary travel writing,
creaming off the very best."   —William Dalrymple, author of *City of Djinns*

Women's Travel

A WOMAN'S EUROPE $17.95
True Stories
Edited by Marybeth Bond
An exhilarating collection of inspirational, adventurous, and entertaining stories by women exploring the romantic continent of Europe. From the bestselling author Marybeth Bond.

WOMEN IN THE WILD $17.95
True Stories of Adventure and Connection
Edited by Lucy McCauley
"A spiritual, moving, and totally female book to take you around the world and back."
—*Mademoiselle*

A MOTHER'S WORLD $14.95
Journeys of the Heart
Edited by Marybeth Bond & Pamela Michael
"These stories remind us that motherhood is one of the great unifying forces in the world."
—*San Francisco Examiner*

A WOMAN'S PATH $16.95
Women's Best Spiritual Travel Writing
Edited by Lucy McCauley, Amy G. Carlson & Jennifer Leo
"A sensitive exploration of women's lives that have been unexpectedly and spiritually touched by travel experiences.... Highly recommended." —*Library Journal*

A WOMAN'S WORLD $18.95
True Stories of World Travel
Edited by Marybeth Bond
Introduction by Dervla Murphy

— ★ ★ ★ —
Lowell Thomas Award
—**Best Travel Book**

A WOMAN'S PASSION FOR TRAVEL $17.95
True Stories of World Wanderlust
Edited by Marybeth Bond & Pamela Michael
"A diverse and gripping series of stories!"
—Arlene Blum, author of
Annapurna: A Woman's Place

Food

ADVENTURES IN WINE $17.95
True Stories of Vineyards and Vintages around the World
Edited by Thom Elkjer
Humanity, community, and brotherhood compose the marvelous virtues of the wine world. This collection toasts the warmth and wonders of this large extended family in stories by travelers who are wine novices and experts alike.

HER FORK IN THE ROAD $16.95
Women Celebrate Food and Travel
Edited by Lisa Bach
A savory sampling of stories by the best writers in and out of the food and travel fields.

FOOD $18.95
A Taste of the Road
Edited by Richard Sterling
Introduction by Margo True

— ★ ★ ★ —
Silver Medal Winner of the Lowell Thomas Award
—**Best Travel Book**

THE ADVENTURE OF FOOD $17.95
True Stories of Eating Everything
Edited by Richard Sterling
"Bound to whet appetites for more than food." —*Publishers Weekly*

HOW TO EAT AROUND THE WORLD $12.95
Tips and Wisdom
By Richard Sterling
Combines practical advice on foodstuffs, habits, and etiquette, with hilarious accounts of others' eating adventures.

Travel Humor

SAND IN MY BRA AND OTHER MISADVENTURES $14.95
Funny Women Write from the Road
Edited by Jennifer L. Leo
"A collection of ridiculous and sublime travel experiences."
— *San Francisco Chronicle*

LAST TROUT IN VENICE $14.95
The Far-Flung Escapades of an Accidental Adventurer
By Doug Lansky
"Traveling with Doug Lansky might result in a considerably shortened life expectancy…but what a way to go."
—Tony Wheeler, Lonely Planet Publications

THERE'S NO TOILET PAPER ON THE ROAD LESS TRAVELED $12.95
The Best of Travel Humor and Misadventure
Edited by Doug Lansky —— ★ ★ ★ ——

—— ★ ★ ★ —— *ForeWord Gold Medal Winner— Humor Book of the Year*
Humor Book of the Year Independent Publisher's Book Award

HYENAS LAUGHED AT ME AND NOW I KNOW WHY $14.95
The Best of Travel Humor and Misadventure
Edited by Sean O'Reilly, Larry Habegger & James O'Reilly
Hilarious, outrageous and reluctant voyagers indulge us with the best misadventures around the world.

NOT SO FUNNY WHEN IT HAPPENED $12.95
The Best of Travel Humor and Misadventure
Edited by Tim Cahill
Laugh with Bill Bryson, Dave Barry, Anne Lamott, Adair Lara, and many more.

WHOSE PANTIES ARE THESE? $14.95
More Misadventures from Funny Women on the Road
Edited by Jennifer L. Leo
Following on the high heels of the award-winning bestseller *Sand in My Bra and other Misadventures* comes another collection of hilarious travel stories by women.

Travelers' Tales Classics

COAST TO COAST $16.95
A Journey Across 1950s America
By Jan Morris
After reporting on the first Everest ascent in 1953, Morris spent a year journeying across the United States. In brilliant prose, Morris records with exuberance and curiosity a time of innocence in the U.S.

THE ROYAL ROAD TO ROMANCE $14.95
By Richard Halliburton
"Laughing at hardships, dreaming of beauty, ardent for adventure, Halliburton has managed to sing into the pages of this glorious book his own exultant spirit of youth and freedom."
— *Chicago Post*

TRADER HORN $16.95
A Young Man's Astounding Adventures in 19th Century Equatorial Africa
By Alfred Aloysius Horn
Here is the stuff of legends—thrills and danger, wild beasts, serpents, and savages. An unforgettable and vivid portrait of a vanished Africa.

UNBEATEN TRACKS IN JAPAN $14.95
By Isabella L. Bird
Isabella Bird was one of the most adventurous women travelers of the 19th century with journeys to Tibet, Canada, Korea, Turkey, Hawaii, and Japan. A fascinating read.

THE RIVERS RAN EAST $16.95
By Leonard Clark
Clark is the original Indiana Jones, telling the breathtaking story of his search for the legendary El Dorado gold in the Amazon.

Spiritual Travel

THE SPIRITUAL GIFTS OF TRAVEL $16.95
The Best of Travelers' Tales
Edited by James O'Reilly & Sean O'Reilly
Favorite stories of transformation on the road that show the myriad ways travel indelibly alters our inner landscapes.

PILGRIMAGE $16.95
Adventures of the Spirit
Edited by Sean O'Reilly & James O'Reilly
Introduction by Phil Cousineau

ForeWord Silver Medal Winner
—Travel Book of the Year

THE ROAD WITHIN $18.95
True Stories of Transformation and the Soul
Edited by Sean O'Reilly, James O'Reilly & Tim O'Reilly

Independent Publisher's Book Award
—Best Travel Book

THE WAY OF THE WANDERER $14.95
Discover Your True Self Through Travel
By David Yeadon
Experience transformation through travel with this delightful, illustrated collection by award-winning author David Yeadon.

A WOMAN'S PATH $16.95
Women's Best Spiritual Travel Writing
Edited by Lucy McCauley, Amy G. Carlson & Jennifer Leo
"A sensitive exploration of women's lives that have been unexpectedly and spiritually touched by travel experiences…. Highly recommended."
      —Library Journal

THE ULTIMATE JOURNEY $17.95
Inspiring Stories of Living and Dying
James O'Reilly, Sean O'Reilly & Richard Sterling
"A glorious collection of writings about the ultimate adventure. A book to keep by one's bedside—and close to one's heart."
      —Philip Zaleski, editor,
      The Best Spiritual Writing series

Special Interest

THE BEST TRAVELERS' TALES 2004 $16.95
True Stories from Around the World
Edited by James O'Reilly, Larry Habegger & Sean O'Reilly
"This book will grace my bedside for years to come."
   —Simon Winchester, from the Introduction

TESTOSTERONE PLANET $17.95
True Stories from a Man's World
Edited by Sean O'Reilly, Larry Habegger & James O'Reilly
Thrills and laughter with some of today's best writers, including Sebastian Junger, Tim Cahill, Bill Bryson, and Jon Krakauer.

THE GIFT OF TRAVEL $14.95
Inspiring Stories from Around the World
Edited by Larry Habegger, James O'Reilly & Sean O'Reilly
"Like gourmet chefs in a French market, the editors of Travelers' Tales pick, sift, and prod their way through the weighty shelves of contemporary travel writing, creaming off the very best."
   —William Dalrymple, author of *City of Djinns*

DANGER! $17.95
True Stories of Trouble and Survival
Edited by James O'Reilly, Larry Habegger & Sean O'Reilly
"Exciting…for those who enjoy living on the edge or prefer to read the survival stories of others, this is a good pick."
      —Library Journal

365 TRAVEL $14.95
A Daily Book of Journeys, Meditations, and Adventures
Edited by Lisa Bach
An illuminating collection of travel wisdom and adventures that reminds us all of the lessons we learn while on the road.

THE GIFT OF RIVERS $14.95
True Stories of Life on the Water
Edited by Pamela Michael
Introduction by Robert Hass
"...a soulful compendium of wonderful stories that illuminate, educate, inspire, and delight."
—David Brower, Chairman of Earth Island Institute

FAMILY TRAVEL $17.95
The Farther You Go, the Closer You Get
Edited by Laura Manske
"This is family travel at its finest."
—*Working Mother*

LOVE & ROMANCE $17.95
True Stories of Passion on the Road
Edited by Judith Babcock Wylie
"A wonderful book to read by a crackling fire."
—*Romantic Traveling*

THE GIFT OF BIRDS $17.95
True Encounters with Avian Spirits
Edited by Larry Habegger & Amy G. Carlson
"These are all wonderful, entertaining stories offering a *bird's-eye view!* of our avian friends."
—*Booklist*

IT'S A DOG'S WORLD $14.95
True Stories of Travel with Man's Best Friend
Edited by Christine Hunsicker
Introduction by Maria Goodavage
Hilarious and heart warming stories of traveling with canine companions.

Travel Advice

THE PENNY PINCHER'S PASSPORT TO LUXURY TRAVEL $14.95
(2ND EDITION)
The Art of Cultivating Preferred Customer Status
By Joel L. Widzer
Completely updated and revised, this 2nd edition of the popular guide to traveling like the rich and famous without being either describes, both philosophically and in practical terms, how to obtain luxurious travel benefits by building relationships with airlines and other travel companies.

SAFETY AND SECURITY $14.95
FOR WOMEN WHO TRAVEL
(2ND EDITION)
By Sheila Swan & Peter Laufer
"A cache of valuable advice."
—*The Christian Science Monitor*

THE FEARLESS SHOPPER $14.95
How to Get the Best Deals on the Planet
By Kathy Borrus
"Anyone who reads *The Fearless Shopper* will come away a smarter, more responsible shopper and a more curious, culturally attuned traveler."
—Jo Mancuso, *The Shopologist*

SHITTING PRETTY $12.95
How to Stay Clean and Healthy While Traveling
By Dr. Jane Wilson-Howarth
A light-hearted book about a serious subject for millions of travelers—staying healthy on the road—written by international health expert, Dr. Jane Wilson-Howarth.

GUTSY WOMEN $12.95
(2ND EDITION)
More Travel Tips and Wisdom for the Road
By Marybeth Bond
Packed with funny, instructive, and inspiring advice for women heading out to see the world.

GUTSY MAMAS $7.95
Travel Tips and Wisdom for Mothers on the Road
By Marybeth Bond
A delightful guide for mothers traveling with their children—or without them!

Destination Titles

ALASKA $18.95
Edited by Bill Sherwonit, Andromeda Romano-Lax, & Ellen Bielawski

AMERICA $19.95
Edited by Fred Setterberg

AMERICAN SOUTHWEST $17.95
Edited by Sean O'Reilly & James O'Reilly

AUSTRALIA $18.95
Edited by Larry Habegger

BRAZIL $18.95
Edited by Annette Haddad & Scott Doggett
Introduction by Alex Shoumatoff

CENTRAL AMERICA $17.95
Edited by Larry Habegger & Natanya Pearlman

CHINA $18.95
Edited by Sean O'Reilly, James O'Reilly & Larry Habegger

CUBA $18.95
Edited by Tom Miller

FRANCE $18.95
Edited by James O'Reilly, Larry Habegger & Sean O'Reilly

GRAND CANYON $17.95
Edited by Sean O'Reilly, James O'Reilly & Larry Habegger

GREECE $18.95
Edited by Larry Habegger, Sean O'Reilly & Brian Alexander

HAWAI'I $17.95
Edited by Rick & Marcie Carroll

HONG KONG $17.95
Edited by James O'Reilly, Larry Habegger & Sean O'Reilly

INDIA $19.95
Edited by James O'Reilly & Larry Habegger

IRELAND $18.95
Edited by James O'Reilly, Larry Habegger & Sean O'Reilly

ITALY $18.95
Edited by Anne Calcagno
Introduction by Jan Morris

JAPAN $17.95
Edited by Donald W. George & Amy G. Carlson

MEXICO $17.95
Edited by James O'Reilly & Larry Habegger

NEPAL $17.95
Edited by Rajendra S. Khadka

PARIS $18.95
Edited by James O'Reilly, Larry Habegger & Sean O'Reilly

PROVENCE $16.95
Edited by James O'Reilly & Tara Austen Weaver

SAN FRANCISCO $18.95
Edited by James O'Reilly, Larry Habegger & Sean O'Reilly

SPAIN $19.95
Edited by Lucy McCauley

THAILAND $18.95
Edited by James O'Reilly & Larry Habegger

TIBET $18.95
Edited by James O'Reilly & Larry Habegger

TURKEY $18.95
Edited by James Villers Jr.

TUSCANY $16.95
Edited by James O'Reilly & Tara Austen Weaver
Introduction by Anne Calcagno

Footsteps Series

THE FIRE NEVER DIES
$14.95
One Man's Raucous Romp Down the Road of Food, Passion, and Adventure
By Richard Sterling
"Sterling's writing is like spitfire, foursquare and jazzy with crackle...." —*Kirkus Reviews*

ONE YEAR OFF
$14.95
Leaving It All Behind for a Round-the-World Journey with Our Children
By David Elliot Cohen
A once-in-a-lifetime adventure generously shared, from the author/editor of *America 24/7* and *A Day in the Life of Africa*

THE WAY OF THE WANDERER
$14.95
Discover Your True Self Through Travel
By David Yeadon
Experience transformation through travel with this delightful, illustrated collection by award-winning author David Yeadon.

TAKE ME WITH YOU
$24.00
A Round-the-World Journey to Invite a Stranger Home
By Brad Newsham
"Newsham is an ideal guide. His journey, at heart, is into humanity." —Pico Iyer, author of *The Global Soul*

KITE STRINGS OF THE SOUTHERN CROSS
$14.95
A Woman's Travel Odyssey
By Laurie Gough
Short-listed for the prestigious Thomas Cook Award, this is an exquisite rendering of a young woman's search for meaning.

ForeWord Silver Medal Winner
— Travel Book of the Year

——— ★ ★ ★ ———

THE SWORD OF HEAVEN
$24.00
A Five Continent Odyssey to Save the World
By Mikkel Aaland
"Few books capture the soul of the road like The *Sword of Heaven,* a sharp-edged, beautifully rendered memoir that will inspire anyone."
—Phil Cousineau, author of *The Art of Pilgrimage*

STORM
$24.00
A Motorcycle Journey of Love, Endurance, and Transformation
By Allen Noren
"Beautiful, tumultuous, deeply engaging and very satisfying. Anyone who looks for truth in travel will find it here."
—Ted Simon, author of *Jupiter's Travels*

ForeWord Gold Medal Winner
— Travel Book of the Year

——— ★ ★ ★ ———